Copyright P. 222-225
136
91-92

Other books by the authors:

Study Smarts
Test-Taking Strategies
How to Improve Damn Near Everything Around Your Home
Homeowner's Book of Lists
Vans
I Can Use Tools
The Magazine Writer's Handbook
Good Writing
Eat Anything Exercise Diet (with Dr. Frank Konishi)
Handbook of Snowmobile Maintenance and Repair
Children's Toys You Can Build Yourself (By Franklynn Peterson)
The Do-It-Yourself Custom Van Book
How to Fix Damn Near Everything (By Franklynn Peterson)
The Build-It-Yourself Custom Furniture Catalog (By Franklynn Peterson)
Stopping Out (By Judi R. Kesselman)
Handbook of Lawn Mower Repair (By Franklynn Peterson)

THE
AUTHOR'S
HANDBOOK

Franklynn Peterson and
Judi Kesselman-Turkel

A SPECTRUM BOOK

PRENTICE-HALL, Inc., Englewood Cliffs, N.J. 07632

808.02
P

Library of Congress Cataloging in Publication Data
Peterson, Franklynn.
   The author's handbook.
   Includes index.
      1. Authorship. I. Kesselman-Turkel, Judi. II. Title.
PN147.P465 1982   808.02   82-9118
ISBN 0-13-053918-X   AACR2
ISBN 0-13-053900-7 (pbk.)

This Spectrum Book is available to businesses and organizations
at a special discount when ordered in large quantities. For
information, contact Prentice-Hall, Inc., General Book Marketing,
Special Sales Division, Englewood Cliffs, N. J. 07632.

Printed in the United States of America

ISBN 0-13-053918-X   131400

ISBN 0-13-053900-7 {PBK.}

Interior design by Linda Huber

Prentice-Hall International, Inc., *London*
Prentice-Hall of Australia Pty. Limited, *Sydney*
Prentice-Hall Canada Inc., *Toronto*
Prentice-Hall of India Private, Limited, *New Delhi*
Prentice-Hall of Japan, Inc., *Tokyo*
Prentice-Hall of Southeast Asia Pte. Ltd., *Singapore*
Whitehall Books Limited, *Wellington, New Zealand*

CONTENTS

PART III The Birth of Your Book

PART IV The Business of Writing

How to Sell
Your Book

Chapter One

A Publishing Primer

A MUTUAL FRIEND SENT MIKE TO US ABOUT A YEAR ago. He sat with us on our front porch and said, "I've written seven novels before this, but they're so bad I wouldn't waste your time even showing them to you. This one is good. I *know* it's good. I can feel it's almost there."

Mike left his 400-page manuscript. We read it. He was right; it was a good novel, but not quite ready to be published. We recommended changes in plot, took apart chapters, suggested new characters, scrapped page after page as one change led to another. Sometimes Mike got pretty discouraged as the wastebasket overflowed. He argued with some of our suggestions and sometimes he was righter than we were. But he never stopped listening and rewriting and testing out ideas . . . until one day we finally said, "Okay. Let's send it out."

Mike's novel wasn't another *Gone with the Wind,* but it was equal to the hundreds of potboilers that keep publishers and writers alive between Nobel Prizes. It's making the rounds of publishing houses now, and several editors have passed it along for second readings—a sure sign we'll sell it soon. In fact, by the time you read this, Mike will most likely be published. And while he was revising this—his eighth—novel, he was plotting and writing a ninth and tenth. "I had to do something while you were tearing apart the other book," he explained. Mike's compulsion to write, which drove him to complete *three* well-structured novels in less than a year, is just like the compulsion that drives half the writers we know. (The other half suffer from chronic writer's block until the month before a deadline.)

Phil, another aspiring writer, attended one of the writing classes we teach at the University of Wisconsin. He turned in a few short stories that might have earned an A or B in most undergraduate creative writing courses. But they fell far short of the professional mark that Phil was shooting for. We directed him toward rewrites, but we never saw any. Instead, he tried parts of novels. Again we steered him toward rewriting, but what we saw next was a magazine article idea. Each new effort was unfinished, unpolished, off-the-top-of-the-head typing. And every time we suggested possible improvements, we'd get not a rewrite but an impassioned or bitter defense of his typewritten words.

Eventually Phil hit on a promising idea; it was in a subject area in which he had some expertise, so the concept was doubly viable. To help Phil shape it into a book that stood a chance of selling, we sent him off to research other published books in that field. Instead, he appeared at our next class with a thin sheaf of papers. "This is my book," he announced. "It's finished."

The class read photocopies of Phil's project and they echoed our evaluation. So again we carefully went over the steps that have to be taken before a nonfiction book can be marketed with any degree of certainty. Seeing no immediate follow-up, we assumed that Phil had dropped this undertaking the way he'd dropped the others. We've learned long ago that you can't push anybody into working hard to become a writer, so we didn't push Phil. But we do try to be candid, so when Phil told us he was quitting his job to write full-time, we suggested that it wasn't a good idea.

Phil wasn't listening, since we weren't saying what he wanted to hear. About six months later the mail brought a somewhat reworked version of his book, with its basic problems still uncorrected. We shipped the manuscript back with a two-page note detailing the problems and again suggesting, more forcefully this time, that maybe writing wasn't for him. Phil is a nice guy, so we worried that we'd been too hard on him.

We shouldn't have. A week later Phil showed up at our office, waving that familiar sheaf of papers and insisting that the book was marketable—*extremely* marketable. He was sure that any publisher would pay a $15,000 advance for it and that we were crazy for not acting as his agent. He tried to badger us into taking on his project. We literally had to shove him out the door.

We doubt that you'll ever see a book with Phil's name on it. Phil, you see, has fallen for that fairy tale that plagues so many beginners: that publishers read every page of their mail every day to discover people whom they can turn into overnight millionaires.

If *you* want to be a published writer—and you must, if you're reading this book—we can do for you what we did for Mike (and tried to do for Phil). We can tell you what the publishing industry is really like and how *you* can tell what's publishable. We can tell you how to go about writing your books. You won't find, in these pages, lots of entertaining jokes. We've left out the inspirational truisms and pep-talks that fill some books on writing. But if, like Mike, you're receptive, we can hold out the realistic promise that—after trial and error, after learning your craft, after the frustration and dejection that come with any totally new endeavor—you're going to publish a book.

Our credentials? We've been writing since 1955, and started writing books in 1972. Since then we've published one college textbook, thirteen nonfiction books for adult readers, and two for children. In addition, we've signed to write one novel and have a second in the works. We've shared what we've learned about the publishing industry by teaching in classes and at writers' conferences, and our students have published both nonfiction books and novels. Our view of the publishers is an *author's* view. Like Lord Byron, who quipped that the larcenous Barabbas must have been a publisher, we're not perfectly unbiased. But our facts are guaranteed accurate.

Let's begin by exploding some of the myths about the publishing industry.

1·1 The Publishing Houses

There are over 6,000 book publishers in the United States, doing a little less than $5 billion worth of business annually. They range in size from the vest-pocket operations that bring out one new title every couple of years, on up to Doubleday, a conglomerate that integrates under one corporate umbrella two very large hard-cover publishers, one huge mass market paperback publisher, and the largest book club as well as several smaller ones.

Whether it regards its books as treasures or considers each manuscript just one more property, *every profit-seeking publisher tries to purchase book manuscripts cheaply and sell finished books at maximum markup.* (Our editor suggested the italics!)

Just this month we spent a day wandering through Chicago's massive McCormick Place convention hall during the annual sales extravaganza of the American Booksellers' Association. Everywhere along the maze of publishers' booths, a wholesaler was trying to entice retailers to place orders for his line. Lyle Stuart was there in person, handing out bottles of Scotch in return for on-the-spot orders (another year it was watches). Whenever star-of-the-moment Ken Follett wasn't on hand, William Morrow's sales force turned on a videotape of Follett pitching *The Key to Rebecca*. Most of the other publishers offered special discounts, prizes, posters, drawings, free books, and authors' autographs. But the hucksterism disturbed us a lot less than the depressing realization that three-quarters of the booths were in the hands of amateurs who were still trying to learn the business. These miniscule publishers each had a booth, a company name, some business cards and order blanks, and a hapless author or two—but no advertising staff or sales force, no professional editors or copy editors, no warehouse or shipping department. They hired outsiders to do all of these essential jobs—when they could afford to. Some of these people have been muddling along this way for years, with a few spectacular successes to keep them going.

A few publishers are owned by admittedly not-for-profit organizations. National church bodies, for example, sponsor publishing houses that bring out books for sale within the church organization, or to spread the church's dogma to the reading public.

A great many universities also sponsor publishing houses. Most university presses, subsidized by the parent schools, are mandated to publish works of important scholarship (usually written by the sponsoring school's professors) that would not be profitable ventures for commercial publishers. Some of the more aggressive university publishers now emulate the for-profit publishers. Brigham Young University Press, for example, put an eye-catching cover on *Roughing It Easy,* Professor Dian Thomas's guide to outdoor cooking, and kept the book on national best-seller lists for months. However, although university presses accounted for 11 percent of all new book titles in 1977, they took in only 1 percent of the industry's overall income.

When it comes to marketing your book ideas, commercial, university, and other not-for-profit publishers differ in important ways. But organizationally, full-service publishing houses are fairly similar.

THE EXECUTIVES

You're not likely to meet the executives at any but the smallest publishing houses. However, it's important that you know what their jobs entail.

At conglomerate-owned publishing houses, the top-level presidents, vice-presidents, and flannel-suited assistants spend their days in conferences designed to maximize profits and minimize costs. A product is a product, and executives who do a good job of maximizing profits for a conglomerate's breakfast cereal division may be asked to do the same thing for its book division. It won't matter if they don't know a noun from a verb or Faith Baldwin from James Baldwin—if they know a roll-over from a discount, they're in charge. Conglomerization has led to Litton Industries, Raytheon, Xerox, and ITT being among the giants in textbook publishing, and to the anomaly that for years Bantam Books was owned by Fiat, the Italian car manufacturer.

Often the effects of conglomerate ownership are subtle. But shortly after ITT took over Bobbs-Merrill, the 150-year-old publisher dropped its venerable fiction line. A conglomerate offshoot's final decision on whether to publish a book depends not on literary merit or benefit to society, but on the bottom line: the book's estimated profit to the company.

THE EDITORIAL DEPARTMENT

In large publishing houses entire labyrinths of editors work in various-sized cubbyholes. In educational and textbook publishing firms those occupying the largest cubbies are called *acquisition editors* because their principal job is to *acquire* book manuscripts. At other houses, people who acquire may be called *senior editors* or simply *editors*. These manuscript buyers occupy the top echelons of editorial departments. Some have worked their way from the bottom of the editorial ladder; others have moved into acquisitions from the sales department.

Regardless of what they're called, acquisition editors are expected to know (or at least find out) what kinds of books will sell the most copies the next year, or the year after. As you will see in later chapters, that's a highly subjective, almost mystical talent. Editors whose hunches prove correct often enough can earn salaries of $50,000 a year—and are worth every nickel of it.

Acquisition editors acquire many of their properties (also called *titles*) as ideas or manuscripts that are submitted to them by authors. But while they're discussing market trends, trying to guess what the reading public may get interested in next year, the editors also generate ideas of their own. Once in a while they seek out authors whose reputations or previous books they know, and ask them to convert the ideas into finished manuscripts.

Notice that what sells a book (in nonfiction, and in most fiction as well!) is not its fine style or unique literary form, but the marketability of its *idea*. Some acquisition editors hardly touch finished manuscripts. They're concerned primarily with locating ideas they can market. Once they're convinced that an author's manuscript satisfies the necessary marketing requirements, they turn over other editorial chores, such as polishing up the writing style, to subalterns. On two of our own books, one generated by an editor's idea, the acquisition editors in question never read the manuscript or finished book!

At publishing houses where senior people are called acquisition or senior editors, employees at other levels are commonly titled simply *editor*. Elsewhere, the second echelon is *associate editor* and the third, *assistant editor*. Associate and assistant editors generally do everything the senior editors do, but have to go through more internal red tape to get it done. On his own, a senior editor may be able to okay a book requiring a $50,000 advance, but an assistant editor might have a $5,000 ceiling and need major decisions approved by a senior editor or an editorial committee. *Editorial associate* or *assistant* is the entry-level job, typically taken by a Smith graduate with a B.A. or M.A. in English who wants to be part of the glamorous publishing world and quickly becomes frustrated at being no more than a typist, go-fer, and protegée all in one. Over the years we've made half a dozen close friends in publishing who, conglomerately, fit this description. All but one have quit and moved out of publishing into less glamorous but more satisfying jobs. The exception is still hanging around at a major house, knowing that her only hope for moving up is to discover some bright, commercially valuable author before her boss does. Her boss is a well-known editor who made her own mark by discovering a best-selling novelist while *she* was an editorial assistant. So these two fine women try to outmaneuver one another to get first crack at each potential new talent that comes along—while the assistant regularly checks the lengthy "People" section of *Publisher's Weekly* to see which assistants have moved to new publishing houses, leaving vacant spots that may be better than the one she's in.

Committees have now invaded all of publishing. More and more decisions are put off until the next editorial meeting, when all the editors suggest projects for acquisition, argue over costs and possible earnings, and together okay or axe each idea.

In the next several chapters we'll help you decide which editors to approach with your book idea. Then in Chapter 13 we'll discuss what various editors are likely to do to your manuscript once you've turned it in.

THE PRODUCTION DEPARTMENT

All the mechanical and editorial procedures that go into converting 300 neatly typed manuscript pages into a 164-page bound book are handled by the production department—copy editors, proofreaders, layout artists, designers, and similar personnel. Very few publishing houses own printing presses or typesetting machinery, so production departments take bids from outside typesetters, printers, and binderies, and supervise delivery by these suppliers. (This is all you need to know about production at the present. Chapter 13 will have more details.)

THE SALES AND PROMOTION DEPARTMENTS

It's hard for neophytes to believe the ragtag way books are sold to the general book-buying public. Imagine General Motors bringing out 100 new car models every spring and fall, printing fancy catalogs to show off each new car—and then paying Ford Motor Company a commission to sell them to dealers. Incredible? Yes, but that's how the majority of new books are actually sold to the bookstores, on whom your royalty and your publisher's profit both depend.

About 40 percent of all book titles are *trade* books, published with bookstores as their major intended market. However, barely one in ten book publishers maintains its own comprehensive sales network. The others rely on different ways of getting their books into the stores.

First there are the *commissioned sales representatives,* a grizzled collection of Willie Lomans. Each has carved out a part of the United States as his turf and regularly visits every major bookstore within his boundaries to pitch new titles and take orders—on behalf of several publishers, most of whom compete with one another for purchase dollars. In return for spending most of his life on the road, the sales rep collects a commission on each order.

The other sales technique is the Ford-selling-General Motors phenomenon. A great many smaller publishers sign *distribution agreements* with larger publishers. In spring 1980, for example, Beacon Press informed booksellers that Harper & Row now represented them to the trade. This meant that the new Beacon book on famous female authors had to be promoted by the same sales force employed to promote Harper & Row's *own* new book on classic female authors. Cornerstone's spring 1980 titles—including a book on women in the business world—were represented by Simon & Schuster's salespeople, who were pushing S & S's own book on women's career decisions.

The above observations are of much more than theoretical interest to authors. One of our first books, aimed expressly (and almost exclusively) at college students, was commissioned by a publisher that planned to hire its own distribution force to sell to college bookstores. After the book was written, distribution was given instead to a company that had no college bookstore outlets at all! It shouldn't be hard to imagine how few copies of that publisher's stepchild were sold.

Recently there's been something new added to bookselling: a network of *book wholesalers.* By buying selected titles from publishers in large quantities, wholesalers can take advantage of high discounts—which, in turn, enable them to sell to local bookstores at *normal* discounts and still profit. Publishers typically take a month or two to deliver books. Since wholesalers deliver orders sometimes within days (at most within a few weeks), stores often prefer to buy through wholesalers. Not only do publishers and wholesalers now compete for orders but, since authors' contracts usually specify a much smaller royalty when books are sold to wholesalers, authors now stand to lose up to 50 percent of their meager earnings.

Superimposed on this Rube Goldberg sales morass is each publisher's promotion staff. It's their job to arrange for the advertising and publicity that, it is hoped, will sell enough copies of enough different books to let the publisher make a profit. Our confidence in them is reflected in the title of Chapter 14: "How to Help Sell Your Own Book."

1·2 Bookstores and Other Outlets

Fewer than half of the half million titles now in print are distributed to bookstores or other retail outlets. Most of the rest (43 percent) go to educational markets, which include classrooms and libraries.

Of the approximately 3,000 U.S. bookstores that belong to the American Booksellers Association, half gross less than $100,000 a year in sales. Their before-tax earnings can be assumed to be under $30,000 each. Small wonder, then, that a third of the stores report they are Mom-and-Pop operations with no salaried employees.

In addition to 8,000 businesses listing themselves as bookstores, the Department of Commerce reports 52,000 drugstores and 38,000 auto and home supply stores that also sell books. Competing for space in one of these nearly 100,000 stores are half a million different book titles, of which about 125,000 are paperbacks. According to Benjamin M. Compaine's study of the book industry, the very largest general bookstores stock up to 30,000 titles, while most stores are limited to between 5,000 and 18,000. Compaine compares that gluttony to the average supermarket's stock of a mere 6,500 different items.

Why do we quote so many dry figures? Not to discourage you (though Judi does get discouraged every time she walks into a bookstore and sees the flood of new titles that will be replaced by another flood next time she goes in). Later in this book you'll find out how to increase the odds that your book will be among the relative few that at least make it onto bookstore shelves so that they have a chance to sell.

1·3 The Books and Their Authors

It's sobering to think that our sixteen published books are only a mere 3/1000ths of 1 percent of the half million book titles now in print. It's more sobering to understand how the price paid for a trade book is divided up among publisher, bookseller, and author. To pay for the costs of editing, typesetting, printing, packaging, and (if you're lucky) promoting, the publisher pockets 50 percent of the cover price. To pay for overhead, salaries, and (rarely) cooperative advertising, the bookseller pockets 40 percent of the cover price. To pay for living expenses incurred during the time it takes to sell and write the book, the author gets around 10 percent of the cover price.

We can't offer you any statistics about the people who write books. Although the publishing industry's publications can tell you many companies' costs and profits, they do not collect data on the success or failure, profits or losses of the authors whose books support the industry. And few authors' groups are representative enough—and rich enough—to undertake accurate surveys.

However, please don't mistake our attitude for despair. It's likely that authors will endure long after the publishers' antediluvian business methods drown them in computer printouts.

In our several decades of full-time free-lance writing, we've luxuriated in its fringe benefits. We spend winters in warm climates now and then, take time off whenever we turn in a manuscript, declare vacation time on impulse to romp with our kids through Wisconsin snowdrifts or to try to catch the elusive muskie.

There are other people we know who abandoned other professions to become full-time writers, and who love it. One dentist got tired of shoving his fingers into people's mouths; now he's writing books he'd always wanted to write, instead of wondering whether patients are going to keep their appointments. A podiatrist who never had enough free time to strap on his air tanks switched to writing—and now gets paid to write about scuba diving.

There's no doubt that this is a fairytale sort of business, and that's half the bait that lures us to it. With each new book you publish, there's a remote chance it'll make you richer, change your life, change others' lives, or accomplish some other goal that most nonwriters stopped aspiring to as teenagers. In addition, there are the more easily obtained rewards: seeing your name in print, going and coming on your own schedule, becoming a bit of a local celebrity. If that sounds appealing, we'll show you the road.

Chapter Two

Can Your Idea Become a Book?

E DITORS SELDOM BUY COMPLETED MANUSCRIPTS— and it's a good thing, too. If authors had to research, organize, and write 400 pages of fiction or nonfiction before they could market it, few could make a living. Authors' closets would be full of unpublished manuscripts, many of them beautifully written and on important topics.

Due to the vagaries of public taste and the importance of the *idea* in today's bookselling, it's all but impossible for authors to predict which books will find publishers. That's why the vast majority of contracts are signed while the books are still little more than ideas. The fact is, finding an idea that'll sell to even *one* editor is a matter of guesswork. With each book we sell, our guesswork becomes more educated. By now, we've learned a few shortcuts we can pass on—but none of them guarantees a sale.

Several weeks ago we were sitting in an editor's office while he was finishing a phone call. His end of the conversation consisted of, "Yes, it sounds interesting, but I'd need to see an outline," and "Yes, the topic is new, but I've got to see the approach." Finally he said curtly, "Brother-in-law or not, I can't tell you what to do with your idea. That's the author's job!" And he hung up.

What editors consider a book idea that's ready for consideration is worlds apart from what many authors hand them. Usually the disparity occurs because the authors don't know what makes a book idea good. There are five fairly universal guidelines for judging whether your idea is sound, though in this, as in all aspects of book publishing, there have been many exceptions.

2·1 Define Your Parameters

The idea must be *clearly defined* in words that can serve as a book title. It must be clear-cut enough that both you and any editor considering it will know exactly what you intend to include and what you intend to leave out.

This is true for both fiction and nonfiction, but it's easier to demonstrate with nonfiction. Take, for example, *a book about children's games*. As presented, that idea is incomplete. Such a book could include every game ever played by children at any time throughout history. Sounds more like a ten-volume encyclopedia, doesn't it?

If clearly defined, this idea could make *several* workable book proposals. A couple of hypothetical examples:

Games played by Pilgrim and other Colonial American children.
Modern children's street games that rely on basic math and logic skills.
A record of modern children's street games that have been played using imaginative play-acting.

But these ideas are still not complete enough to market. To evaluate ideas, editors want to know more than just the parameters of the objective information. They also ask for the author's subjective approach. When expanded to incorporate viewpoint, these three ideas could become:

How games played by Colonial American children helped shape their outlook on life.
Modern children's street games that can help slow learners acquire and reinforce math and logic skills.
A record of actual modern children's street games that were played using imaginative play-acting, and a discussion of how they helped these particular children cope with the problems of growing up.

Notice that once the topic and approach for an idea are clearly defined in a comprehensive sentence, the sentence makes an excellent working title. If you keep it clearly in mind during every step of your writing, it'll be hard to wander off the topic, as so many beginners do. With our own nonfiction, we generally use our working title as a long subtitle all the way through, until the publisher makes the final title decision. Our *Do-It-Yourself Custom Van Book* kept its working title right on into print.

In fiction, the idea embodies the kind of novel or the theme as well as the subject, and it may have nothing to do with the title at all. For examples, William Blatty's *The Exorcist* is a supernatural tale about a girl who's possessed, and Marilyn French's *The Women's Room* is a woman's novel about self-awareness and a change in identity. Jill Ross Klevin's *The Summer of the Sky-Blue Bikini* is a teenage romance about how people change as they grow up. Of course, these thimble-tip sketches are clichéd; they *have* to be because most editors feel comfortable when they can see a novel filling a niche in the season's list: one romance, two psychological dramas, and so forth. Your chances of a sale increase if you show immediately whether your story is a thriller, a romance, a family saga, or science fiction.

Of course, novels may combine several genres or themes. But usually an editor must fit a book into a single category so the sales force can sell it. *You* must decide on that category before you begin to market it.

2·2 Consider Your Length

Here's one test for whether your idea is book material: could you write at least 250 double-spaced pages on the topic without becoming repetitious, boring, or trite? More important, would adult book buyers want to read 250 pages or more on your topic? If not, your idea would probably not make a successful book for adults. Novellas are not in vogue right now; adult novels generally run upwards of 300 pages. With books for older children, you can use 100 pages as a guide.

On the other hand, if you think you'd have trouble covering a nonfiction topic adequately in fewer than 500 manuscript pages— 125,000 words—your parameters are probably much too broad. These days, even textbooks are held to about 400 pages whenever possible, because of the high cost of paper and composition. (Throughout this book, we'll refer only to *manuscript* pages of about 250 words each, not finished book pages, unless we alert you to the contrary.)

It's tough for beginning authors to visualize how long their proposed books might be. Since we've found that most nonfiction hopefuls have made a stab at writing for magazines, here's a shortcut. Sketch out a rough, tentative table of contents. If you end up with ten subtopics, would each of them make an interesting chapter twenty pages in length? If you come up with twenty subtopics, decide whether you can expect to cover them adequately in about ten pages each.

If you're an embryonic novelist, too long is much less of a problem than too short. If Thomas Wolfe could stand to see a million-word manuscript hacksawed into *Of Time and the River,* you too will be able to weather some heavy blue-penciling.

2·3   Determine Your Timeliness

Your idea may be interesting and timely today, but will it remain so for several more years? If not, it may be a news item or magazine feature and not suitable for a book.

First, selling the idea to an editor will require at least several months. (The average beginner's first sale takes closer to two years.) Writing the book can take from several months up to several years depending on how much spare time you can devote, how much research you have to do, and how fast you work. After your completed manuscript is turned in, the production crew can take up to a year to convert your stack of pages into a bound book. So years may elapse from the time your idea is conceived until your book is in the stores. Therefore, take a long, hard look at your idea. Can you *realistically* expect readers to be interested in this topic that long from now?

You must consider one other aspect of timeliness: publishers prefer to acquire books that can remain on sale for several years. Paradoxically, most hard-cover books now vanish from the shelves after six months. Still, of the half million books in print, barely 10 percent were released as new titles within the past year. So you'd be wise to assess whether your idea will still seem timely five, ten, or even a dozen years from now. All of our sixteen published books are still in print. The publishers who recognized the books' timeliness are still earning profits—and we still receive royalties. We've yet to see a book of ours remaindered—that last small ignominy before a book is taken out of print. (The only thing more ego-deflating than seeing a book *by* you among the remainder piles is seeing a book *about* you in that bargain-basement display.)

One exception to the time factor consideration is the often-headlined *instant book.* The first of its kind appeared when Bantam Books rushed into print the book-length Warren Commission Report on the Kennedy Assassination only weeks after the Commission released its now-disputed findings. Bantam and other publishers have so streamlined production that they can actually ship finished books within a few days of receiving the manuscripts. But few instant books are published compared to the thousands of general books brought out every year. They're usually nonfiction, pegged to attention-riveting disasters. Also, since the stakes in these costly gambles are very high, they're usually written by teams of pros well-known to the publishers.

An exception to the timeliness rule is the movie novelization, published in paperback to flame and fade with what's hoped to be a blockbuster film. This is also a written-to-order genre, usually reserved for writer friends of the filmmaker or editor.

The nonfiction equivalent of the movie novelization is the phenomenon of fad books. When Americans jump onto some band-wagon such as transcendental roller skating or disco meditation, you can be sure that publishers will jump on six months later. Every editor seems to dream of having a book come out in the opening weeks of a new national craze; that's why over a dozen different titles appear, one after another, pandering to each passing phase. If you have an inside track on what promises to be a major fad *and* can churn out a book that contributes something new to interested readers, then it might be worth the effort to devote all your energies nonstop to selling the idea.

Examples of recent fads that sold millions of books come readily to mind: est, crock-pot cookery, fiber diets, T.A., assertiveness training, tummy-tightening, ecology, jogging. Hal Higdon discov-ered his own joys in running long before the rest of us, and his 1971 book *On the Run from Dogs and People* may have been the first on the subject. Never a best seller, it did nonetheless establish Hal as a surefooted jogging writer. Later on, when the fad hit, he quickly sold *The Beginner's Running Guide, The Runner's Cookbook* and, since he's put on a few years since his first effort, *Fitness After Forty*. He's been jogging to the bank ever since.

2·4 Pinpoint Your Prospective Readers

The mere fact that you can write 250 pages of lively fact or fiction on your chosen theme doesn't guarantee that anybody will want to read it. Only a book with a pool of waiting readers is worthwhile for a publisher to print and sell. Even scholarly presses generally balk at taking on a book unless they feel certain that several thousand people will want to buy copies. But how can you second-guess publishers as to whether a market exists for your topic?

Any well-stocked library or bookstore relies on several reference guides to help it order books, and they can aid you in figuring out the audience for what you have to say.

Books in Print and *Paperback Books in Print* are annual volumes that list almost every book that every American publisher has (or expects to have) on sale during the year. Neither guide includes once-in-print books that have been discontinued. Both have separate title, author, and subject indexes and include such information as publisher, year of issue, and price. For nonfiction authors trying to identify whether an audience exists for a book idea, the subject guides are a good first stop. For example, if three books on learning disabilities have been published within the last year, those publishers believed a market existed. (The next step is to try to find out from your friendly bookseller how *well* those books sold—and whether they whetted or satiated the book buyers' urge to know more.)

Since people in publishing are insecure about investing thousands of dollars in an untested subject area, it is important to collect proof that publishers have sold books on a subject similar to yours. If you find a dozen or more books on the same general subject, but none that exactly duplicates *your* specific idea, you've got two good selling points. Even if you find some titles that *seem* similar to what you want to write, don't give up your idea just yet. Study the books; they may not be what their titles make you think they are—or as informative as they should be.

From your research in *BIP,* you will discover the names of any publishers that specialize in publishing your kind of book. What if you can't find *any* books at all in your idea's genre? We'll talk about that quandary later in this chapter.

Publishers' Trade List Annual is arranged alphabetically by publisher. Following each company's name and address is a complete listing of the books and authors in that publisher's current catalog. Some publishers carve out special subject areas. Doubleday has a line of popular religious books; Lyle Stuart iconoclastic exposés; Abrams expensive art books; Schocken Judaica; and Farrar, Straus & Giroux literary novels. For such special areas, authors often consult *PTLA* early in their research. Since this reference's editors work strictly from publishers' catalogs, forthcoming books are listed as well as *backlist* books; that is, previously published books that have sold well enough to be still in print.

Many booksellers and librarians also subscribe to *Publisher's Weekly* and *Library Journal.* In these periodicals, publishers advertise to promote books they hope will have wide readership, so the clever author can feel the pulse of the market by reading the journals regularly. Bookstores and libraries also receive publishers' announcements and catalogs, and some file their copies for reference.

A lot of writers have trouble deciding when a book idea is *too* similar to something in existence. For instance, when Jay Anson's *The*

Amityville Horror clung to best-seller lists for months, you might have thought he exhausted the market for books about haunted houses in that small New York suburb. Still, before Anson's cobwebs cleared, *Publishers Weekly* announced (12/10/79) that Hans Holzer had sold a book with the working title *Murder in Amityville* and Harvey Aronson had sold one with the working title *Murder at Amityville;* both books detailed the grisly deaths that preceded the events in Anson's epic. Obviously, the editors who contracted those two books felt that Anson had not sated his readers' curiosity. Instead, as often happens, they were seen as an identifiable market who probably wanted to read more on the topic.

2·5 Study Books Whose Ideas Are Similar to Yours

After you have identified books that are similar to the one you have in mind, browse through them at a library or bookstore. (In fact, help support your fellow writer: buy a few. Their cost is deductible from your taxes.) Identify how the concept behind each book is similar to your idea and how it differs in various aspects:

    title
    contents
    approach
    sources of information

By studying the books, you will learn how *your* book has to be focused to make it clearly different from—or improved over—your existing competition.

Why, you may ask, does your book have to be different or better than Publisher A's? Why can't you sell your almost identical book to Publisher B? The reason is one of the ill-explained etiquettes of publishing. If an editor at Publisher B knows that Publisher A has already contracted a book on your topic, it's unlikely that she'll want to touch your idea. If you refocus the idea to emphasize something that's newer or better than what exists, then it's a different book.

What about those two Amityville follow-ups? Editors don't *always* know that a competitor has signed a book on the same topic. And once in a while they decide that a topic is so hot that there's room for several books—as when the Mets won the pennant and *five* books glutted the bookstores.

In doing your market research, keep in mind that your aim is to appeal to the book-buying audience you've identified. To summarize, your goal is to establish (1) that the readers exist, and (2) that some aspects of the subject have not yet been published for that audience.

To illustrate the art of pinpointing nonfiction markets, we've pulled out a small stack of somewhat similar home improvement books, all published during 1978 and 1979 by Prentice-Hall. Stanley Schuler's *Handyman's Guide to Home Remodeling* concentrates on ways to add space and value to one's home. Carmen and Brownlee Waschek's *Your Guide to Good Shelter* is subtitled: "How to plan, build, or convert for energy conservation." Floyd Hickok's entry, *Your Energy Efficient Home,* is subtitled: "Improvements to save utility dollars." This might seem to overlap the Waschek title, but casual perusal reveals that Hickok limits his book exclusively to *existing* homes and to stopping heat loss; the Waschek volume covers new *and* old homes and designs for entire comfort and safety, not just energy efficiency. A fourth Prentice-Hall entry into housing efficiency, George R. Drake's *Weatherizing Your Home,* differs from the others primarily by sticking almost entirely to do-it-yourself techniques. (The other two volumes help you get the job done by professionals.)

If you had analyzed books on energy-efficient housing, would you now rule out Prentice-Hall for your projected book on the same topic? Or would you make that publisher a prime candidate because it displays real interest in reaching that particular audience? We'd count them in for books on designs for passive solar heating, do-it-yourself energy-saving greenhouses and vestibules, window improvements that cut heat loss and enhance solar effects, and similar concepts. On the other hand, we'd forget about doing a book for them on do-it-yourself insulating and weather-stripping or general home remodeling unless we had enough new information to offer an improved or different design (or if their books on the subject had become outdated and gone out of print).

As you browse through each book on your list, here are some things to look for to help you identify (1) the audience the book hoped to capture, and (2) how it's similar to or different from your project.

TITLE
Does it aim at a clearly defined readership or a diverse population? Does it tease or inform? Is it fact or speculation? Is it scholarly or light reading? Does it appeal to intellect or emotion?

AUTHOR
Is he an expert or scholar in the field, or does he play some role in the story being told? Does he have a reputation? Are his credentials or involvement stressed on the front cover?

COVER AND JACKET BLURBS
The synopses and little biographies on dust jackets or back covers are, in truth, designed to lure readers to buy the books. Read critically; they provide valuable clues to what audience the editors and salespeople had in mind.

TABLE OF CONTENTS
What is its approach to the subject? Personal? Authoritative? How detailed is the coverage? What aspects are included and what left out? At what points in the subject does the book begin and end?

APPROACH
Is the reader assumed to know nothing about the subject, or a little, or a great deal? What is the expected educational level? The sex? The age range? Is the book told as a personal narrative, or impersonally, or is it a mixture of the two? Is it full of anecdotes or long on facts and figures?

SOURCES OF INFORMATION
Where did the author's information come from? Are sources cited prominently, or are the contributions of outsiders played down?

With a handful of volumes, we'll illustrate just how we analyze books when we're leaning against a wall in Moseley's, Waldenbooks, or the University Bookstore.

Men in Love by Nancy Friday (hard-cover nonfiction): The title is in type three times the size of the author's name, leading us to surmise that Delacorte Press believed that her subjects were still better box office than her own byline. Still, right under her name is *"Author of My Mother/My Self"*—a reminder to readers who liked her biggest best seller.

The title is vaguely titillating, aimed at all men *and* women and counting on an emotional response. So is the very explicit subtitle: "Men's sexual fantasies: the triumph of love over rage." Neither has a scholarly ring to it. The dust jacket quotes from two other authors, an M.D. and a psychoanalyst, lending additional authority to the book. The publisher's own copywriter has added the words "groundbreaking study," "based on thousands of candid responses from men aged fourteen through their sixties," and "thought-provoking—and loving. . . ."

The table of contents tells us more about the subject and anticipated readership. The 22 chapter titles start with "the masculine conflict" and proceed via "oral sex," "fetishism," "water sports," and "transvestites" to the climax, "virgins." They seem to cover all aspects of sex and all ages of men from puberty to the grave. Despite the title, we discover little pertaining to romantic love. If *we* were selling a book about men in love, we'd make that point in our proposal.

Leafing through the back, we find a collection of loosely organized, informal anecdotes acquired by mail and strung together with analyses that have been bolstered by consultation with psychologists and psychiatrists. The author gives her experts plenty of credit. Her analyses incorporate a great many personal reflections, such as, "I remember a summer weekend when I was single. I woke in the night to find my lover was not in bed."

The Third Wave by Alvin Toffler (hard-cover nonfiction): Al's name is two-thirds as big as his title. That tells us that William Morrow believed his name sells books. Immediately under Al's byline the editor reminds potential buyers that he is "Author of *Future Shock*."

The Third Wave's table of contents reveals 28 long chapters, each subdivided into catchy but lofty-sounding topics like "The technological womb," "The reassurance ritual," "Blip culture," and "A destiny to create." We see, too, such scholarly accoutrements as acknowledgments, notes, bibliography, and a highly detailed index.

Scanning *The Third Wave*'s pages, we find exposition almost unrelieved by quotation or anecdote. Al doesn't city sources for well-accepted information, but does credit the originator of each important concept he refers to or borrows. His messianic prose takes full responsibility for his expansive reinterpretation of civilization's wobbling progress.

The cover blurb is as straightforward as the text itself. There's no leaning on outside authority, only bold underlining of Al's reputation, his book's premise, and its most dramatic points: ". . . another explosive book that will dramatically alter the way we view ourselves and the world around us." "This Third Wave civilization is challenging the power elites in both capitalist and socialist societies." "*The Third Wave* prepares us to cope with a future that is already here."

The Book of Daniel by E. L. Doctorow (paperback fiction): The cover seems to reach for several audiences at once, since three different elements are about equally eye-catching: (1) The word "Daniel" in the title is large, ornate, and set in metallic gold type. Maybe the editor (or his marketing associates) hoped to attract readers looking for warm, personal stories. (2) The cover painting features a young man and woman, serious and looking forward to the horizon, surrounded by a montage of 1970's counterculture—hippies, flag desecration, and demonstrations. It promises youth, romance, and conflict in modern America. (3) Doctorow's name is as prominent as the other two elements. It must have been a vital selling point of this edition.

The blurb on this 1979 edition of *The Book of Daniel* is teasingly low-key: "The central figure of this novel is a young man whose parents were executed for conspiring to steal atomic secrets," which could lead you to conclude that the book is a work of "faction" about the Rosenberg family. It continues, "It is a book of memories . . . about the nature of guilt and innocence." We are warned that the novel isn't just light reading but has a message.

Fiction isn't as easy to scan as nonfiction. Short of actually reading *The Book of Daniel,* you can draw only tentative conclusions about Doctorow's style and approach. But a glance at the copyright page makes us privy to interesting market data: the Random House hard-cover edition came out in 1971, but the Book of the Month Club didn't offer the book until 1975. Soon thereafter came a third printing and the Bantam paperback edition. Why the book club's long delay? A bit of research tells us that *Ragtime* was published in 1975, quickly became better known than Doctorow's previous novels, and tugged *The Book of Daniel* along with it. So, we suspect, it may not be the subject matter but the author who became trendy.

2·6 How to Identify Your Audience When There Are No Similar Books

If you've failed to find a book in any way similar to what you'd like to write about, talk to a good librarian—preferably one who specializes in your general area, be it business, social science, or science and technology. Often, novices fail to find what they're looking for because they don't look in the right places or under the right headings. If your librarian assures you that you've hit on something very new, an untapped market may exist. But you're going to have to convince an editor of that.

Cynthia Orenberg told us she wanted to write a book exposing how the hazardous drug D.E.S. had been misused in the United States. Hundreds of popular medical books had already been published, but none of them on D.E.S. Why, we wanted to know, anticipating editors' questions, should thousands of people want to buy the book? Cynthia uncovered statistics that indicated a solid potential market for the new, shocking information she'd be presenting: an estimated 6 million women alive today had been given the drug, and all their daughters and sons risk cancer because of it. The weight of Cynthia's statistics about her potential readers, along with her well-written proposal, convinced St. Martin's Press to offer a contract. (*DES: The Complete Story* was published in October 1981.)

It isn't always so easy to document a potential audience. When Al Toffler became intrigued with the impact of our rapidly changing technology, he couldn't convince book publishers that a market existed for *Future Shock* until there was widespread discussion of his article for the magazine *Horizon,* in which he coined the term. Likewise, Betty Friedan's efforts to sell *The Feminine Mystique,* a book about feminism instead of the more generally accepted femininity, remained frustrated until she demonstrated via an article in *Harper's* that people wanted to read about the subject. *People* magazine remarked that Betty's book has had "greater impact than most presidents." Still, without a demonstrated readership it might never have found a publisher.

Murray Teigh Bloom also likes to focus on social issues before the publishing business discovers their potential audiences. He did it in his best-selling *The Trouble with Lawyers.* Murray once remarked, "Many of us regard magazine writing as some sort of investment, hoping that every so many articles results in a profitable book contract. Otherwise, frankly, I lose money writing most magazine pieces."

If your fiction doesn't fit into a popular genre—gothic, romance, adventure, mystery, message novel, or the like—it will be very difficult to convince a publisher to take you on. An editor once told us, "It's a good thing James Joyce wasn't trying to write in the United States in the 1980s. He'd probably have starved before he found a publisher brave enough to risk his experimental writing." If you're out to break entirely new ground, your best chance for a reading is to write as beautifully and meaningfully as the best writers in history and submit your *entire* novel to one of the few publishing houses that still delight in discovering unique talent.

Ironically, most of what we've said in this chapter applies to textbooks, too. Educational publishers love to plunge into a field that's been proven lucrative by several earlier texts from competing houses. But few like their *own* texts to compete with one another. If you can create a new text that's similar to the best-selling ones, but jazzier, you've found a potential gold mine. But as a rule, you'd better have some experience in teaching the subject yourself.

Even editors at scholarly presses are influenced by markets. Once their subsidies were pinched, the scholarly press people quickly turned from disparaging commercial publishers to studying their methods. A professor's employer's press might consider only his book's *scholarly* contribution, but once the prof mails his book to another campus, editors there want to know how many other scholars and libraries are likely to buy it.

Chapter Three

How to Find a Publisher for Your Book

W E'VE HEARD DOZENS OF SECRETS AND SURE-FIRE formulas for how to sell book ideas to editors: make up a great title, know the editor personally, appear absolutely gorgeous, get a big-name literary agent, adopt a personal trademark such as always wearing a white Panama suit. We've never been told that the casting-couch technique helped sell a book—but if we heard it we wouldn't be surprised.

What all these legendary formulas have in common is their simplistic nature. Each applies in a limited case or two. All overlook the one factor common to the vast majority of book sales: persistence.

Before an editor will buy your book idea (or, in the case of a scholarly publisher, your manuscript), she has to think it's interesting, believe there's a market for it, trust in your ability to write the book, persuade the company's executives to take a chance on you, and make many other totally subjective conclusions peculiar to the book business. Obviously, the odds are very high against all elements being present to any one editor's satisfaction as she reviews your proposal. You have to present your idea to the maximum possible number of editors, in order to stand the best chance of ending up holding a full house. That takes persistence. If you've done your homework and identified the market for your project, then persistence will sell it for you.

To demonstrate our point, take Frank's book *How to Fix Damn Near Everything*. It went to 24 different publishers, all of whom said, "No thanks." But the twenty-fifth said yes, and it proved to be a steady money-maker for both Frank and Prentice-Hall. Each of the 24 turndowns was for a very good reason. A number of publishers thought 600 or so pages seemed just too long. For many, the book's numerous photos, drawings, and diagrams were prohibitively expensive to reproduce. Several already had fix-it books in their lines that were still selling nicely, even if the information wasn't as up-to-date as Frank's. Some of the editors couldn't put their fingers on any reason for nixing the book—it was gut reaction, pure and simple. (The reasons editors give for saying no, we've discovered, are rarely universal and not generally helpful.) What is important is that publisher number 25 did buy the book.

Novelist Mary Higgins Clark told us that one of her earlier stories didn't sell until her fortieth submission. If she had become bored and discouraged and had stopped taking her package back to the post office, she might never have found her work on the best-seller lists.

Experiences like Frank's and Mary's are the ones to remember as you set out to find a publisher.

3·1 Tools for Nurturing Persistence

The technique of persistence reduces to a simple procedure: find the name and address of every possible publisher of books similar to the one you want to write, and send your proposal to every one of them. If that fails to work, send it to every one of them *again*. This is true even if your idea is for a textbook or a scholarly work. But where do you actually line up all the possible specific names and addresses of actual customers?

PUBLISHERS WEEKLY

If your idea is for anything other than a textbook, your first stop ought to be the publishing industry's bible, *PW*. Each August an inch-thick issue heralds the autumn lines of the most significant publishers; in January an equally heavy volume announces the spring releases. Throughout the year special issues are devoted to religious books, children's books, and other specific areas of interest.

Most libraries of any size subscribe to *PW*. By studying the ads, particularly in special issues, you can make a fairly comprehensive list of publishing houses interested in your general subject or theme. Don't count on *PW* for addresses, however: the ones given are for bookstore orders. The *editorial* offices you need are often across town or in another city altogether.

LITERARY MARKET PLACE

LMP is an annual reference written for book industry professionals. Every major library has a copy or two in its reference collection. Here's where to find the proper name, address, and telephone number of every publisher. Also listed, for most publishers, is the name of at least one editor. Copy down his name and title; it's your key to the magic door.

We cannot overstress how important it is to address all correspondence and submissions to a real, living, breathing *individual* who may feel personally responsible for reading, evaluating, and safeguarding your precious offering. Otherwise, your letter or manuscript goes on the slush pile (that pile of unsolicited manuscripts that's read by the lowliest clerk on the worst day she's had all month). Even if the *targeted* person decides to reject your idea, with a small bit of luck he may feel personally enough involved to share a reason for the rejection and guide you to other sales avenues. There are lots of printed rejection slips in the book business, but they're almost never used for authors whose manner of presentation suggests they may be pros. Even our earliest efforts—half-formed esoteric ideas born of youth and innocence— always brought personal notes from the editors unlucky enough to have been singled out of *LMP*.

How do you pick a likely editor from a list of a dozen or more who work for some of the larger houses? *Don't* choose the editor-in-chief or executive editor, who has little time to look at incoming mail. If the staff is divided into senior editors and associates, it's a toss-up. Senior editors have more clout, but their minds are often on developing tried-and-true authors. Associate editors haven't as much power or prestige, but they're hungry to discover new talent in the day's in-box. In a company with several divisions, select an editor from the one that publishes your type of book. For example, Little, Brown lists a trade division, children's division, law division, medical division, college text division, and education division. To find out whether your idea fits the college text or the education division, you'd have to consult Little, Brown's catalog or *Publisher's Trade List Annual* (see Chapter 2).

Some publishers list only one editor, some just a publisher and no editor at all. But any name and title is better than none.

OTHER TOOLS

Many libraries stock *Writer's Market,* a useful reference book published annually. It includes company names, addresses, phone numbers, and names of editors. Use its thumbnail sketches of publishers' interests, terms, and recent successes to make preliminary decisions for further research in *PW* and *PTLA*. For editors' names, *LMP* is a more complete guide.

Browsing in bookstores can also provide you with good leads to who's publishing what. Studying library shelves is misleading: you can't tell just by the covers what's new, what's ten years old, and what's long out of print. If the American Booksellers' Association's annual convention ever comes near your home, we suggest you spend several days ogling the publishers' booths and buttonholing the salespeople, market staffs, promotion personnel, and sprinkling of editors who line them. You'll learn quickly who is publishing what lines and with what vigor they're selling their products. And maybe somebody will even tell you, "Send that idea to me."

3·2 The Technique of Polite Persistence

It's tough to send out your book proposal a tenth time when you've been rejected by the first nine publishers. But the thing is, they *haven't* rejected either you or your idea. They haven't said anything about you personally; they haven't said your book isn't publishable. They haven't even said it's not their kind of book (unless you have received specific words to that effect—and if you've done your homework as we suggested, this is very unlikely). They have said only that they are not able to publish your book in the current market or along with their current offerings. Again, there are any number of reasons for an editor's decision not to publish a particular book. If you've been in a bookstore lately, you know that the quality of the idea and the quality of the writing are not the most important of those reasons.

Therefore, after you've finished compiling your list of possible publishers, devise a marketing plan. Take into account your temperament, your financial resources, and every one of your strengths and weaknesses, but your goal should be to reach as many different book editors in as short a time as possible, making good use of whatever tips you pick up from editors along the way.

What follows is a strategy we've devised. Like all models, it's an ideal that must be modified to suit your personality and your needs.

TEST MARKET
Make a test mailing to about 10 percent of the names on your list. Choose the publishers you'd especially like to sell to. Send your book proposal with a brief covering letter. Explain that the idea is being sent to a few editors who are your preferred choices and that you don't intend to submit the idea to any other publisher until some specific date about four or five weeks hence (or several weeks after that, if you're not submitting by first-class mail).

If you can afford it, do use first-class mail. In fact, if you live in

Phone Call

the same city, deliver your parcel by hand to the company's mailroom —but *not* to the editor, which is a sure way of starting out on the wrong foot. Enclose stamped, self-addressed envelopes as a professional courtesy. (Courtesy sometimes speeds decisions.)

(If your submission is a scholarly book, send just a brief letter that explains your project and asks whether the editor would like to see the entire manuscript. Always use first-class mail for this.)

FOLLOW UP

Within a few days after the deadline date given in your covering letter, phone each editor you haven't heard from. (People submitting to university presses rarely give deadlines. After a month or so, phone anyway.) Courteously explain that you are getting ready to make a second mailing and were wondering whether the editor was still trying to decide, in which case you'd like to answer any questions he has. If the editor says he simply hasn't gotten to your idea because of being inundated with work, say, "I still think you're the publisher for me, but I'm going to have to mail it to others." Your confidence may impress him enough to pull your offering from the bottom of the pile and put it at the top.

Right now, every editor reading this chapter must be shaking her head over our advice to telephone. Frankly, we were torn as to whether to be forthright with our readers or cautious with the temperaments of the editors we, too, have to sell to. Despite everything we tell you about how to select publishable ideas, some of you are going to fasten onto ideas that are completely unsaleable in today's market or completely useless to the particular editors you single out. We shudder at suggesting that you waste any more of the editor's time than you're already wasting. We hope enough of you have on-target ideas, good research skills, and outstanding writing ability to convince the editors that the found bits of treasure are worth the time spent throwing back useless junk.

ENTER SECOND PHASE

Gather together all your letters of reply and notes from follow-up phone calls. Take into account any constructive comments that can help you improve on your idea or its presentation. File and forget—for now—all unconstructive correspondence. (Later, you'll want to know the names of the editors who signed them.)

After you've made the necessary refinements or changes, mail the revised offering to the best 25 percent of the remainder of your list.

Again include a subtly worded deadline in each covering letter and send stamped, self-addressed envelopes.

FOLLOW UP AGAIN
Make follow-up phone calls. Get to know the likes and dislikes of as many editors as possible, and reinforce in their minds that you are a serious writer with good ideas. Even if this is the only book you ever intend to write, its sales will depend to a great extent on whether you behave professionally in marketing it.

TEST MARKET AGAIN
If any editors have offered comments that led you to revise your idea or its execution, send them copies of your improved proposal, along with covering letters that point out that—thanks to their interest and advice—you have made revisions that you'd like them to look at. If any test-market editor has specifically asked to see an improved version, by all means mention that fact in your covering letter. (Editors who ask for another look don't expect you to include prestamped return envelopes.)

ENTER THIRD PHASE
Duplicate your second-wave mailing and follow-up for half the remaining names (about one-third of your total list).

ENTER FOURTH PHASE
After you've again revised to take into account constructive changes, mail to the rest of your list.

DO IT ALL OVER AGAIN!
This step, which separates the doers from the dreamers, requires that you take a long, hard, critical look at your basic idea or story, your proposal for it, and even the list of publishers you've chosen. Study all the correspondence you've received, as well as all the notes from your phone conversations. Then revise all your material again and go through the first seven steps once more. Sure it's frustrating if you haven't sold a book by this time. We can't blame you for wanting to throw in the towel—but giving up a project you believe in can be even more frustrating. One of our favorite ideas for a medical book has gone through this marketing merry-go-round *three* times. When we started, it was the only idea of its kind on the market, and far ahead of its time. By this point, we've heard of at least three somewhat similar proposals

being circulated by other authors. But we've honed and polished ours until it reads like a jewel, and we still keep it moving. We believe it's a highly saleable idea with a wide audience of readers out there—if it can only get past the conservatism of editors. Somewhere, we know, is an editor who's just beginning to agree.

Chapter Four

How to Package a Dynamite Book Proposal

R*IDDLE:* WHAT'S POWERFUL ENOUGH TO MAKE an editor hand over at least $5,000 to a total stranger?

Answer: A great book proposal.

The sheaf of papers describing your book idea, which goes to every editor on your marketing list along with your covering letter, is commonly called a proposal. The vast mystique that has grown up around book proposals gets in the way of seasoned writers as well as beginners. With rare exceptions, editors contract novels and nonfiction after seeing only proposals, not finished manuscripts. Your ability to write a book is tested primarily by your skill at packaging a proposal. Only if you do a bang-up job at that are you likely to get anyone to read your finished manuscript.

We've deliberately used the ad copywriters' term "package" instead of "write." As Chapter 1 makes clear, selling a book is a commercial venture. Editors who buy book ideas know they're dealing in commerce, and if you want your book to get serious consideration, you must view its submission as a sales effort and prepare as attractive a sales package as you can.

We've also deliberately avoided the term "book outline," sometimes used to describe what this chapter is all about. Calling it an "outline" has led many would-be authors to merely sketch in a few rough strokes on a book idea and put it into the mail. But a dynamite book proposal includes much more than just an outline.

Over the years, we've evolved a fairly standard book proposal form. Many colleagues have sold their book ideas with proposals that were less comprehensive. On the other hand, some authors with more books to their credit asked us how we could sell books on both magazine writing and book writing when they'd been trying unsuccessfully for years. The editor who commissioned our *Magazine Writer's Handbook* told us that our proposal was the seventeenth she'd seen on the subject, and that she grabbed it when it came in "because it was long enough to demonstrate that you knew the subject as well as the market and that you knew how to write about it."

4·1 The Six Purposes of Every Book Proposal

A literary agent once asked if we would (for a sizable fee) draft a book proposal for one of his important clients. Until then, we hadn't realized that our proposals had established a benchmark among agents and editors who'd seen them. Since then, we've heard that copies have been passed around as examples of what authors ought to shoot for. What's the magic we use? Simply the attitude that writing is our *business*. When IBM draws up a proposal to sell new computers, certain basic elements are always included. Why should a sales effort be any different simply because it's Frank Peterson and Judi Kesselman-Turkel trying to sell some new books?

While writing every book proposal, there are six aims to keep in mind:

AIM 1: SELL AN EDITOR

As a writer, you like to think of yourself as an artist. That's why so many of you resist a selling approach. But every editor who reads a proposal knows that the publishing company will have to part with some cash to publish it. (It may surprise you that few professional writers begin actual book manuscripts until they have some of the publishers' money in hand. How much you can expect in advance, and how you should go about getting it, will be covered in Chapter 6.)

The editor has more faith in a writer who is confidently businesslike than in a stereotypic artist. Therefore everything that you put into your book proposal should contribute to its sale. What doesn't help sell the idea doesn't belong. Telling how many unsold manuscripts are in your drawer, or promising that you've got lots of other ideas for novels, is irrelevant. But it is good sales strategy to include any limitations to your product. For instance, if another publisher has just commissioned a book similar to yours, the editor will appreciate your honesty and realistic approach to the market—and may decide to go ahead anyway. When we wrote the proposal for this book, we told as much as we knew about its competitors, describing not just how it would be different, but where it would overlap. We were told that our realistic self-confidence helped sell the proposal.

AIM 2: OUTLINE YOUR TOPIC OR STORY

A book proposal is a promise to deliver. An editor needs a concise description of your book so he can first picture in his *own* head what you plan to deliver, and then talk about it knowledgeably to other editors or to his superiors.

How to Package a Dynamite Book Proposal

With nonfiction, a paragraph plus a tentative table of contents is sometimes enough to show what you intend to include, what you'll leave out, and whether you're going to approach the topic as history, how-to-do-it, personal experience, exposé, or what. In our proposal for *The Magazine Writer's Handbook,* we named the five major titles on magazine writing then in print and added, "These books are all easy to read and filled with tips and anecdotes. But none of them is a *textbook.*" Then we detailed what we would include that would make our approach different from the rest.

For fiction, a complete and detailed story outline is required, sometimes amounting to as many as 25 or more typewritten pages.

AIM 3: IDENTIFY YOUR BOOK'S AUDIENCE

One of the first things an editor wants to know is the size of the market for your topic or story. She'll do her own checking, but she'd like to feel that you have marketing in mind too. In your proposal, tell *who* you think will buy your book, and why. For fiction it may be "the millions of historical romance fans who can't get enough Mary Stewart books" or the "small but steady readership for serious fiction who make John Barth's novels sell into fifth and sixth editions." For nonfiction, it can range from the "100,000 who own crock pots" to the "4 million families who had babies this year."

In our proposal for *The Magazine Writer's Handbook* we pinpointed the audience with a subtitle: "A one-volume course for free-lancers, staff writers, and students." In a proposal for another how-to-write book we spelled out the market more precisely: "350,000 college professors, 1 million engineers, 250,000 doctors, 175,000 physical and life scientists, 90,000 social scientists, and 250,000 lawyers and judges."

AIM 4: ILLUSTRATE THE DEPTH OF DETAIL IN THE FINISHED BOOK

Every editor wants a solid, substantial book. It's important to show that your book will have some meat in it.

Obviously, you can't include many details for *every* topic or scene, or you'll end up writing a book instead of a proposal. But for at least one or two topics or subtopics of a nonfiction work, and for the main characters and events in a novel, it's good to offer detailed facts or description, quotes or dialogue, anecdotes or scenes to show that you know what you're talking about and that you've put in enough thought and research to deliver a weighty manuscript.

For example, in the proposal for our *Magazine Writer's Handbook,* in a page of detail that fleshed out one of our chapters, we subheaded one section, "How magazines pay free-lance writers," and offered a lengthy anecdote to show the type of example we would use. Elsewhere, we named friends and colleagues whose experiences we intended to quote. In actually writing the book, we called on only half the people on that list but added more than enough tips and comments from other friends. In reading our proposal, the editor knew we were simply providing examples and would probably deviate from them once the book took actual form.

In another place in the same proposal, we stated that our book would include real examples of query letters, research notes, first drafts, and edited manuscript pages, and we inserted two illustrations to show exactly what we were talking about. In another proposal we included a Xerox of an article we had written on the topic, not just as an example of our writing style, but as a quick and easy way of telling the editor how much detailed knowledge we already possessed.

AIM 5: ESTABLISH YOUR CREDENTIALS AND SOURCES

For novels, credentials are not of paramount importance, though if you've had fiction published, it's a selling point. If your fiction is based on facts, it helps to mention that. For example, one of our students based a science fiction novel on a seemingly outlandish premise. Actually, it was a theory advanced by a highly respected scientist. That made the entire story line suddenly credible to editors who read the proposal.

With nonfiction, you must convince the editor that you know something about the subject you want to turn into a book. You may think that you're a great writer who can write about darn near anything. (We think that too.) But few editors share that faith. So your proposal has to contain your *specific* qualifications for tackling the subject at hand. Not pertinent are the writing courses you've taken, nor what Norman Mailer once said about your prose at a seminar. Pertinent are the facts that, when reduced to a blurb on the dust jacket, sell books. If you've written a previous book, its sale to even a tiny book club or a second printing before publication date (even if you know it was only 857 copies) impresses an editor more than several favorable reviews.

Here's where you must throw false modesty to the winds. If you're the self-effacing type, try writing in the third person. In our magazine book proposal we led off our credentials with "Kesselman-Turkel and Peterson are not only professional, award-winning writers, they have been teaching magazine article writing, and their students have *sold*." The editor liked that line so much she used it at every meeting that involved our book. We also put in, "As writers, the authors have made their living by writing for magazines ranging from . . ." and listed some of our more impressive titles. We included professional association memberships and schools where we'd taught, and by presenting this pertinent information matter-of-factly, without embellishment, we sounded like businesspeople, not braggarts. (In most of our other book proposals, we've never mentioned the magazines we've written for because that information had nothing to do with writing or selling a book.)

But *The Magazine Writer's Handbook* was to be based not just on our own experience, but on that of the writers we'd learned a great deal from. We pointed out in our proposal that we planned to draw heavily on them. If your proposed book depends on accurate and up-to-date facts, you'll be expected to show in your proposal that you know by name some of the important resources in your field and that you plan to make full use of their expertise.

AIM 6: SHOW YOU CAN WRITE

Admittedly, some editors can't tell a gerund from a gerbil. If your proposal appeals to one of them, you've probably made a sale no matter how weak your command of English. Other editors will skim every third sentence, hardly reading your proposal at all. However, there are still plenty of acquisition editors who know and love lively, lyrical language. Should a carelessly written proposal fall into their clutches, they assume that it represents the writer's best effort (as it *should*) and that if they sign him up, they'll get a badly written manuscript to edit.

Even though your proposal has to concentrate factually on sales potential, you can't neglect your writing skills. Every word has to be correctly spelled. *Every word.* Every sentence has to be well constructed and carefully punctuated. *Every sentence.* There should be no uncorrected typos, *none.* And in addition, your unique style should peek from every page.

4·2 How to Package Your Proposal

It's appearance, as well as content, that sells a book to would-be readers. Editors are used to looking at books as packages. They know that the cover, type face, and white space on a page all add to a book's sales potential. Take advantage of their frames of reference, and package your proposal as effectively as they try to package their books.

We have evolved a proposal package that begins each new major selling point on a separate page, boldly headlined, and with a big margin at the top. That way the editor can quickly locate specific information without having to reread the entire proposal. For nonfiction, the book's table of contents is on a page of its own. Then we spend a page or two discussing each chapter's contents. (For fiction, we use either chapter-by-chapter outlines or a flowing treatment that doesn't delineate separate chapters.) One of our typical proposals can run 25 pages. We'll describe it in detail, with the hope that you'll modify it to express your own particular style.

THE COVER

Just as every book needs a cover, so does every book proposal, fiction as well as nonfiction. We often make ours out of colored paper, and use the same paper for a back cover to protect the last typewritten page. On the front cover goes the title as well as our byline. Somewhere near the bottom (where it can be found easily without getting in the way of a dramatic first impression) is our address and phone number. Some agents prefer that their clients type in the agent's name and address instead. In any case, if you have an agent, her name and address should be somewhere on the cover.

We pick out one important sales pitch to make on our front cover, something we hope will excite the editor to read the proposal at once from beginning to end. For our *Magazine Writer's Handbook* we selected a subtitle: "A one-volume course for free-lancers, staff writers, students." For our make-it book proposals we often use one of the designs our book demonstrates. We once tried to sell an as-told-to book based on the antics and advice of a small-town hustler who had amassed $50 million in real estate speculation. As a teaser, we left the cover completely blank and cut a rectangular hole in it to reveal the figure "$50,000,000.00" typed on the next page. We never did sell that project, but nobody who saw our proposal has forgotten it.

TENTATIVE TABLE OF CONTENTS (USUALLY NONFICTION)

By giving tentative titles to the ten to twenty chapters of your nonfiction book, you provide editors with a thumbnail sketch of the book's parameters, approach, depth of coverage, and similar attributes. Including the word "tentative" in your heading indicates that the editor's input is welcome, as well as the fact that the design may change or improve as you write the actual book.

Take time to construct chapter titles that will help sell the book. If you envision subchapters, or see larger units that include several chapters, this is the place to signal that. If your book does not have chapters—for example, if it's a short book for children, a dictionary, or an alphabetized handbook—you may have to take an introductory paragraph or two to explain what the book is to look like visually.

INTRODUCTORY SALES PITCH

The sales pitch incorporates all the points discussed in section 4·1. It can vary in design from straight exposition to question-and-answer format, lists of points, or any other eye-catching device. Your goal is to make it as attractive and easy to skim as possible.

In our *Magazine Writer's Handbook* proposal we presented our aims in four major sections and headlined each section in capital letters:

"*The Magazine Writer's Handbook* IS BEING WRITTEN TO FILL A NEED." We outlined here the groups that make up the major potential market for the book.

"AREN'T THERE ANY BOOKS AVAILABLE?" Here we listed the five major competitors in print and demonstrated that none did what our book would do.

"*Magazine Writer's Handbook* WILL INCLUDE . . ." Here we described briefly our approach, our content, and our sources.

"HOW DO WE KNOW ALL THIS IS NEEDED?" This is where we demonstrated our expertise by listing our credentials.

CREDENTIALS

Some books' successes depend on the authors' credentials. For example, a medical book needs the expertise of a doctor. A how-to-fix-your-car author should have proof that he's fixed a lot of cars. It's important to put your relevant credentials up near the front of your proposal, either within your introductory sales pitch or under a separate heading. If you want to *downplay* sparse credentials, it might help to bury them within your sales pitch. Remember that even if your credentials are many and impressive, include only those that are pertinent. (Our fix-it proposals have mentioned all the fix-it projects we've successfully accomplished, but that information doesn't appear in any of our proposals for books on writing.)

ANNOTATED TABLE OF CONTENTS (NONFICTION)

For nonfiction proposals we devote a page or more to each chapter. Few of our chapter write-ups fill the entire page; for most, we merely sketch in salient generalizations. For a few, we incorporate anecdotes or a substantial amount of detail. These highlighted chapter write-ups are the ones for which we already have enough information in our heads or in our files to illustrate our approach, style, and expertise; they run two or three pages long. Editors don't expect you to have done all the research needed to write a complete manuscript, but they are entitled to know the kind of job you're prepared to turn in. We've found that this approach is one of the most convincing methods to accomplish that goal.

ILLUSTRATIONS

If your book is going to require illustrations, your proposal should include samples. For example, the proposal for Frank's *Children's Toys You Can Build Yourself* included simple line drawings of some of the finished toys, plus some of the step-by-step diagrams he planned to submit with the finished book. Art directors are as wary of amateur artists as editors are of amateur writers, so if graphics are important to your project, give these sketches your very best effort, or work with a pro whose work will receive the Art director's okay. In a proposal, one good picture is worth a thousand duds. (Chapter 12 will discuss how to negotiate for the cost of illustrations and will help you obtain low-cost art.)

If photographs are essential, your best bet is to include a few 8 × 10-inch black-and-white prints as part of your proposal. You might like to economize by sending along smaller prints, but if you do you'll risk looking amateurish: pros regard the 8 × 10 size as standard.

A word of warning is in order about drawings and photographs. They're expensive to produce in a book. In fact, *color* photographs are rarely considered any more except in high-price travel or art books, which are usually assigned to an author/photographer with a proven track record. So don't suggest drawings or photos unless you're convinced you must have them. When in doubt, include a few sketches or photos prominently identified as *samples* of what's available *if* the editor and marketing division decide that they are a useful addition to the book.

BOOK PROPOSAL GRAPHICS

If you feel comfortable and competent dabbling with artists' tools or typesetting materials, you can dress up the appearance of your proposal to make it look slick, clever, and unforgettable. We sometimes use Letraset or other type-transfer sheets purchased at art supply stores, to set our cover titles in large, bold type. We sometimes set a big bold number for each annotated chapter or, using other transfer devices, call attention to each section of our proposal. For example, we livened selected pages of our *Eat Anything Exercise Diet* proposal (originally titled *The Diet and Exercise Handbook* and reproduced at the end of this chapter) with art-transfer golfers, tennis players, swimmers, and other exercisers. (Production considerations prevent us from reproducing those illustrations here.) For our *Magazine Writer's Handbook* we clipped miniature magazine covers from ads and small logos from actual magazines, and pasted them liberally on the cover and throughout the 25 pages. For *How to Heat Your Home for Less Next Winter* (which still hasn't found a buyer at our price) we created, near each topic heading, an abstract heat-wasting house from a large arrow and some wavy lines.

Sometimes we use colored paper for some of the inside pages— preferably a light color that complements the brighter tones we've chosen for the cover. We use it only if it enhances the overall presentation, and we stick with colors on which black type is easily legible. For example, we may use light yellow for our charts or drawings to separate them from our text, or light green for a magazine article that we've reproduced as part of the proposal. But if the colors get in the way of the words, we stick with white paper throughout.

Unlike manuscripts, proposals should be fastened together with staples or some other device. We usually put two staples at the left edge, booklet style. On occasion we use plastic folders with colored strips of springy plastic binders at the left edge.

Editors are accustomed to reviewing photocopies of proposals, and they prefer a clean Xerox copy to the easy-erase typewriter paper that smudges. Count on making copies, on a good copier that uses regular bond paper, even if you plan to send your ideas to one editor at a time. (The copier we use copies onto colored paper, too, for a cent or two more per sheet.) We never send our original, but keep it to ensure that we'll always be able to make another clean, crisp copy. You'll get the best copies if you start typing the original with clean keys and a new ribbon. (We greatly prefer carbon film ribbons.)

If the editor is not sure you can deliver what your proposal promises, you may be asked to prepare one or more sample chapters. However, the more complete and exciting the proposal, the more likely this chore can be avoided.

4·3 How to Package Your Novel's Outline and Sample Chapters

So far, most of what we've said applies to fiction and nonfiction alike. But there are some real differences between the two that must be reflected in the book proposal. Nonfiction authors have to sell an editor on an exciting *idea,* but novelists have to convince him that they've got an exciting *story.* Instead of a tentative table of contents and annotated chapter summaries, you should include a tentative story outline and several sample chapters.

A proposed novel's story outline can be anywhere from 5 to 50 pages long. More important than length is whether the outline presents the story, important characters, and settings to the fullest. Many authors like to give capsule information about characters in a separate cast list, but it's usually more effective to introduce them as they enter the story. Some writers signal a new character's entrance by typing his name in capital letters or by underlining it, in order to help foundering editors find people they may have missed in a quick skim.

We've found that novelists have a hard time making their outlines detailed enough, especially if they've already completed first drafts. To overcome that problem, ask a trusted friend to read with an eye to picking out all the gaps, inconsistencies, and shadowy character-izations.

Besides the outline, editors expect to see about a hundred pages of the completed novel. Most want the *first* hundred pages, because that's where the eventual reader will have to start. (Novels that don't start well are very hard to market.) Do choose a hundred consecutive pages, not a potpourri. If the novel has chapters, don't stop at the hundredth page but include the entire chapter.

Ordinary staples don't safely hold together the 150 pages of a fiction presentation. Many editors prefer to get them unbound, in a sturdy box, so they can be shuffled during reading. Stationery stores stock heavy binders that hold thick manuscripts; some are hinged on the side and some on top. If you want one, buy it before you do your final typing so you're sure to make your margins wide enough to take binding into account. Some copy centers offer inexpensive adhesive binding. But don't bind unless you feel you must. Your only goals should be (1) to make your presentation look professional and well designed (and remain in one package while being shuffled on a paper-piled desk or transported home in a crowded subway) and (2) to get it into the hands of as many editors as possible, at a cost you can afford. The ultimate object is to sell your book.

Ill. 4·1 ————————————————————————————————

A Book Proposal That Sold, and Was Published As *Eat Anything Exercise Diet*

THE DIET AND EXERCISE HANDBOOK
by Dr. Frank Konishi
with Judi R. Kesselman and Franklynn Peterson

30X6 G. Street
Madison, Wisconsin 53711
(608) 23X13X5

2

THE DIET AND EXERCISE HANDBOOK

Tentative Table of Contents

3

45

How to Package a Dynamite Book Proposal

THE DIET AND EXERCISE HANDBOOK

Control Your Weight

Yourself . . .

Easily . . .

Quickly . . .

No Gimmicks,

No Pills,

No Starvation!

FOR LOSING WEIGHT	"The significance of proper exercise is frequently minimalized."
	    Dr. Frank Konishi
	    Southern Illinois University

FOR LONGER LIFE	"A person 65 and over who is put on an exercise program can gain back at least 15% of his or her physical fitness."
	    Dr. Everett Smith
	    University of Wisconsin Medical School
	
	"A diet of undernourishment can significantly increase a person's life span."
	    Dr. Leonard Hayflick
	    world—famous gerontologist

FOR REMISSION OF ILLNESS	"The scientific community is buzzing over the growing number of reports that a drastically low—fat diet plus planned exercise is curing heart disease." *New York* magazine, 11/8/76

THE DIET AND EXERCISE HANDBOOK

CHAPTER 1

The Diet and Exercise Formula

This chapter begins by pointing out that the problem with most diets is that they severely limit one food or another. That's why, although they work for a short while, they can't be followed over the long haul. The *reward foods* are the usual no-nos in most diets. Yet it is an undisputed fact that it is sometimes as important to eat for fun or reward or compensation as it is to eat for nourishment. (We'll describe some of the fascinating research that proves this.)

Being able to eat for fun is one reason why the exercise-diet that is explained in this book works. The simple basic principle of the book is that you can substitute exercise equivalents for your reward foods. Choose your favorite reward food; choose your favorite exercise; then go ahead and enjoy them.

For example, if you're worried that a 209-calorie bar of Hershey chocolate will make you gain 5 pounds, you can go ahead and eat the chocolate anyway. If you take a half-hour bike ride or a 40-minute walk, you'll totally expend those 209 calories.

In most diets, losing weight is easy. But holding the weight down there isn't. With the diet-exercise plan in this book, *staying* at the correct weight is a cinch if you'll simply get into the habit of doing your favorite exercise regularly. Once you begin exercising, the pleasure derived from *that* provides incentive not only to keep on, but to increase the exercise time—which itself adds measurably to the success of the weight-maintenance program.

THE DIET AND EXERCISE HANDBOOK

CHAPTER 2

How to Choose Your Diet

In the spirit of free choice, you can pick out a diet of your own choosing. First you must figure out your optimum calorie intake. With charts and examples, we'll show how to do it.

There will be *updated* tables of suggested weights for men and women by height and body frame, tables of recommended calories per day for men and women by weight and age, and charts for calculating body frame types *objectively*. We'll also explain the pinch test for determining how overweight you really are.

Once you know your *optimum* calorie intake and have determined your *usual* calorie intake, you can decide whether you want an intensive diet program or a modified one. We'll describe both plans using as our model the fine New York City Board of Health diet plans which are the basis of such successful weight—reduction programs as Weight Watchers.

This chapter will also cover the importance of attitude in the success of any diet plan. And we'll give well—proven tips for successful attitude development to help in successful dieting.

6

THE DIET AND EXERCISE HANDBOOK

CHAPTER 3

Exercise—the Big PLUS in the Health Formula

Exercise erases the anxiety that often attends weight—reduction. It curbs the appetite and that helps dieters too. It firms up flab.

But the diet—exercise formula is not only a boon for dieters. It is a life prolonger . . . and we'll explain how. It is a curative for heart disease . . . and we'll explain how. It can help smokers or drinkers kick their habits . . . and we'll explain how. Better still, we'll let anecdotes from typical men and women explain and encourage at the same time.

Alone, exercise has many healthful ramifications, which we'll enumerate and exemplify. But in concert with a careful diet reduction or maintenance program, its healthful effect is synergistic. We will show through statistics and anecdotes how moderate exercise combined with judicious diet brings rewards beyond what anybody might expect.

We're not proposing strenuous exercise over long periods of time, something many people would reject at once. You don't even have to stick to the same exercise all the time. Mix 'em up if you prefer.

    walking
    bicycling
    swimming
    jogging
    tennis
    stepping
    canoeing
    sex
    mountain climbing

THE DIET AND EXERCISE HANDBOOK

CHAPTER 4

A Consistent Exercise and Diet Program

The best way to use this book, for most people, is in a consistent daily diet plus exercise program—life-long. We'll explain how to do that and how to get started at it.

In essence, start with what you like to eat, chart it, and then determine your usual calorie intake. Now figure out how much you *should* be getting in daily calories to keep your weight down to where you want it. Subtract one number from the other, and that's how much exercise you need to do every day if you don't want to give up any food at all.

We'll make many points via an "actual case record" and diagrams. The final step—again diagrammed—is to use our charts to figure out which exercising and how much. Then keep a record so you make sure you hold to your own program.

We'll design worksheets for this chapter so the reader can use them in designing an individualized program.

THE DIET AND EXERCISE HANDBOOK

CHAPTER 5

A Now-and-then Exercise & Diet Program

You may be prone to binges, and need only sporadic weight control. Or you may be able to keep to your preferred diet with only an occasional break for some "reward" or "compensation" food. In either case, you can use this book another way.

Before you eat the no-no, look up an exercise equivalent and DO IT FIRST. You might find that just looking up the equivalent stops you from eating the extra food. That's OK too since you have made a conscious decision that you don't need the extra food that badly. But if it doesn't, you get the food without getting the extra pounds. (OK, it can be used after a no-exercise binge too, whenever required.)

Here again, we'll let "actual case histories" demonstrate the techniques.

THE DIET AND EXERCISE HANDBOOK

CHAPTER 6

How to Choose Your Exercise Route

OK, we've already talked about how exercise fits into the health formula. Now it's time to explain the mathematics as well as the practicalities of the various exercises you can choose from.

> walking
> jogging
> swimming
> going up stairs
> racquetball
> hiking
> canoeing
> waterskiing
> bicycling
> golf
> tennis
> mountain climbing
> etc., etc., etc.

We'll show the relative efficiency of the various exercises as calorie-consumers. Also, how to perform each exercise for maximum weight loss. For example, running fast doesn't necessarily burn up more calories than running slowly. But bicycling uphill will burn more than bicycling downhill. And a poor swimmer actually burns more calories than a good one.

In general, here are some exercise equivalents:

walking	5 Calories per minute
bicycling	6 Calories per minute
stepping	8 Calories per minute
swimming	9 Calories per minute
jogging	10 Calories per minute

There are other questions to answer as well. Do you burn more by exercising in hot weather? Do you burn more by hiking with a pack or a youngster on your back? What exercises don't burn any calories to speak of?

For each exercise discussed, we'll have pointers from professionals about how to get started, how to get the most exercise as well as enjoyment out of it, and enough lore to make them exciting. Also, we'll want a few medical provisos regarding how much exercise of various kinds is

1 D

safe, and for whom. (No great problems at all. We simply want to reassure readers and ourselves that it's covered.)
As part of Chapter 6, we'll include at least six tables. The first one will help the reader figure out the number of days required to lose from 5 to 25 pounds by reducing daily caloric intake by varying amounts from very little to a great deal; "*no exercise*" is taken into consideration. Then we'll show the charts that'll be much more popular than the first, the ones that help you figure the number of days required to lose the same amount of weight through combined diet plus exercise programs: One *abbreviated* chart follows:

THE DIET AND EXERCISE HANDBOOK

Days required to lose 5 to 25 pounds by
BICYCLING and lowering daily calorie intake

MINUTES OF BIKING	+ CALORIE REDUCTION PER DAY =	DAYS TO LOSE . . .				
		5 lbs.	10 lbs.	15 lbs.	20 lbs.	25 lbs.
30	400	25	50	75	100	125
30	600	19	38	57	76	95
30	1,000	13	26	39	52	65
45	800	14	28	42	56	70
60	400	19	38	57	76	95
60	800	13	26	39	52	65
60	1 000	11	22	33	44	55

An abbreviated chart.
Bicycling calculated at 6.5 Cal/min,
at approximately 7 mph.

THE DIET AND EXERCISE HANDBOOK

The Charts: Exercise Equivalents of Food Calories

A comprehensive appendix, at least 45 pages in length,
graphically shows the reader exactly how many minutes of
doing five representative exercises are equivalent to the
calories ingested in over 500 common foods. Foods are
organized into major groupings, and within that,
alphabetically. For double clarity, the index includes
food names and the appropriate page number.
    Only five exercises are given comprehensive treatment
to avoid an encyclopedic volume. Preceding the listing
we'll include an exercise evaluation chart which tells you
how to relate your own chosen exercise to the tables if
it's not one of the five included in the giant listing.
    An *abbreviated* sampling of entries follows:

How to Sell Your Book

THE DIET AND EXERCISE HANDBOOK

FOOD	WEIGHT (gm.) 1 oz. = 30 gm.	CALORIES	WALKING (Minutes)	BICYCLING (Minutes)	STEPPING (Minutes)	SWIMMING (Minutes)	JOGGING (Minutes)
ALCOHOLIC BEVERAGES							
Beer (8 oz. glass)	240	115	22	18	15	14	12
Brandy (1 br' pony)	30	75	14	12	10	9	8
Daiquiri (1 glass)	100	125	24	19	17	15	13
Scotch (1½ oz.)	45	105	20	16	14	12	11
CANDY							
Almond bar (1¼ oz.)	38	310	60	46	41	36	31
Hershey bar (1⅜ oz.)	40	209	40	31	27	25	21
Milky Way (1¾ oz.)	52	192	37	29	26	23	19
CEREAL PRODUCTS							
Macaroni or pasta, (cooked, 1 cup)	140	205	39	31	27	24	21
Macaroni & cheese (cooked, 1 cup)	225	505	97	76	67	59	51
Popcorn, butter & salt (1 cup)	18	82	16	12	11	10	8
EGGS							
Boiled or poached	48	78	15	12	10	9	8
Fried or scrambled	53	108	21	16	14	13	11
FRUITS							
Apple, raw (2½" diam.)	150	87	17	13	12	10	9
Apple, baked	150	188	36	28	25	22	19
Applesauce (⅓ cup)	100	90	17	14	12	11	9
MEATS							
Beef club steak (3 oz.)	90	175	33	26	23	21	18
Hamburger (3" × 1")	85	224	43	34	30	27	22
Frankfurter (8 / lb.)	56	170	32	26	22	20	17
Liver (2 slices)	75	170	33	26	23	20	17

13/

THE DIET AND EXERCISE HANDBOOK

Judi R. Kesselman & *Franklynn Peterson*, singly or
together, have written six self-help books:

> Children's Toys You Can Build Yourself
>   (Prentice-Hall, 1978)
> The Do-It-Yourself Custom Van Book
>   (Contemporary Books, 1977,
>   Hard cover and paper, 2nd printing)
> How to Fix Damn Near Everything
>   (Prentice-Hall, 1977,
>   Hard cover and paper, 2nd printing)
> Stopping Out: A Guide to Leaving College &
> ' Getting Back In
>   (Evans, 1976)
> The Build-It-Yourself Furniture Catalog
>   (Prentice-Hall, Hard cover 1976,
>   paperback 1977)
> Handbook of Lawn Mower Repair
>   Emerson (hard cover 1975, in 5th printing)
>   Hawthorn (paperback 1978)

Dr. Frank Konishi is a professor in the Dept. of Food and
Nutrition at the University of Illinois-Carbondale. He is
the author of numerous scholarly studies for prestigious
journals dealing with nutrition and exercise.

Ill. 4·2

A Book Proposal That Sold, and Was Published As
The Do-It-Yourself Custom Van Book

How to Get on the Van Wagon
by Franklynn Peterson
and Judi R. Kesselman

TENTATIVE TABLE OF CONTENTS

1 / The Van and What to Do With It

2 / How, When, Where and Why to Buy a Van

3 / Designing a Van Interior

4 / Sitting in a Van

5 / Sleeping in a Van

6 / Eating in a Van

7 / Other Essentials

8 / Van Electronics

9 / Decorating Your Van

10 / Vanning

AUTHORS Peterson and Kesselman are experienced pros in the how—to—do—it and youth culture fields. Peterson's first two books in print were acquired by the Popular Science Book Club, two more are in production with 1977 publication dates, and a fifth is nearly written. He has written several hundred how—to—do—it and investigative articles for major popular magazines, illustrating most of them himself. Kesselman's first book, STOPPING OUT, won spontaneous praise from the education community and brought unsolicited requests for newspaper, radio and TV interviews. A former fan magazine editor, Ms. Kesselman has written two hundred stories for popular magazines.

HOW TO GET ON THE VAN WAGON

How do we get. . . .

HOW TO GET ON THE VAN WAGON

. . . . in on time?

Assuming that the publisher wants to get this book out by next spring when van interest is expected to peak again, deadlines promise to loom important. And we deliver on time! That's true even when deadlines are, by editors' own admissions, damned near impossible.

During August, we're going cross country in our own customized van. We'll use the time to look at plenty of other vans and study how they were built. More important, we'll decide how we can show readers how to build intriguing aspects in them. The trip will also afford a chance for us to photograph hundreds of vans, their interiors, their owners.'. . . Later we can decide how many of which ones to include. Color photos are OK with us if they're OK with the book's budget.

During September and October we could write and illustrate the book. November 1, 1976, we could deliver manuscript and pictures, given adequate incentive to put off or reschedule other profitable assignments we're already scheduling for that period from magazines we supply regularly.

If you doubt the deadline's feasibility, check with these people:

Jim Hoffman, editor of FAMILY HEALTH. We've delivered on time every time. We even brought home a story he'd inherited. Jim discovered, to his horror, that covers at the printer promised an article based on interviews with 25 doctors. Five days later he had the story.

Larry Reich, Associate Editor of Metropolitan Sunday Newspaper Group. Since the 1960's, we've met their exacting standards, and on time.

Barry Feiden, publisher of Emerson Books who wrote up a contract calling for a one month deadline on the first how—to—fix—your—lawnmower ever written. He admitted later that he doubted it could be done on time. But on deadline day, manuscript and pictures were delivered. Did quality suffer? Well, it's the second—bestselling title his company has ever published!

Shirley Stein, former hard—working production editor at Prentice—Hall, Inc. often asked for short deadlines; I would drive across that big bridge to save the time of mailing proofs and dummies both ways.

This proposal, for example, was available in rough draft 24 hours after it was requested. Art and copy polishing were done during the next 24 hours.

HOW TO GET ON THE VAN WAGON

WHY VANS?

In 1976, the van became the object of a whole, affluent subculture. Dealers bemoaned the fact they couldn't get thousands more of them to sell. Detroit plans to turn over as much of its 1977 and 1978 production to vans as possible . . . but nobody really expects the supply to equal the demand. We've spoken to over a dozen dealers, all of whom are afraid that Detroit won't be able to turn out as many vans as dealers can sell. Which means it's a sellers' market . . . book sellers' market too, since van-buyers aren't poor hippies but generally well off, well schooled younger people, roving retired people, working people who can afford vans as second cars. . . .

Anybody who invests $6,000 and more in a van isn't likely to lose interest in it overnight. With a lifespan of five or more years per van, the van culture promises to be around awhile, bringing in new recruits every year.

Sticker prices for new vans range from $5,000 upwards to about $10,000, thanks to air conditioning, special windows, nifty interiors, super-seats, etc. Then most van culturists spend additional money in customizing the back to suit their choice of living arrangements. The playboy set builds bars and beds out of plush velvet. Families build bunk beds and iceboxes. Companies have sprung up to customize vans to order (for prices which sometimes top $10,000). But most people prefer to do it on their own. And from what we've seen, they need help. Some of their jobs aren't safe. Most are needlessly expensive. Some don't use space as efficiently as possible. HOW TO GET ON THE VAN WAGON meets those needs.

B 5

HOW TO GET ON THE VAN WAGON

THE VAN

A primer for the uninitiated

Van: noun.

1) a small delivery truck;
2) an amazingly efficient vehicle about as long as a full-sized station wagon, slightly wider and much higher. Its engine is underneath, leaving almost 100% of its front to rear and side to side space available for productive use;
3) a customized and personalized recreational vehicle with mobility of a jeep, luxury and spaciousness of a small house trailer, the sound system of a discotheque, and the excitement of a stagecoach plying the trails of the rooting, tooting Old West;
4) a subculture which captured America's imagination about 1976, complete with ritual, language, art forms and flat tires.

HOW TO GET ON THE VAN WAGON

CHAPTER 1 / *The Van and What to Do With It*

An introduction to the van.
　+their relative costs,
　　+styles available,
　　　+how they're used by different people,

and plenty of van lore such as
　+the story about the New York couple who parked their van
in a secluded spot (they thought) one night, only to awake
in the middle of a Boy Scout jamboree!
　　+the story about the world's most expensive van!
　　　+the van which is a traveling photo studio,
　　　complete with darkroom, sinks and bed.
　　　　+famous (among van fans) art painted or
　　　　stenciled on the sides of vans
　　　　　+and more.

HOW TO GET ON THE VAN WAGON

CHAPTER 2 / How, When, Where and Why to Buy a Van

New or used van? Is the spring or the fall best? Which accessories are worth the dealers' prices, which ones are not?

Van buyers can get their best deals by shopping around, but it's nothing like the new car market yet; it's still a sellers' market. Even at that, much of the shopping around for a new van is not in search of a better basic price but shopping around for a dealer who has in stock a van with features the buyer most wants or needs. A lot of money can be needlessly spent when buyers need a van off the dealers' showroom floor, but end up taking one with more built-in features than they want or need. One answer to that problem is planning ahead—ordering a van with exactly the features desired. Delivery time? Generally a couple of months.

Used vans are a risk, maybe more of a risk than used cars. Buying from a private owner who has grown tired of the van life is OK. It's probably a good chance to save a lot of money, assuming the van has what the new van owner wants in the way of space, features and looks. Buying a van from a delivery service is certainly buying trouble; they don't sell them unless there isn't a minute's worth of economical life left. If the price is very good, if the buyer knows how to fix cars or can get one fixed cheaply, or if cost is more important than reliability, then a second-hand van can be converted to personal use. The telephone company, in some parts of the country, sells its used vans for $100!

At the same time, let's spend some time discussing the van in comparison to other recreational vehicles:

campers
trailers
jeeps
self-contained campers

HOW TO GET ON THE VAN WAGON

CHAPTER 3 / Designing a Van Interior

A Chinese restaurant menu of features we've seen on vans or we'd like to see on vans, and which readers might like to use themselves. Then we'll discuss how each feature fits into the overall living scheme as well as the mechanics of building (or buying) the feature. This section in particular can be highly illustrated with photos of existing features along with sketches of how to create the feature. Here are some examples:
+what do you do with the spare tire?
+clothing storage made simple (trunk, bags, drawers, hammocks. . . .)
+bed which doubles as seat by day and triples as trunk–like storage area all the time
+chemical toilet (buy one or build one)
+stove: pros and cons of various types
+icebox or refrigerator: build or buy, safe or unsafe, handy or not. . . .
+hi–fi: tape, radio, mono or stereo, where to place the speakers, . . .
+CB radio and the antennae
+table: screw–in top and pedestal which store out of the way after use
+shades and/or curtains: heat control, people control, beauty. . . .
+benches and chairs
+upholstered, painted, wood–paneled walls
+carpeted, tiled, padded (for sleeping) floors. . . .
+two–room suites or bunks
It's a design chapter, not a construction unit. Only enough how–to–make–it details will be included to let readers decide if it fits their skills and matches their other choices for interiors. After digesting this chapter, the how–to–make–it material takes over.

β9

HOW TO GET ON THE VAN WAGON

CHAPTER 4 / Sitting in a Van

What kinds of seats come with a van. What kind of
options can be had at a price. Often a van enthusiast buys a
stripped van and builds or buys seats separately. But
especially important to van novices is *how to secure seats
(and seat belts) to the floor.* We've found a lot of unsafe
seats in vans.
Some of the build—it—yourself van seats convert to
beds. We'll probably cover them in the next chapter.
Anybody who is willing to bolt and unbolt eight pieces of
hardware nightly can remove the seat from most vans.
Playboy types, we've seen, go for richly padded interiors
where bed and bench are one with the walls, floors, ceiling
and. . . . well, we'll have to leave some of the rest to
fertile imaginations. But in any event, since people use
vans for many hours, thousands of miles of intense
traveling, sitting is just as important as armchair
editors might imagine.

HOW TO GET ON THE VAN WAGON

CHAPTER 5 / Sleeping in a Van

     Some people are content to rough it, even in a van.
They leave a maximum of space uncluttered by chairs,
chests, cabinets and such. Then, whenever bedtime
arrives, they simply throw sleeping bags on the floor and
shut their eyes. Others prefer the Ritz. Single beds,
double beds, bunk beds, hammocks, sofa
convertibles . . . they're all in vogue. There's even a
"penthouse" tent-type sleeping loft which sits on top of
a van. It folds flat by day, flips up at night. And they'll
all be illustrated here along with photos or simple
how-to-build'em sketches and text.* We expect to liven
this chapter with plenty of off the road anecdotes.

*Our proposal contains several representative sketches

B11

HOW TO GET ON THE VAN WAGON

CHAPTER 6 / Eating in a Van

Refrigerators cost well over $50 and run on electricity or gas. Iceboxes cost less and can be handmade if a van fan is handy. Most will prefer to buy an icebox.

Since so many motels have ice making machines these days, when the ice runs out—every 3 or 4 days—van trippers can help themselves to some new cooling power. Or they can stop at a coin operated ice machine to buy cooling power.

Stoves vary from the very elaborate to the very simple. It is possible to connect a radar range inside a van. A two-burner gas camp stove is popular. Some prefer simply to toss open the rear doors and light up a simple hibachi charcoal grill. Simplest of all? Wrap your meal in aluminum foil and securely tie it under the hood. Over the exhaust manifold, 25 miles of driving are required for a rare steak. Well done takes 50 miles. After reading about our experiences, other van fans may want to build a simple warming box under their hood too.

We're going to warn against hooking up the big tanks of cooking gas so popular on many trailers. First, there is some doubt about their safety on the highway. Second, they're prohibited in many tunnels.

We can even offer comments on menus since space and facility limitations give cooking in a van a whole new flavor.

HOW TO GET ON THE VAN WAGON

CHAPTER 7 / Other Essentials

Don't forget the chemical toilet if children are
involved. You can buy fancy ones which actually flush.
Other store bought models simply store deposits in a
sanitary, sealed bucket (under chemical treatment). The
lid is odor—tight.

We'll give details for building one model, complete
with outside vents—something the store—bought models
don't feature. Ours doubles as a car seat and, to utilize
space really efficiently, the padded top serves as one
portion of the overall Queen—sized—bed—sized sleeping
area.

Running water isn't hard to include in a van. The
question is, is it needed? If so, we'll show how to buy the
hardware and what to do with it—and where. Portable camp
sinks which store their own supply of water in a compact
unit are easily adapted to van use.

Mosquito netting is something nobody forgets more than
once if they plan to sleep out in a van near the woods.
Unfortunately the Detroit makers don't offer screens
ready—made. Fortunately it's easy to cut and install
either screens or mosquito netting via Velcro, magnet
strips and similar devices.

Sometimes a family decides months too late, "Gosh we
should'a bought air conditioning too!" In a van, unlike a
car, it's relatively easy to add on air conditioning. In
fact, the add—on units are often more efficient than the
factory—installed coolers. We'll show how to go about
doing it or having it done.

B 13

HOW TO GET ON THE VAN WAGON

CHAPTER 8 / Van Electronics

In buying a van, we recommend that advance consideration be given to electrical demands. For most people, the van should be ordered with a battery *double* the capacity Detroit usually sticks in. That allows them to keep the lights and radio running for 8 to 10 hours after the engine is turned off. People with heftier demands— such as an electric refrigerator or other big power eaters—might want an even bigger battery. And for that, the engine needs an even bigger alternator, but that's a fairly common accessory item.

Lights are important for readers and youngsters who don't want to share their bedroom with tigers at night. With slight modification of the van's basic wiring system, it's easy to add lights almost anywhere and in almost any brightness. It's easy to improvise, possible to add as many plugs around the side walls of the van as desired—whichever route the reader prefers.

A CB radio is almost standard equipment in the van culture. And you know what? It really is useful. Forget about the ratchet jawing (in English, "gabbing") on most channels. We stick to the truckers' channel 19. On 19, there's a constant parade of travel information about speed condition Smokey reports (tips about speed traps), traffic pileups, accidents, and—for chauvinists only—beaver reports (tidbits about where the girls are). When things get dull, the truckers' channel makes lively listening. We'll let readers in on an obscure book which lists all of the great music radio stations around the country by frequency and location.

We recommend buying a van without radio, then going to a discount store for a great radio and speakers. Many vans have stereo, so we'll show how to place speakers. We'll show how to wire up headphones so the driver can tune in on CB or the latest tapes while others sleep in peace.

HOW TO GET ON THE VAN WAGON

CHAPTER 9 / *Decorating Your Van*

Everything from adhesives to zippers goes here.

Foam rubber: what kind is both tough and fire retardant; what size is both comfortable and compact; what sits best; how do you mount it. . . .

Fabric: vinyl, cotton, corduroy, velvet, burlap work great; how do you protect it from greasy hands; how do you upholster with it. . . .

Carpeting or tile: which works best and where; how do you clean it; how do you install it. . . .

Curtains or shades: how to make them; how to make them reflective and heat repelling; how to keep them safe but beautiful; how they insure privacy both from within the van as well as from outside. . . .

This chapter deserves lots of photos to show off the finished vans and styles. Ardent van lovers will appreciate all the tidbits right down to and including advice about finding out the color of a van's interior when it left the factory. Customizers often want to touch up nicks or paint an entire new feature to match the original paint job. But Detroit has a zillion different colors. They're all available in cheap spray cans and bottles, but they won't be cheap if a reader has to try out half a dozen similar colors before locating the right shade.

Underlying much of the decorating information are design tricks for making the van not only beautiful but quiet, cool, private, safe and rugged. Some of the fanciest looking decorating schemes, by design standards are also the most practical and effective. And on top of that, some of them are easiest for novices to tackle.

HOW TO GET ON THE VAN WAGON

CHAPTER 10 / Vanning

A blend of van legend, personal experiences, lore and lively tips, all aimed at letting readers either plan in advance or vicariously savor life in a van. In most how—to—do—it books, we can safely assume that readers know *why* they have a lawn mower, *why* they want to build furniture and *what* to do with it once it's built, and *who* they might see on a trip to Grand Canyon if it matters). But with vans, a lot of readers won't have a van, might never get one, and are likely to be very curious about what van living is like. In the format of a do—it—yourself book, we can satisfy the curiosity of the would—be van buyer. And that ought to expand our market substantially.

Topics?

+where to park for the night: some states don't allow overnight camping in highway rest areas, but they think vans are OK. In an if—you—can't—beat—them—join—them spirit, motels often permit vans to park overnight for a modest fee. Garages likewise.

+how do you keep drivers from going bananas on long trips?

+how do you keep kids interested (read quiet) in case the scenery doesn't? Answer to both questions above is easier in a van than in a car or a trailer since a van—if you buy it that way—is all windows and there's scenery on all four sides, often different scenery. CB radio is a source of amusement by itself if all else fails. With a table, kids can play board games when bored.

+does a van family have to feel out of place in a campground used mainly by tenters? (nonsense!)

+what's wrong with parking in a cemetery overnight?

+warning: a van isn't a jeep or an amphibious craft. It can't climb like a mule or swim like a turtle. But you can pick out hard trails like a horse.

Chapter Five

How, When, and Why to Look for an Agent

I F YOU'VE NEVER HAD AN AGENT, YOU PROBABLY think getting one will guarantee that you pass the publishers' monopoly on "Go" and collect $200 many times over. Once you do get one, you'll wonder how he can live in a New York mansion and send his kids to private school on his 10 percent of everything you earn, while you're struggling to pay off a tract split-level in Piscataway, New Jersey.

The ideal literary agent is a cross between Humphrey Bogart and Loretta Young—tough enough to talk wily publishers out of high advance payments and long deadlines, yet supportive enough to nurse dejected writers back to literary health and happiness. Unfortunately there are no ideal agents. The best you can hope for is a Peter Sellers attempting the many disguises of Inspector Clouseau.

Basically, a *good* literary agent helps his authors sell. He helps sell books to publishers by rigorously pursuing the eight steps in selling that were outlined in Chapter 3, thus leaving you free to think up more salesworthy ideas and prepare more dynamite book proposals. In return he earns 10 percent of all the income from those books. But there's much more to being an agent than that basic role. He often helps sell magazine and newspaper condensations or serializations based on his authors' books, taking 10 percent of those proceeds too. He may also help sell book club rights, paperback rights to hard-cover books, hard-cover rights to paperback books, and similar subsidiary rights, again in return for a 10 percent cut of the income. For novels, he may get involved in dramatic rights, though these deals are often complicated by the fact that most literary agents who specialize in books are clustered about the East Coast, whereas most agents who specialize in movie sales are in California. Most East Coast agents use the services of West Coast agents when they want to sell movie rights, and since half of 10 percent looks unattractive to them both, they usually insist that authors part with at least 15 percent. Likewise, when American agents sell foreign rights, agents with offices abroad are often brought into the picture, and then a 15 or even 20 percent commission is common.

Up to 20 percent looks like a lot for spending a few hours (spread over several months) peddling a work that may take you several *years* full-time; that's why writers are rarely satisfied with agents who seem to do no more than mail out their manuscripts and proofread contracts. And now many agents charge more than the traditional 10 percent which has remained the basic commission for generations.

Submitting without an agent, very much as we outlined in Chapter 3, Nancy Hanson of Bismarck, North Dakota, successfully sold her first book, *How You Can Make Twenty Thousand Dollars a Year Writing: No Matter Where You Live.* After readers bought 30,000 copies early in the first year in print, she thought an agent might help her sell even bigger and better. She methodically went through *LMP* and singled out twenty literary agents, then wrote each of them a letter delineating her credentials and some good book ideas.

Some agencies replied that they were not taking on any new clients. Others said they would read and evaluate her future manuscripts in return for hefty reading fees. Most answered that they wanted to work with Nancy, and quoted fees of from 12 to 15 percent. Shocked, she told us about it. We could only reply that we'd heard some agents were asking 20 percent. Naturally, Nancy wanted to know what agents could be expected to do to merit 10 percent, and what they ought to do if they wanted more. She had additional questions about agents, and because most writers ask the same questions, we'll answer them here.

WHAT CAN AN AGENT DO FOR A WRITER?

Although Nancy asked it first, this is usually the *last* question writers ask, because as a rule, writers have little business sense. And that's the primary value of an agent: to be your business manager.

You should handle the research and writing and talk to your editor about editorial matters. Your agent should be responsible for all financial discussions with your editor, and he should be directly in charge of selling your book ideas, although you should be ready to share with him names of any publishers you think are likely candidates for buying your book. The two of you should brainstorm together—in person, on the phone, or by mail—each new book idea you're thinking of working up into a proposal or chapters.

Because your agent is in daily contact with editors who are supposed to keep sensitive ears to the ground, he should keep you abreast of market trends. If a lot of editors seem to be losing faith in how-to-do-it books but are getting interested once again in popular psychology, that information may help you make a sale. If novelized psychological examinations of women in crisis have run their course in favor of heavily researched, fact-based historical dramas, your agent should help you find your way into the new genre or suggest alternatives you can handle.

Unfortunately, most agents who know what editors are looking for use that information only to go through their authors' piles of proposals and pick out some that may earn them fast commissions. Few think to pass on this vital information to their authors. So if you expect an agent to do that continuously for you, you are probably going to be frustrated.

Agent Elsie Goodman once said that you can't find the perfect agent—that you should estimate the areas of your greatest needs and concentrate on finding an agent who fills those needs. Mystery and adventure writer Warren Murphy responded that this would give you about as much chance of finding an agent you were happy with as "reading the entrails of a pig."

I'VE GOT THIS IDEA FOR A BOOK.
HOW DO I GET AN AGENT TO SELL IT FOR ME?

You probably can't. Agents prefer, and are set up, to handle *authors* rather than individual books. Although most do take on individual projects if the subjects are personally intriguing, finding an agent who is intrigued by your particular subject might take more time than finding a publisher.

I'VE SOLD SOME MAGAZINE ARTICLES. NOW CAN I GET AN AGENT?

Probably not. Agents almost never handle magazine sales these days (unless it's an excerpt from a complete book) and they don't see that writing for magazines is much of an apprenticeship for writing books. They may be right.

THEN HOW DO I GET AN AGENT?

The absolutely best way is by referral through a mutual friend or professional acquaintance. The *worst* possible way is to approach with the same conciliatory attitude you'd bring to a potential employer, or to a publisher whom you want to buy your book. After all, you can be sure that any agent who takes you on believes that she will make money with your talent. Whether she will be creative, tough, and persistent enough to *earn* her 10 (or more) percent commission remains to be proven after you begin working together.

Engage an agent as carefully as you would a spouse. You should like each other personally, trust each other's honesty, value each other's intellects, and lean on each other's strengths. Never make a long-term agreement, formally or on a handshake, until you're sure your literary marriage has a good chance of working out. That's usually not until you've been through at least one book sale together. Unwisely consecrated, this partnership can cause more pain and cost than any rocky marital scene.

When introduced to the one agent we stayed with for years, we told him, "We don't like agents. We've never seen one who was worth his ten percent to us. You seem bright, eager, and worth the risk. So here are two projects we haven't yet been able to sell ourselves; see what *you* can do." He sold them fast, got nice advances from good publishers, and proved reliable enough to work with long-term. A business deal became a good relationship. That's the best way to get an agent.

WHO'S IN CHARGE, ME OR MY AGENT?
You are. He's working for you, not the other way around. You have to decide what you want to write, although he should provide plenty of guidance to what the editors are looking for these days. You have to decide how much cash you need to live on while you write, and he should get that much in advance for your project or have a good explanation why he can't.

HOW MUCH SHOULD AN AGENT CHARGE?
Some agents are trying to up their incomes by pressuring their authors for bigger cuts, instead of pushing the publishers to sell more books. No agent should charge you more than these following percentages unless she's doing something extraordinary and valuable for the money. The industry norms are:

10 percent of the proceeds in the sale of a book to a U.S. publisher.

10 percent of the proceeds in the sale of subsidiary rights in your book including such things as magazine sales, newspaper syndication, and the like, but excluding foreign and film sales.

20 percent of the money earned in the sale of foreign rights for a book if another literary agency helps make the deal and splits the fee; 15 percent if no other agency, domestic or foreign, is used to make the sale.

15 to 20 percent of the money earned in the sale of movie rights in a

book if a second literary agency enters the deal and splits the fee; otherwise the standard 10 percent commission should apply.

5 to 10 percent in addition to the above fees if the agent makes a substantial and time-consuming editorial contribution to your book. If he merely suggests improvements to your proposal, reads your book and makes suggestions, and provides similar sales-enhancing help, that's part of the job; he is not entitled to a bonus. However, an agent who makes page-by-page editorial comments for a major rewrite, or gets heavily involved in the planning, organizing, writing, and editing of a book can ethically ask for an extra percentage of that book's income. How much depends on how much of his time and expertise are used, compared with the amount of *your* time and expertise.

THIS AGENT I KNOW WANTS TO COLLECT ALL OF HIS MONEY IN ADVANCE FOR TRYING TO SELL MY BOOK. IS THAT OKAY?
When you get yours, he gets his. Period.

ANOTHER AGENT I KNOW WANTS TO CHARGE A READING FEE TO DECIDE IF MY BOOK IS PUBLISHABLE. IS THAT OKAY?
No, it's not. Either you're not yet professionally ready to have an agent, or the agent in question is not professional enough to represent you.

Let's face it, it takes an agent as much time to sell a small, special-interest book to a low-end publisher for a $1,000 advance as it does to sell a standard potboiler to a major publisher for a $10,000 advance. The difference is that the larger advance earns a $1,000 commission, more than enough to cover her overhead. The smaller project is a money-losing proposition. Many entry-level authors work on these small-advance projects, which is why some agents cover their time by asking for reading fees.

Nevertheless, agents looking for new writers to represent should be willing to gamble some time to read what you're working on. If they see some talent in you that's worth developing, they should welcome you into the fold and help you move up to projects that net the two of you more money. (You, on the other hand, should stick with agents like that at least long enough for them to get back their investment in you.)

As a rule, agents who charge reading fees are seldom worthwhile. The readers, for the most part, are not the agents themselves but kids fresh out of college who are learning the business or—as a friend of ours was—housewives who may have once sold a few hard-core porno novels. Sometimes your "manuscript report" is little more than an individually typed form letter full of platitudes and carefully drafted sales pitches to lead you into paying more reading fees.

HOW CAN I, A BEGINNER IN THE FIELD, GET A GOOD AGENT?

You probably can't. Instead of trying to find one, spend your time trying to find a publisher for your books. After you've compiled a track record that separates you from the dilettantes and rank beginners, you'll be able to talk to agents as one pro to another. It has to be that way for the author-agent relationship to work.

NOW THAT I'VE WRITTEN A BOOK OR TWO, RECEIVED FAIRLY GOOD REVIEWS, AND MADE SOME MONEY, HOW DO I FIND AN AGENT?

By this stage of your career, you've probably met other authors, some of whom have agents. (The best way to meet other authors is to join and attend meetings of a writer's group like the American Society of Journalists and Authors.) Ask your colleagues what they think of their agents. If you like what you hear, ask for introductions. Meet a few in person if you can; at the very least, talk to each of them on the phone. Would you trust this one to baby-sit with your children? Would you lend that one your car? Would you ask any of them to lend you some money until your next royalty check is due? Would you enjoy having any of them come to your dinner parties? As in a marriage, how well your personalities mesh is as important as what you think of each other's talent.

IS THAT THE ONLY WAY TO FIND AN AGENT?

None of the other ways is as satisfactory as meeting an agent through an already satisfied author. Book editors know a great many agents, of course. The trouble is, you wouldn't ask a car salesman to recommend a tough consumer advocate. Will any editor recommend a tough bargaining representative for you?

LMP lists agents and notes whether they are members of the Society of Authors' Representatives. SAR members tend to be the bigger, longer-established agencies, and SAR itself sets stricter standards for members than the other agents' organization, the Independent Literary Agents Association. *Writer's Market* also lists agents along with some general information about their interests, their commissions, and whether they charge reading fees.

Before Judi had written a book, an article of hers appeared in *The*

New York Times. Soon thereafter, a top agency contacted her by mail. Flattered, she did as the letter suggested and made an appointment to see the head of the agency. During her interview she knew enough to ask a direct question: "Will you represent me, or will one of your staff members?"

He had to admit that she would be handled by a young assistant who was just learning the business. Judi was aware that being represented by the great man himself or by his assistant were two very different things. She declined the offer, and nothing she's learned since has made her regret her decision.

Make sure that you too check out not just the reputation of the literary agency that's recommended to you, but the person there who'll be in charge of selling your books.

DON'T AGENTS OFTEN FIND AUTHORS TO WRITE BOOKS THAT EDITORS WANT WRITTEN?

On rare occasion, an editor says casually to an agent, "Hey, I've always wanted to do a book about . . ." and the unusually alert agent says, "Why, I have an author-client who specializes in that." On even rarer occasion, an editor tells an agent, "Look, we've got this series in the works and we need someone who can write about . . . ." In that case, the agent may examine his stable of authors to find one who can handle the job. On the other hand, he may use the knowledge to seek more profitable clients. Just last week we were approached by an agent who knew that Dell was looking for an expert to write a particular how-to book—and he wanted us to submit a proposal through him. We had never heard of the agent and asked him to name some of his clients. He named several writers of how-to material.

The upshot is, you can't expect a newly acquired agent to find work for you, though that's a notion shared by a great many novices. A local magazine writer recently asked us for an introduction to our agent because, she told us, she thought she wanted to write a book. "What do you want to write about?" we asked. "I'll let the agent tell me that," she replied. Of the twelve books our agent negotiated for us, two were ideas initiated by him. One teamed us up with an expert who wasn't a writer. The other idea was suggested by an editor—who didn't want it enough, after all, to pay what we needed. Happily, another editor did.

DON'T AGENTS AUCTION OFF BOOK IDEAS FOR LOTS OF MONEY?

Auctions are the way that literary superstars get sold. Maybe one book out of every several hundred gets auctioned, and though a few each year net their lucky authors hundreds of thousands of dollars, some bids bring in only a few thousand. Sometimes in the past, publishers have stayed out of auctions on books they otherwise had some interest in, for fear of seeming like cheapskates if the prices ended up much higher than they could pay—and the proposals have sold to nobody at all. (We know the logic here doesn't makes sense, but you can't make sense of the publishing business.) So the auction, a double-edged sword, has to be wielded by someone with a good sense of what your book idea may *realistically* be worth. And don't let an agent's success in auctioning another book convince you that he can do it for yours.

CAN'T AGENTS SELL BOOKS THAT I'D HAVE TROUBLE SELLING ON MY OWN?

If you don't have a good idea, backed up by a good proposal, neither you nor an agent will be able to make a sale. If you have a good idea *and* a good proposal, either you or an agent can sell it—if any publishers are currently interested in the idea. Where the agent *may* have an advantage is in reputation: if you're unknown but your agent is known as an honest person who represents other competent authors, then that reputation may help pull through your marginal project—but only if the agent's willing to stake her reputation on you and your book idea.

SO WHY IS AN AGENT REALLY NECESSARY AT ALL?

If you experience difficulty speaking to people and negotiating for yourself, then you may decide an agent is worth his 10 percent. If you have a full-time job and don't have the time to sell and negotiate book ideas during normal business hours, an agent may be worth his 10 percent. Some of our friends feel they need agents to sort out the legalese in publishers' contracts; others prefer to use lawyers with some literary expertise. By now, we can negotiate most of the language in our contracts, and we hope that after you read the next chapter, you'll be able to too.

Some of our friends feel their agents get them higher advances for book ideas than they'd be able to get on their own. On the other hand, we've recently found that *we* made more money on deals we negotiated and then turned over to our agent to finalize. That's when we decided to try living without agents for a while.

Reputation

Chapter Six

Book Contracts: How to Read and Negotiate Them

YOUR FIRST BOOK CONTRACT IS LIKE YOUR FIRST day of school and your first home mortgage rolled into one. The language is strange, the terms vague, the demands stringent, the threatened punishments harsh. Even most local attorneys are hard-put to make sense of the legalities and terminology peculiar to the business of writing and selling books. In fact, the most valuable service literary agents offer is their specialized understanding of contracts, gained through years of servicing authors. (That's why, in general, an experienced agent is preferable to a beginner.)

Most book deals are made orally before the contract is prepared. The editors and you (or your agent if you have one) agree on the figure for your guarantee against royalties and on the percentage of the cover price you'll receive for each book sold. You'll agree on the manuscript deadline, the length of the book, and whether you're to supply illustrations. Perhaps you'll discuss one or two other points. But when the contract finally is mailed to you (or your agent) it will contain at least a hundred other points on which you and the publisher must agree.

Lots of negotiation should take place *after* the contract has been sent to you or your agent, because any contract prepared by the publisher is naturally slanted very much in his favor. The revisions you are able to write into the printed contract may be the most rewarding words you will ever write. We can't make you a crackerjack negotiator in one chapter, but we can offer you a cram course in understanding a contract and dealing with an editor. We can give you the benefit of our experience on sixteen contracts, and the experience of our colleagues who shared their successes and sticking-points with us. Armed with all this, you'll be better equipped than most beginning agents.

As befits a romantic industry, contract negotiation in the publishing world has the aura of moonlight and mystery. Authors often share the results of their negotiations with close friends, but they don't want posterity to know how well—or poorly—they came out in their book deals. We've used our friends' experiences by promising

79

anonymity, and that's why you won't see any author's name mentioned in this chapter.

We do make frequent reference to the Authors Guild, which has done more for getting authors' protections into contracts than anybody including literary agents' trade associations. The Guild prepared its own model contract, and some of the author-protection clauses it wrote in were later adopted in most publishers' printed contracts. With your help, we'll get more model clauses accepted as industry norms within the near future. To that end, we include them in our discussion.

6·1 The Art of Negotiating a Contract

Simply stated, negotiating is demanding what you want most while being prepared to give up in exchange the things you want least. All publishers' contracts contain a few clauses you can expect to get changed with little effort, and some that Swifty Lazar would be hard put to alter. If you know which are which, you'll spend your negotiating energies more efficiently. Your aim should be to get as much as you can while wrapping up negotiations within a reasonable time—so you can start writing while the editor is still excited about buying the book.

To understand the basics of book negotiating, you have to know some basic publishing economics. Theoretically, you will be paid a royalty for every copy of your book that's sold. Depending on the kind of book (hard or soft cover) and publisher, that can range from 6 to 15 percent of the retail price. Since your first royalty statement (and therefore your first royalty check) will arrive no sooner than four months after your work is shipped to the bookstores, you could work for at least two years without seeing a penny for your labors. Since few of us could manage so frugal an existence, the publishing industry developed one of its greatest misnomers: *the advance.*

In poorly drafted contracts, the advance amounts to a loan against anticipated royalties. If you do not protect yourself in your contract, your publisher could theoretically force you to pay back whatever part of the advance your book fails to earn back in royalties—even if the publisher's inept handling has caused the shortfall. Fortunately, authors have progressively negotiated tougher and tougher clauses on advances to where the entire sum is virtually unrecoverable unless you fail to turn in an acceptable manuscript. Even if you turn in what is deemed to be an unacceptable product, most contracts permit you to keep part of the advance as acknowledgment of the effort you put in.

In short, the advance is no longer an advance but a guarantee.

That's how it ought to be. And authors should universally stop accepting advances and begin demanding guarantees.

Whichever it is, the guarantee or advance, it is paid to the author in several installments. Most common is doling out half the amount on receipt of the signed contract and half on delivery of the manuscript. If you're a beginner, or if the editor has some other reason for being uncertain that you can complete your promised book by the agreed-on deadline, the advance may be divided into several smaller payments that are sent out as you deliver chapters or sections of the book.

When you and your editor agree on basic terms, one of the most important figures is the amount of your guarantee or advance. Although you can count on its being deducted from the royalties and other income that your book later earns for you, you'll be able to count on having reaped at least this guarantee money if the book doesn't earn enough to repay the advance. For most books, the guarantee or advance is the *only* substantial money the writer earns, so you can see why you should put your greatest effort into getting the largest guarantee possible.

Negotiating begins almost as soon as an editor says, "I like the book. I think I'll buy it." Instead of a grateful thank you, you ought to counter with, "How much can you pay?" meaning, in professional parlance, "What's the proffered advance?" But because beginners are afraid of losing that first precious sale, talking money is the hardest thing for them to do, and that's why so many want agents. To get past your natural fears, just remember that talking money is a professional thing to do.

Seasoned friends agree that no matter *what* figure the editor comes up with, you should ask, "Is that your best offer?" At that point you might hear the classic hard-luck story about how bad the book business has been and how many restrictions management imposes. On the other hand, the editor might actually raise the offer. If he suggests only that the amount is negotiable, immediately make your own counteroffer: "I was counting on at least . . ."

If you get the amount you ask for, kick yourself and remember to ask for more next time. But your counterproposal will probably be turned down. In that case, be prepared to answer, "Well, that'll have to do, but in return I'm going to expect some good percentages on royalties and subsidiary rights, including an escalation clause on the royalties." Guidelines in this chapter will help you choose the specific percentages to hold out for.

Before closing on this tentative verbal deal, make sure that the editor is aware that you know enough about publishing to expect to continue negotiating *after* you see what his company's contract offers. Never forget that until it's signed by *both* you and the publisher, that piece of paper is merely your editor's written offer. He fully expects to see it changed as you negotiate.

Unlike your oral negotiations, points in the written contract cannot usually be agreed on in a single session. We hope you're going to want some substantial changes written in, and your editor will not want to give you an instant yes or no. Even if he has the authority to make the final decision on the changes you ask for, he may tell you that he must consult company specialists, in the hope that his relationship with you can remain warm, cordial, literary, and unbusinesslike.

If you have an agent negotiating for you, review the contract yourself after all the changes are made. We never used to do that, but then we discovered too late that our busy agent overlooked a percentage that should have been changed. The oversight wound up costing us several thousand dollars in subsidiary rights.

When *you* negotiate your contract, start with the clauses that are *easiest* to change. (They're discussed in the next section.) Score a few points for your side; gain the editor's respect. Then move into the tougher areas (which we'll explain next). It's important to keep in mind that you're asking for what you're *entitled* to as an author—and what you need in order to earn a decent living at your work. Fight to get as much as you can in the clauses that are most important to you. On the least important, don't push too long or too hard. Listen to what the editor is saying; he has some needs and priorities too, and if you're sensitive to his, you can more easily demand that he be more sensitive to yours. On the other hand, be careful not to assume the tough guy posture taken by too many yearling negotiators we've watched. If you try to get every contract clause turned around just to prove you can, negotiations will degenerate and the editor will turn to more tractable authors. Since the editor always holds the high card, you may find you've lost the contract for your book.

6·2 Contract Clauses That Are Generally Easy to Change

The following are usually among the easiest clauses to get added, deleted, or altered in your favor. It makes good negotiating sense to assume that your editor will okay the changes without too much pressure. If you do run into opposition, it's fair to ask why this publisher is so much at odds with industry norms.

OPTION CLAUSE

Almost every printed contract includes a clause giving the publisher an option on your next book. In fact, the standard Prentice-Hall contract requested an option on our next two books. You might feel flattered that your publisher wants to publish your next book or two, but hold on: the wording doesn't say it *will* publish, only—to use Prentice-Hall's language—that "the options *may be* exercised by the publisher by written notice to the author of its election to publish, given within 60 days after receipt of the *complete and final* manuscripts of such works."

We've italicized the key words. If you had blithely signed that contract, on the next two book ideas you wanted to sell you'd be obliged to write complete manuscripts and offer them to this publisher first (whether or not it's the best publisher for that book). Then it could decide at leisure whether it wanted the books.

When you get to be a best-selling author who commands six-figure advances, you'll have considerable trouble getting rid of an option clause. But now you should be able to get it stricken totally. If not, there are several modifications you should try:

1. The publisher should agree to an option clause that specifies that you turn in not a completed manuscript, but a comprehensive proposal no more than 25 pages long.

2. Terms for the optioned book should be mutually agreeable to both parties. Many printed option clauses offer terms identical to those in the contract you are negotiating at the moment. Some leave out terms entirely, and you're free to turn down any unacceptable offer (otherwise it's a violation of the Fourteenth Amendment to the Constitution, which outlawed slavery). Your publisher should be content with "first right of refusal" to your next book on your terms.

3. As an editor we know says, "If we don't want to do business with each other again, we won't, so what's the point of an option clause anyway?" You should have the right to make the publisher exercise its option when *you're* ready with your next idea—not, as is typical of option clauses, only after acceptance or publication of the present manuscript. This way, you can begin to sell your next book before the editor finally okays your latest manuscript. One manuscript we turned in sat on an editor's desk three or four months before she finally read it to see if it was acceptable. Another took three years from acceptance until publication.

4. Your publisher's response time, in accepting or declining your next

work, should be limited to 30 days. Thereafter, you should be entitled to take it elsewhere.

RECOVERABLE ADVANCE

Some contracts lead the unwary to agree that if a book fails to earn enough royalties to repay the advance, the publisher can ask the author to refund the difference. That just isn't done, *ever*. Don't sign such an agreement without making a mighty hue and cry, and only after you've tried every possible publisher without success.

Most contracts permit publishers to recover advance money if you don't produce a manuscript within a reasonable time after the agreed-on deadline. That's fair. But if this is your second book for the same publisher, be wary of clauses that let it recover its money from a book you have *already* written under a previous contract. It sounds like a small point, but several publishers we know have held up money legitimately earned on an earlier book in order to play tough in a legal or economic dispute over a later book. Protect yourself by separating the money earned from each of your books.

If the book you're about to write depends on some timely event or living person, what happens if the person dies—or if the event ceases to be timely? If you can't complete the book through no fault of your own, would you have to repay the entire advance? Yes, under the language found in most unrevised contracts. If your book falls into this category, protect yourself by striking out as many parts of the advance recovery clause as your publisher can be made to agree to.

BANKRUPTCY

Incredible though it sounds, many publishers' contracts do not protect authors against the company's possible financial demise. It is relatively easy to get an editor to insert such protection. The standard wording that we use is:

> If the Publisher shall become bankrupt or file a petition for an arrangement under the Federal Bankruptcy Acts or if it shall make a general assignment for the benefit of its creditors or if a receiver or a trustee shall be appointed of all or substantially all of Publisher's assets or if Publisher shall take advantage of any insolvency law of any state of the United States, or shall commence the liquidation of its business, then immediately upon the happening of any of the said events, upon written notice by the Author, Publisher's rights under this agreement shall terminate.

This frees you to promptly sell the work again elsewhere (assuming you can find a second buyer).

Don't assume that protection like this is only theoretical. When a friend of ours read about a bankruptcy action against his publisher, he acted quickly to recover rights in his published paperback novels, and resold all six of them in a package to a solvent publisher—for more of an advance than he had received the first time.

OUT-OF-PRINT CLAUSE

If the publisher doesn't keep your book in print, there's small chance you can earn royalties on it, and you should be free to find a new publisher. Most reasonable publishers whose contracts don't already contain such protection for you will agree to put it in. The language we've seen inserted is:

> If the book shall go out of print and off sale for six (6) months or more in all editions, including reprints, whether over imprint of the Publisher or another imprint, and if there is no contract for any impending edition, and upon notification from the Author, if the publisher does not agree to reprint the work within six months, this agreement shall terminate and all rights of the Publisher in connection with the book shall revert to the Author. Such termination shall in no way affect any rights granted to third parties prior to such termination date or the right of the Author or the Publisher to participate in the proceeds therefrom as hereinabove set forth.

The same clause of the printed contract also usually provides that when the book goes out of print, the author can buy the plates, negatives, and unsold copies at cost. Some clauses also permit the writer to bid on, or to buy at a price equal to the highest bid, all copies that are to be remaindered.

6·3 Contract Clauses Worth Working to Change

Depending on how tough a negotiator you are and how much the publisher needs your book at the agreed-upon advance, you may be able to make worthwhile changes in some of the tougher contract areas. You'll never know unless you try.

ROYALTIES

Most publishers have fairly fixed limits as to how much royalty they're prepared to pay you. Unless you've built up some clout, you may have trouble increasing the basic percentage. But you should succeed at getting an escalation clause built in so that if sales do nicely, you'll get a higher percentage after the first printing is sold out.

For adult hard-cover trade books, the most common royalty schedule is:

> 10% for the first 5,000 copies sold,
> 12½% for the next 5,000 copies sold,
> 15% on all copies thereafter.

Some negotiators have obtained 12½ percent for the next 2,500 copies and then 15 percent for the rest. A few have gotten 15 percent for all books sold. On the other hand, on books with lots of four-color pictures that make reprints expensive, there are contracts written for as little as 7½ percent royalty across the board.

Almost all royalties are figured on retail or *list* price. In other words, a 10 percent royalty on a book with a cover price of $9.95 is 99½ cents. A few publishers try to pay royalties based on *net* price. Since standard discounts range from 40 to 50 percent, a net arrangement pays you royalties on only 50 to 60 percent of the books' cover price. We've signed agreements like that when we've been convinced that *that* publisher would sell more than twice as many books as any other, so we're not suggesting you turn down such deals—just understand what you're getting before you sign.

Paperback royalties are less standardized than hard-cover. We've seen them range from 6 to 20 percent of list. On trade paperbacks, percentages are sometimes identical to hard-cover royalties, but often lower. The Authors Guild recommends a minimum of 6 percent for the first 150,000 copies sold and a minimum of 8 percent thereafter.

The Guild's most recent survey of mass market paperback royalties showed that the most usual figure was 10 percent on all copies. Other common arrangements were 10 percent for the first 50,000 with 12½ percent for sales beyond that; 8 percent, often with an escalation clause to 10 percent; 12½ percent; and 15 percent. These figures are high for the industry but most of the respondents were probably seasoned authors.

100%

SUBSIDIARY RIGHTS

Subsidiary rights are those sold or licensed to magazines, newspapers, cassette manufacturers, and so forth who want to reproduce excerpts, condensations, recordings, or serializations of the book. For these rights, the buyers usually pay the publisher. Your contract haggling should be restricted to how that income is to be split. Many contracts come with printed or typed-in figures that share *all* subsidiary income 50–50, and many authors (especially of nonfiction books) tend to ignore the figures and expend their negotiating energies on other parts of the contracts. This is dangerous, for two important reasons: first, many sleepers earn a great deal of subsidiary income. Frank's *Build-It-Yourself Furniture Catalog* earned more money from subsidiary rights sold to magazines and book clubs than from bookstore royalties. Second, if you allow the 50–50 split to remain in your early contracts with a particular publisher, you're establishing a precedent which may be tough to break later on when you decide that you want your fair share of subsidiary rights income.

Here are the percentages suggested by the Authors Guild:

First serial sales (magazine, newspaper, and similar abridgments made before publication of the book): The author should retain 100 percent unless the publisher arranges the first serial sale, in which case it is entitled to the agent's standard 10 percent commission.

Paperback licenses, book club licenses, and second serializations (which are magazine, newspaper, and similar abridgments made *after* publication of the book):

Author 50%, publisher 50% on the first $10,000 of gross income,
Author 60%, publisher 40% on the next $10,000,
Author 70%, publisher 30% above $20,000.

Stage, motion picture, TV, radio, and similar rights: It's customary for established authors to retain 100 percent of the money earned from the sale of these rights. However, if you do not have an agent, the publisher can expect a 10 percent agent's commission for selling them for you. Some publishers feel entitled to 20 percent, others even hold out for an outrageous 50 percent. To quote the Guild: "Authors . . . who concede a large share to the publisher on the theory that the rights will never sell sometimes live to regret it." (If you think nonfiction book ideas don't sell to the movies, consider *Everything You Always Wanted to Know About Sex but Were Afraid to Ask.*)

FOREIGN PUBLICATION   75%

For sales made to the British commonwealth, the publisher should never expect more than a 20 percent share; elsewhere, no more than a 25 percent cut. Quite commonly, the author keeps 100 percent of this income.

d. OTHER RIGHTS

Authors typically retain 100 percent of the income from the sale of other subsidiary "novelty" rights such as commercial exploitation with toys and tee-shirts.

REVERSION OF SUBSIDIARY RIGHTS

If your publisher has made no sale of subsidiary rights for you within the twelve or eighteen months after publication date, then all interest in those rights should revert to you. You (or your agent) will then be in charge of making whatever sales you can, and you'll enjoy 100 percent of any income from them.

RESERVE AGAINST RETURNS

Many contracts have clauses that permit the publisher to reserve up to 50 percent of your earned royalties for a year or two past the time you have a right to the money, as a cushion against possible bookstore returns. For a friend who had a runaway best seller, that clause cost him a year's interest on $50,000. Try to get the clause deleted or at least reduced to a 20 percent figure. (Normal returns are about 20 percent.)

OFFSETS

When it comes to repaying the advance, try to separate the subsidiary rights income from your royalties. The publisher should recoup its advance *only* from the royalties on the sale of your book, not from offsets—a financial term that, in this context, means setting the subsidiary rights income due you into the column marked "royalties" and deducting it from your advance.

In all fairness, you should be paid your subsidiary rights income whether or not book sales have chalked up enough royalty to repay the advance. Your publisher's primary agreement with you was to work as hard as possible to sell your books. If you can't entirely stop an offset, you may be able to negotiate a limitation such as: "No more than 25 percent of subsidiary rights income may be offset to cover repayment of the advance."

FLOW-THROUGHS

Your share of the money paid to your publisher for subsidiary rights sales, such as from book clubs, should "flow through," or be paid to you as soon as the publisher receives it. Otherwise it sits in the publisher's bank, collecting interest until the next accounting period, which can be as long as nine months away. Companies in business to publish books are more likely to agree to flow-throughs; those that act more like finance lenders are hard to budge.

EXPENSES NOT PART OF ADVANCE OR ROYALTIES

If your book involves extensive or expensive research and travel, you may be able to negotiate an expense account as part of your contract. Typically, this expense money is not considered part of your advance and is not recoverable from your book's income. On the other hand, expense money is easiest to negotiate if it *is* recoverable from royalties or subsidiary rights sales. Which arrangement you get depends in part on your negotiating skills.

When you are putting together a book that depends on other authors' excerpted works, it is sometimes possible to get an additional permission budget so that payment for using their writing doesn't come out of your advance or royalty. For a book that includes illustration expense, see the beginning of Chapter 12.

FREE COPIES

Any publisher that contractually offers fewer than ten free author's copies is an unconscionable cheapskate—a fact you will no doubt learn from his other clauses as well. We've negotiated for as many as 60 free copies of a hard-cover book (in return for helping to publicize the book), and friends have been able to get up to several hundred copies of their paperbacks.

DEADLINE FOR THE COMPLETE MANUSCRIPT

Don't be too sanguine about how little time it takes to write a book, especially if this is your first attempt. And don't believe the too-often-whispered rumor among neophytes that publishing deadlines don't count. Almost without exception, your editor will expect your final manuscript by the deadline that's in your contract. Editors are under considerable pressure to get books in on time, and often a book appears in the publisher's catalog while the author is still working on the manuscript. If you suspect that time may become a problem, get the deadline changed before you sign.

As more and more publishers pay advances more and more slowly, we've been changing the deadline entry. Instead of accepting a firm date, we calculate the number of days (or months) between the contract signing and the expected completion date and offer as our deadline "X days after receipt of the first payment of the advance." That tactic either encourages prompt payment or wins an automatic extension in the deadline. Either way, we've placed some of the onus for promptness onto the publisher's shoulders too. On the first contract in which we used this ploy, the publisher's tight-fingered accountants extended our deadline by almost three months. Needing the extra time after all, we turned in the manuscript three months later than the editor had hoped for—and were able to point out that we were indeed on time.

UNSATISFACTORY MANUSCRIPT
As drafted by publishers' attorneys, contracts usually cite no deadlines for the crucial matters that are in the publishers' hands. For example, most contracts require that your manuscript be deemed "satisfactory" before it's accepted and your final advance payment is issued. But there's no deadline by which the editor must decide whether it's satisfactory. With most professional authors and editors, that's no problem. But what if the sales force decides there is little interest in the book, and the publisher wants to dump it? What's to stop the company from arbitrarily declaring your writing unsatisfactory long after you've turned in the book? Absolutely nothing unless you thought ahead to write in a deadline of 30 to 90 days for the publisher to inform you if it finds your manuscript unsatisfactory.

If the editor *does* say your book is unsatisfactory, even after you've made all the revisions requested, she may ask for all or part of your advance money. We don't think she's entitled to any of it. The Authors Guild doesn't think so either. But your publisher will, so get the amount of recoverable advance for an unsatisfactory manuscript limited right in the contract. The Authors Guild feels that if you can't limit it to zero, 30 percent should be the maximum permitted.

PUBLICATION DEADLINE
To protect you and other authors against production and editorial delays (which can ruin your book's sale if a competing book comes out, and at the very least can hold up monetary returns on your writing-time investment), the Authors Guild model contract includes a clause holding the publisher accountable for getting your book into print within twelve months after you deliver the manuscript. Of course, exceptions are made for war, fire, and other disasters, but even in these extreme circumstances, publication must take place within 24 months of the manuscript's delivery (or within six months after the disaster's end). If your publisher agrees to this clause, you can recoup all rights if publication is delayed longer. Whether you have to pay back all or even

part of the advance depends on your negotiating skill. Certainly, the publisher should have to forfeit something for keeping your manuscript for that period of time.

Neophytes wonder why anybody who's worked so hard to sell a book in the first place would want it back to sell it all over again. First of all, you don't *have* to take back all your rights—you just have the authority to do so if you want. In fact, you can renegotiate a new contract with the same publisher if you think you'll get a better deal the second time around. But the mere presence of a clause like this is often enough to keep you from having to exercise its options.

Two of our friends, one a novelist and the other a recognized science writer, are kicking themselves for not fighting for this clause. Over three years ago each wrote a book for one of the biggest paperback publishers. Both books were accepted by the editors and paid for by company accountants. Since then, whenever either book is scheduled for publication, another more exciting project comes along and shoves it off the calendar.

6·4 Contract Clauses Very Hard to Change— but Worth Fighting For

Several of the standard contract clauses are extremely detrimental to authors. Established writers have been struggling for years to pry away at these coffin nails. We hope you'll join in the fight with every contract you negotiate. If we *all* hold out long enough, and combine that effort with organizational clout from groups like the Authors Guild and the American Society of Journalists and Authors, we'll achieve some modification of these unacceptable paragraphs.

INDEMNITY CLAUSE
Under most publishers' standard indemnity clauses, you agree to turn in a book that is *totally* original, drawn from sources that are neither copyrighted, invasive of anyone's privacy, libelous, slanderous, obscene, nor in some other way legally bothersome. If anybody decides to challenge your book in court by suing you and your publisher, the publisher reserves the right to hire the lawyer while you foot the bill. If you read that in a novel, you'd consider it ludicrous. But this real-life indemnity clause has proven a hardship to the good, careful, *successful* authors who've been hit with all kinds of expensive nuisance suits only

to find that their publishers' legal divisions have become equally grievous nuisances.

To insert fairness, there are several steps you should take during contract negotiations. Begin by insisting that the publisher's language be entirely replaced by the appropriate clause in the Authors Guild model contract, which is fair to both author and publisher. It holds the author accountable for his mistakes but frees him from blame for materials added to the book at the publisher's insistence. This model clause, outlined below, also contains additional valuable protections. If you can't get the clause inserted in its entirety, strive to get as much of it as possible:

1. It holds the author liable for damages for breaches of the warranties such as libel, copyright infringement, and violation of privacy that are sustained by *final* court judgment (after all appeals), but not for out-of-court settlements that publishers otherwise are likely to favor.
2. It limits the author's liability to a percentage of the total money payable under the contract. (The Authors Guild recommends 30 percent.)
3. It permits the author to hire his own lawyer, and if he does, to be exempt from paying the publisher's attorney fees and court costs.
4. It limits the amount of earned royalties and subsidiary rights income due the author that the publisher can hold in escrow (in its own account) if someone files suit. (The Authors Guild model recommends 30 percent as a maximum, but adds that there never should be more held than the amount claimed in any lawsuit.)

QUARTERLY STATEMENTS

If you pick up the telephone and ask your editor to tell you how many total copies of your book have been shipped to date, he or she will usually be able to give you a computerized read-out that's accurate as of 9 A.M. that same day. When it comes to paying up the royalties your book has earned, however, your editor has to defer to an office full of myopic ladies and gentlemen who twice a year key-punch incomprehensible figures onto your royalty statement, which is then sent by Pony Express to the other end of the continent, where a check is issued. Consequently, the publisher has free use of your money for from three to ten months after your book legitimately earns it.

As one modest step toward getting what is due you with a bit more speed, the Authors Guild model contract calls for quarterly (instead of semiannual) reckoning and payment. If you'd like to hear a really spirited defense of antiquated accounting methods (even though most publishers' royalties *are* computerized), demand that your contract grant you quarterly royalty statements and payments.

PROMOTION BUDGET

Editors are past masters at promising authors that they'll advertise, publicize, and otherwise ensure the popularity of the books they sign. But if you like controversy, just try to reduce those promises to a contract clause. A promotion budget is considered a matter of faith and, like most faith, has a habit of forsaking those who need it.

Hundreds of underpromoted authors are now strenuously suggesting that a minimum dollars-and-sense promotion budget be written into every contract. A few publishers have actually agreed to our demands.

6·5 How to Make a Contract Conform to Negotiated Changes

Type in negotiated additions either at the appropriate place or, with asterisks or other symbols of reference, elsewhere on the page. Cross out all negotiated deletions in ink. Wherever changes have taken place in a printed or typed contract, both parties are supposed to write their initials in the margin to show that they've read and agreed to the changes. Since book contracts are typically filled with alterations, we've seen them go through without the initialing, but we suggest you play safe and insist that this customary formality be practiced by both you and the publisher.

You will receive several copies of your contract, all unsigned. After you negotiate and make the agreed-on changes, and you (and sometimes a witness) sign all the copies, return them all. You should receive one copy for your files, signed by an executive of the publishing house. (Before mailing back the contracts, we make a Xerox copy for our files in case the editor wants to reopen negotiations at that point.)

When you open the envelope that has your legally binding contract inside, if you're lucky a check for the first part of your advance will fall out. Pick it up and get to work. You're an author now.

How to Write Your Book

Chapter Seven

How to Organize and Do Research

A REPORTER WE KNOW DECIDED TO WRITE A BOOK based on his experience with Army Intelligence in Ethiopia. He spent six years, on and off, researching Ethiopia's history, geography, and current affairs; studying everything written about the workings of Army Intelligence; and taping interviews with all his Army buddies. When he finally came to us for help, he was struggling under a mountain of facts and opinions.

We suggested that he sit down and write the book proposal he should have written *before* beginning his intensive research. That forced him to isolate (for the first time) the aspects of the subject that he wanted to write about. We'll never forget his rueful grimace when he told us, "You know, most of the material I've collected has nothing to do with the book."

If you're writing nonfiction, you'll probably have to do some background research along the way to support your facts and contentions. Even novels depend for much of their believability on correct details, especially historical novels built around actual events. Margaret Mitchell's *Gone With the Wind* and E. L. Doctorow's *Ragtime* are examples that come quickly to mind. Detective stories, westerns, and science fiction yarns also depend on proven facts of physics and chemistry as well as authentic dress, speech, and behavior.

Even autobiography requires research. "Memories can fool you," says dramatist and film producer Dore Schary. He tells how Eleanor Roosevelt read his play, *Sunrise at Campobello,* before it opened, and offered the correction that FDR had been on canes when he'd nominated Al Smith in 1924. "I had to tell her she was wrong. He was on canes in 1928, when he nominated Smith the second time. In 1924 he was using crutches."

All too often, beginning writers rely strictly on their own knowledge and experience—and produce thin, insubstantial manuscripts; or else they drown themselves in too much premature research, as our reporter friend did. To keep from either extreme, it's important to begin by deciding what you need, where you'll research it, and how you'll keep track of it—and to begin the research *after* you have your specific book idea firmly in mind.

7·1 How to Make a Research Plan

If you've followed the steps outlined in Part I, you've already narrowed the scope of your project and prepared a story outline (if it's fiction) or a tentative table of contents (if it's nonfiction). For many novels that use facts only for atmosphere, it's wise to write the entire first draft before doing much research. But if your novel is based on facts, or if you're writing nonfiction, you'll save a lot of time and paper if you research before attempting a word of the actual manuscript.

PREPARE A TOPIC LIST
The first step is to prepare a list of topics to be researched. Some people work in loose-leaf notebooks or spiral pads; others like scraps of paper and clipboards. We prefer 5 × 8 inch file cards. The easiest starting point for your list of topics is your tentative table of contents (or story outline). For our nonfiction, we list each chapter topic on a separate card and, under it, every subtopic we can think of that we expect to cover in the chapter. We assign each subtopic a number or letter and then put that on the pertinent research note or Xerox copy. That way, each fact we find is immediately assigned a tentative place—though its position may change as we write and revise.

You may find a method that's easier for you. The important thing is to write down the bulk of your topics before you begin to research in earnest.

DECIDE WHAT RESOURCES YOU'LL NEED TO TAP
There are two basic kinds of research. If you get your information indirectly, from a newspaper, magazine, report, journal, paper, book, or film, that's a *secondary* source. If you obtain it directly from a live person or through the written report of an eyewitness, that's a *primary source*. Go down your list of research topics now, and decide which ones need the authority or immediacy of primary sources and which don't.

For much of your information you can rely on published material. But for the anecdotes that make a book come alive (for example, the one about our reporter friend), and for up-to-date, complicated, or controversial facts or opinions, it is best to talk directly with the people involved. The next chapter will show you how to find people and interview and poll them by mail, by phone, or in person.

There's a third kind of research that Grace Halsell, author of *The Illegals, Bessie Yellowhair,* and *Soul Sister,* calls "more primary than primary." For those books, she actually took on the identity of a Mexican, an Indian, and a black woman. For most books, happily, it's not necessary to live your research 24 hours a day.

MAKE A TIMETABLE

When Judi sold her book idea for *Stopping Out,* she agreed to a six-month deadline. Her research included a mail poll of 200 colleges, live interviews with a dozen educators, letter interviews with three dozen administrators, and secondary research of books, articles, and pamphlets in her local library and of reports and papers in the files of several educational institutions. She completed all her research, except for a few odds and ends, within the three months she had allotted herself. She did it by making and sticking to a timetable.

Not all books require a great deal of research. Frank wrote *Children's Toys You Can Build Yourself* after trips to half a dozen toy and craft stores. We researched our *Do-It-Yourself Custom Van Book,* and took most of its several dozen photos, at two weekend van shows. On the other hand, Alex Haley spent many years researching *Roots* in the libraries of America and the jungle villages of Africa. How long your research takes should depend on your topic and your deadline. To get it done in time, we suggest you make a timetable.

You'll probably need a certain amount of background research before you contact your primary sources. This will help you prepare all the questions that can't be answered elsewhere. So decide how much preliminary research you need, and do only that much.

Next, prepare your polls, mail interviews, and requests for material that must be mailed to you. (See Chapter 8 for guidelines.) Begin to set up your face-to-face interviews. Establish a ballpark budget for research expenses. (Caroline Bird, author of numerous books including *The Two-Paycheck Marriage* and *What Women Want,* says she spends about a third of her advance on research. We average substantially less.) Arrange for any needed and affordable travel. If you find you *must* travel and can't cover the cost, talk to your editor—preferably before you sign the contract.

Then, while waiting for appointments to materialize and requests to be filled, do the rest of your secondary research. For every fact you copy, be sure to jot down its source: the author, the title of the article or book, the page number, the publisher, the volume number, and the date. Make sure you have all the information you might need for a complete footnote. Even if your book is to have no footnotes, the extra time you take to write down all this information is time well spent. It will save you hours and hours later, trying to retrace the source of the one fact your publisher queries or challenges. Be careful to put into quotes every directly copied statement, so that when you write the book, you can attribute the words or else change them sufficiently to make them your own.

Caroline Bird is one of the many successful authors who employ students to help with research. We feel it's a good idea only if you can afford it, if you can detail exactly what the researcher is to look for, and if you don't mind missing the one serendipitous observation that may deepen your investigation or alter it entirely. While researching a children's biography of Eleanor Roosevelt, author Doris Faber came across boxes of letters a friend had written to that famous lady. Out of curiosity, she scanned the letters—and what she found caused her to forget her children's book and sign to write a revelatory adult biography, *The Life of Lorena Hickok, E. R.'s Friend.* "Anyone could have found what I did," says Faber. "In fact, other people were looking through the boxes while I was there." But sometimes it takes an author's eye to recognize the nuggets of gold in stacks of rubble.

7·2 A Guide to Printed Information Sources

You'd have to take several years of courses to learn everything librarians know about the thousands of secondary and printed primary sources in the United States alone. Even then, you'd have barely scratched the surface of information retrieval. For descriptions of specific research materials, there are several good books, including Alden Todd's revised edition of *Finding Facts Fast* and our own *Research Shortcuts* (Contemporary Books, Fall 1982). Here we'll concentrate on some tips that are of special help to authors.

LEARN THE LIBRARY'S REFERENCE SECTION
Every year or so we teach a short course in research techniques, and its most useful part is the two hours we make our students spend using the tools of the library's reference section. The amazed response is always, "We never dreamed there were all these specific resources."

Few people guess how many reference tools are available at the local library. A typical researcher enters, heads for the card catalog, looks up the subject, checks out some books, and calls it a day. But circulating books are rarely useful. By the time a book is written, printed, and tucked away on a library shelf—as you'll discover when your book finally comes out—its information is usually at least a couple of years old.

A more enterprising neophyte adds *Readers' Guide to Periodical Literature* or its equivalent. But magazine writers—and printers—don't work overnight. Information published tomorrow in a popular monthly magazine is usually at least a half year old.

The reference collection has other, more helpful resources: noncirculating directories of authoritative and famous people, compilations of facts on subjects you wouldn't dream were of interest to anyone but you, bibliographies, catalogs, and dictionaries of all kinds. In its vertical files are pamphlets on a variety of topics. Become familiar with these files and see what's there in your subject area. When Judi was writing *Stopping Out,* much of her research data came from the education drawers in the Great Neck (New York) Public Library's well-stocked vertical files.

The reference collection also includes newspapers and periodicals, not just the microfilmed *New York Times* and popular magazines, but professional, trade, and scholarly journals. These special publications often contain the keys to current thinking and latest research. Some libraries' collections of technical periodicals are extensive, some inadequate for our needs, but most libraries now have interloan facilities for getting needed titles within weeks, and many libraries keep lists of other libraries in the state that subscribe to the magazines and newspapers you need.

The reference collection also contains indexes to and abstracts of newspapers and professional journals. The more familiar ones are the *New York Times Index, Psychological Abstracts, Publications of the Modern Language Association, Index Medicus,* and *Dissertation Abstracts.* There's an index or abstract for nearly every field of endeavor, and it's one of the first places you should check. Aside from providing new, unrehashed facts and figures, the journals also tell where to locate their authors, the people doing the current research in the field.

Indexes are merely categorized lists of articles' titles or topics plus authors' names, but abstracts include thumbnail summations of the salient points covered in each indexed article. The summations generally save you from having to skim dozens of articles to locate the two or three you need. Depending on how much detail you need, the abstracts are sometimes comprehensive enough that you can work from them and not have to read the articles at all.

Before you begin your library research, spend a few hours becoming familiar with the reference tools that specifically help you. It'll save you many days later on.

FIND THE WISEST LIBRARIAN

After you've learned a little about the library's reference collection, seek out its wisest librarian. The reference librarian is usually the one. Cultivate his friendship and learn his work hours. Then, if you can, do your library research when he's there. Each day when you come in with your list of topics to be researched, head straight for him. Tell him precisely what you're looking for and why. Follow him as he finds the information for you. Often, he will lead you to shelves or files you hadn't thought of going to, or to several nearby sources you never knew existed. Take the resource from him and examine it: recheck the fact and read the surrounding material. He's wise but you're the author; *you're* accountable for the information. Besides, in the paragraph right after the one he found may be a fact that's even better for your purposes.

REACH OUT TO OTHER INFORMATION BANKS

Years ago, librarians realized that even the best-budgeted libraries were not going to be able to purchase every book published, and they developed interlibrary loan systems. Depending on where you live, you may have easy access to almost any nonrare book or periodical in almost any public or academic library in the United States. Many states maintain special central collections of books that are mailed to smaller libraries on request. Even part of the Library of Congress's collection busily circulates to libraries across the country. Before you get into a major research project, learn about your library's interloan procedure.

More and more libraries are linking up to computerized data banks that store and sort out information for researchers. For a fee of from $10 to $100 or more (depending on the service you need), your library may be able to provide you with a computer-printed index or set of abstracts to journal articles on the topics of your research.

The type of information available on computers is growing all the time. For example, Lockheed Information Systems' Lockheed/Dialog claims to be the world's leading on-line information system. Its data banks, housed in Palo Alto, California, include such subjects as medicine, business, art, music, and history. It has over 25 million separate items, received from over 70 libraries, of computer information (called *data bases* in computer talk) and provides references from three times as many periodicals as are listed in *Readers' Guide,* along with such newspapers as *The New York Times, Wall Street Journal,* and *Christian Science Monitor.* (It even rates books, plays, concerts, phonograph records, and restaurants from A to F, based on its files of assorted reviews.)

The New York Times has its own data bank, and you can subscribe just to its computer search service. In 1980 it could cost as little as $15 an hour, or as much as $130, depending on the data bank chosen. A thorough search in preparation for a book could run to about $500. Medline, on the other hand, is a medical search service that is 50 percent government subsidized. Our search of Medline for *Eat Anything Exercise Diet,* planned carefully with a knowledgeable librarian, cost less than $50 and saved us about 35 hours of library time.

College libraries are important resources for the serious researcher. The larger the institution, as a rule, the larger its collection. Most publicly run colleges permit citizens of their state or city free use of library facilities, although if you want to check out books, a nominal deposit may be required. Many private colleges allow outsiders to use their libraries, although there's sometimes a fee. Most colleges have more than one library, a fact that we've seen too many authors overlook. At the University of Wisconsin, for example, Memorial Library is the major library, but the Schools of Engineering, Medicine, and Agriculture each have large libraries as well, and a number of individual departments, such as geology and Afro-American Studies, maintain smaller, specialized libraries. The librarians at such places know their respective fields intimately and can be valuable guides to resources and authoritative people.

Don't overlook corporation libraries, either. American Metal Climax, Inc., in New York City, maintains for its staff a library of 10,000 books, 1,000 journals, plus sundry reports and other backup information on exotic metals, mining, and places its executives are interested in. It makes all these resources available to serious researchers and is even willing to make interlibrary loans. The Zator Company in Cambridge, Massachusetts, also welcomes serious researchers to its library of 4,000 technical reports, 400 books, 350 volumes of journals, and other data on artificial intelligence, computer programming languages, information storage and retrieval, and so forth. A great many other corporations maintain in-house libraries for staff purposes, and most permit limited access to researchers. There are several directories to these special libraries; ask your librarian to help you locate one.

Trade associations of professionals, businesses, and activists— from the Administrative Management Society in Pennsylvania to Zero Population Growth, Inc., in California—all maintain libraries of their own. Most of them feel obliged to help researchers. Your public library should have indexes to these special libraries, too.

Morgues are what newspapers call their libraries. Morgue employees clip and file their own printed editions, and sometimes other newspapers as well, on a topic-by-topic, name-by-name basis. Very few newspapers refuse authors access to morgue files. Most also handle short requests by phone, and some answer mailed requests by photocopying shorter files—usually for a fee.

7·3 How to Organize Your Researched Material

If you're like most novice authors, the sheer weight of your resource material can stagger you. Don't let it terrify you into inaction—and don't become so involved in orchestrating your wealth of statistics, anecdotes, and quotes that you overlook or drift away from your book's original purpose. In your proposal you promised the publisher a particular book. You must deliver pretty much what you proposed, or else discuss the changes with your editor. In the event she agrees to the changes, make sure you have a written agreement on them in case your original editor leaves (as happens all too often) and the replacement tries to hold you to the original proposal. (Even a letter from you to your editor in which you recount a phone conversation about agreed-upon changes can get you out of later contractual hot water.)

Do be flexible in considering changes in direction. Sometimes research does change the premise of a chapter or even an entire book. Before he began researching *An American Death,* Gerold Frank assumed that Dr. King's assassination was a conspiracy. His findings changed his mind—and the thrust of his book.

In fiction the facts gathered in research are blended into the story, normally without attribution to their sources. Nonfiction, however, should identify the sources of its facts unless there's an overriding reason not to. Furthermore, the development of the chapters is governed less by the preliminary outline suggested in the proposal than by the results of the research.

Once you've done all your interviewing (see next chapter) and have everything you need to start the book, separate it into workable bundles. The way we've found most efficient is to make a separate file folder for each chapter and to put each piece of information—Xerox copies, pamphlet, index card reference, or the like—into the folder for the chapter in which we expect to use it. For data that seem to apply to several chapters, we select the first conceivable chapter, put them there, and move them on after completing that chapter. After all the material is in folders, we prepare an outline for each chapter and organize and cue each file's contents according to the outline.

With nonfiction you can jot down formal chapter outlines or make just a few notes, whichever works best for you, but you must begin with an unclouded perspective of exactly how a chapter's first draft is to proceed. Once you've typed the draft, you may see relationships that weren't clear before, or discover that an anecdote or fact fits better somewhere else or leads to a different conclusion. But unless you begin with a plan, you'll come out with a hodgepodge of long notes, not a first draft.

Very often the subject matter itself dictates the most logical sequence for writing. Some chapters beg chronological or step-by-step organization. Often you must impose logical order on your ideas, such as a point-by-point sequence or a succession of pros and cons. Many chapters include several types of organization, but as a rule, one main organizational pattern weaves the material together from start to finish. For example, let's look at this chapter's first three large sections (before research, during research, and after research). They're arranged chronologically—the easiest sequence to write in and the one used for most chapters in fiction. Within the first section, organization is again chronological (although subthemes are arranged point by point). Our second section (sources of research) is arranged roughly from most to least familiar. The section you're reading now is again essentially chronological, in the order in which you, the reader, need to know the information.

When the various topics you plan to write about don't fall into chronological sequence, you still have to arrange them sensibly so that the reader follows easily from topic to topic or from event to event. Some arrangements to consider for nonfiction are: from a general point to its specific aspects, from easy concepts to more difficult ones, from least to most controversial, from least to most complicated, from theoretical to practical. When several techniques are combined—for example, if you decide to move from least to most controversial points and, within each point, from theoretical to practical examples—the reader must, at all times, be able to follow you and to understand the general point your specifics are making. Poor organization is one of the most glaring problems we've seen in the books of first-time authors.

Authors of fiction who watch a lot of modern movies and television often have trouble organizing their chapters into sequences a reader can follow. The visual media can handle sudden shifts in time, place, and point of view with a deftness that the author of books cannot rely on. For the beginner, old rules are generally best: stick to one point of view within a chapter (and maybe within the entire book); keep the time frame of each chapter (and maybe of the entire book) fairly condensed; and, generally, move from place to place along with the movement of a character.

In our earlier thumbnail sketch of this chapter's organization, we left out one small but important section: the introduction. Every nonfiction book chapter has one, although it may be as short as a sentence or two. It usually serves three functions: to interest the reader in the chapter's topic, to explain what the topic is, and to show its relationship to the theme of the book. (In fiction there are comparable, though infinitely subtler, statements of chapter theme and relationship to overall theme near the beginning of each chapter.)

Every chapter in fiction and nonfiction also has an ending sentence, paragraph, or group of paragraphs that tie together the theme of that chapter and, often, make the reader want to turn to the next one. The best way to learn how to write effective introductions and endings is to study the best authors in the field of your writing.

7·4 How to Evaluate Your Researched Material

It is important to evaluate your research rather than accept it blindly as fact, as Dore Schary discovered when he was researching his *Heyday: An Autobiography*. He realized that even the notes he'd made during important meetings weren't entirely factual. Reading them much later, he found that "what I'd put down made me much more articulate than I was."

Readers and writers alike employ five criteria in assessing a statement:

ACCURACY
If you see an event happen and report it carefully, you and your readers assume you've reported accurately. However, six eyewitnesses to an

accident may render six conflicting reports; thus an "accurate" report may not always reflect precisely what happened. Since total accuracy is so seldom achieved, this criterion is the least useful of the five.

AUTHENTICITY

Not to be confused with accuracy, authenticity is what you get automatically from a primary source. It comes from the horse's mouth—the logical, natural origin for the chosen information. If you can't confirm your data, you must be careful to present them as authentic statements and not verified facts.

The best case for showing the distinction between authenticity and accuracy is the Pentagon. It's about the only team in town that has *authentic* information about U.S. missile strength. When asking for money, it claims there aren't enough missiles; when it's bragging about the good job it's doing, there are suddenly more than enough missiles planted in the ground. That's why sharp writers report that the missile-strength statements coming from the Pentagon are authentic, but inevitably leave their accuracy in doubt.

CREDIBILITY

The source's way of telling his facts and backing them up, or the source's proven track record, may lead you to the subjective conclusion that the source is credible and his facts can be believed. And *that's* how to present the information to your readers.

PLAUSIBILITY

You may conclude that, subjectively, the fact makes sense to you and presumably to other people. That's how you'll write it—not as verified fact, but as plausible consideration.

CORROBORATION

You may obtain information from a separate, also believable source, that substantiates the first source's facts. Then you will have objectively demonstrated, if not the accuracy, at least the honesty of your source. In reporting the fact, you will probably tell the reader of the corroboration, although that is not always necessary.

Few statements meet all five of the above criteria, but those that meet several make the strongest supports for your arguments. On the surface, they all sound like nonfiction devices but just read carefully any horror story like William Blatty's *The Exorcist* or any historical romance like Colleen McCullough's *The Thorn Birds* and see how the criteria are used by skillful authors to make their readers *believe*.

Especially in nonfiction, the facts you choose should be not only accurate, but plentiful. One of the most frequent reasons given by editors for rejecting commissioned manuscripts is that the author has tried to stretch too little research across too many pages. Nonfiction writers must often spend more time researching than actually writing. We make it a rule to collect more details than we think we need, so we can choose the best and most applicable in making our points. Furthermore, we stick to dependable sources and keep conscientious track of who they are. There are at least three practical reasons for this method:

IT'S MORE EFFICIENT

Let's say that you're researching a chapter on railroad-related deaths and injuries. From a chart of statistics, you extrapolate that 3,392 people are killed or injured at railroad crossings every year. Then, while organizing or writing the chapter, you decide it's more effective to separate how many were killed from how many were injured. You'll waste a lot of time relocating the source of your information unless you also made note of its location: U.S. Federal Railroad Administration's *Accident Bulletin* reprinted in the 1973 *U.S. Statistical Abstract,* p. 561. (We also jot down the name of the library we've used and the reference book's call number.)

IT'S MORE BELIEVABLE

One nonfiction author writes that "3,392 people are killed or hurt at railroad crossings every year." Another writes: "The Federal Railroad Administration tallied 3,392 deaths and injuries last year." Which sounds more like a fact? Which sounds more dramatic? If the source of your fact is authoritative, include it to heighten credibility.

IT'S SAFER

If you write that 3,392 people a year are killed or hurt at railroad crossings, without attributing the number to anyone, you personally stand behind the statement's accuracy. If, instead, you include the source of your information, you are reporting it. Aside from being more authoritative, citing the source also leaves you practically in the clear if somebody else got the numbers wrong.

Never forget that your researched facts are only as good as their sources. So, in writing nonfiction, follow three general guidelines:

1. Always report your information accurately and, unless there's an overriding reason, identify the source.
2. When using a secondary source, try to double check with at least one independent secondary source.
3. Whenever the facts are controversial, incredible, or important to bolster the statements you've chosen to make, try to use primary sources.

Because living primary sources are so important to both fiction and nonfiction authors, we devote the entire next chapter to finding and using them.

Chapter Eight

How to Collect First-Hand Information

WHEN MARILYN FRENCH WROTE HER NOVEL *THE Women's Room,* she used mainly her own first-hand experiences, augmented by many she'd witnessed happening to her friends. When Nancy Friday wrote her nonfiction collection of male fantasies, *Men in Love,* she used 3,000 mailed responses to an invitation she'd placed at the end of her previous book, *Forbidden Flowers.* When the late Mort Weisinger wrote his novel *The Contest,* he began with his own experiences as judge of Miss America contests and then did a great deal of interviewing of judges and contestants to collect facts and feelings. When Don and Joan German wrote their two-volume nonfiction work *Tested Techniques in Bank Marketing,* their information came entirely from telephone interviews with bank executives.

Some books, fiction and nonfiction, have been written solely from the authors' own experiences and observations, although the most successful of them have shown extraordinary powers of observation and recall. Some books—for instance, new interpretations of old events—have succeeded while relying completely on secondary sources, information reported in books and pamphlets. But the majority of writers research their books from primary sources.

The primary information contained in documents, letters, and autobiographical writings entrusted to libraries and other research facilities is generally of great use to writers of historical fiction and nonfiction, but the rest obtain their new data—the stuff that makes their books say something that hasn't been said before—direct from the people who have done what they're writing about. As Gay Talese, author of *Thy Neighbor's Wife* and *Honor Thy Father,* said, "Part of the challenge of nonfiction is getting close enough to human nature to describe what it's like." If you have a mountain scene in your novel and never climbed a mountain, you'll want to interview someone who did. If your nonfiction gives advice on direct-mail advertising, and you've done little direct-mail advertising, you'll need input from the experts. A good author is not expected to be proficient in everything he writes about, but he is expected to be an intermediary and interpreter between those who know and those who want to know.

The information you seek may be as straightforward as answers to yes-or-no questions (using the technique of poll or questionnaire, for example), or as unstructured as Nancy Friday's "tell-me-your-fantasies" solicitations. Whether to get your first-hand information by mail, phone, or personal interview often depends on the depth of response you need. Mailed replies are usually superficial and should be used only when you know exactly what you're looking for. Phone interviews are more pliable and able to elicit deeper and clearer responses. And though face-to-face meetings require a great deal more time and possible travel expense, they extract by far the most information and richest details.

8·1 Finding First-Hand Sources

Where do book authors get the names, addresses, and phone numbers of first-hand sources? If it's just anyone you want, like Friday's fantasy-sharers, place an ad in a likely publication or on a well-read bulletin board, or ask around among your friends. But if you're looking for a person with particular expertise, it's a bit more challenging. We have several favorite aids.

WHO'S WHOS AND OTHER BIOGRAPHICAL DIRECTORIES
Almost every field of endeavor—science, medicine, psychology, even journalism—has its own biographical directory. Often addresses and phone numbers are included along with achievements. Many libraries maintain at least small collections of these tools in their reference sections. Some even list home addresses of the movie stars (though the best way to reach celebrities is through their public relations representatives).

COLLEGE CATALOGS AND DIRECTORIES
Shelved in most college libraries and many public libraries, the catalogs tell you who's teaching what and where. It's a good bet that these people are authoritative and up-to-date. Public relations offices of the larger colleges prepare directories of experts and mail them free to authors who request them. These are even better than college catalogs.

JOURNAL ARTICLES
After reading an article, we sometimes get in touch with its author. It's easy to find his address: it's care of the institution listed (along with his name and title) at the beginning or end of the article.

TRADE AND PROFESSIONAL ASSOCIATIONS
Executive directors of most associations know which of their members
are experts; many volunteer to contact the experts themselves and have
them phone us. Often, the sources don't bother to call collect.

PUBLIC RELATIONS
Manufacturers and sellers of everything from nuts to education,
hospital care, and peace are all out to promote their products. Many
produce free press kits and press releases for authors and pamphlets,
booklets, and such for the general public. These secondary materials
often provide clues to resident expertise. To find the experts, telephone
or write the public relations help that these public and private
corporate bodies hire to get their names into print. They will get your
questions answered, often by having the best authority they can find
phone you at their expense. (If an outside agency handles the firm's
public relations, the switchboard operator usually has the name and
phone number.)

You must, however, evaluate the credibility of information
provided by organizations eager to promote products and causes. Don't
expect a P.R. employee to volunteer data that reflect badly on his boss
or client. Sometimes you can get information that's not entirely
favorable, but you'll probably have to ask—or in some cases, demand
it.

Because of the credibility gap, authors should avoid quoting
public relations people. In fact, even their experts' opinions should be
carefully weighed. At a recent meeting of the American Society of
Journalists and Authors, a P.R. representative revealed how subtly an
organization can work to get its message across. He told of a woman
who'd written a book on toys, and afterwards "has been touring with us
for four years. We pay her per diem, and we pay all her expenses. We
smooth the way and book stations for her . . . as an author and an
authority on toys. Of course, she happens to be traveling with our toys.
When she talks about a good or a bad toy, the good toy is our toy."

FEDERAL, STATE, AND LOCAL GOVERNMENT PERSONNEL
One of the largest sources of primary (as well as secondary) information
is the federal government. The annual *U.S. Government Manual* is
available at most libraries; you can buy it for under $10. Detailed
though it is, it just grazes the tip of the information iceberg. The
names it lists tend to be department heads and subheads who can refer
you to knowledgeable subalterns.

State governments, too, inevitably have matrices of informed individuals tucked into their political superstructures. If you can locate them—generally via public information officers of the various government divisions—they're a ready source of up-to-date information and leads to other sources. Local governments sometimes have these good resource people too.

In using government sources, keep in mind your readers as well as the scope of the subject. Quotes from federal officials have fairly universal applicability: if a U.S. Department of Agriculture expert talks about green potatoes, you can use his data as the basis for nationwide generalizations. But if you choose a state agricultural officer to be your authority, her comments on green potatoes may carry little universality. For additional safety, keep in mind that readers these days don't tolerate excessive reliance on government sources. When it comes to potatoes, weather, and census figures, you're on sure footing; but start to base an argument in the area of employment, taxes, or housing on government officials' figures and opinions, and you may lack credibility. If you were *reading* instead of writing the book, would you have confidence in the bearer of the information?

8·2 The Kinds of Data That First-Hand Sources Provide

First-hand sources are able to provide six kinds of objective and subjective data. Before you contact a source—whether by mail, by phone, or in person—figure out which of these data you're looking for. That way, you'll be able to phrase questions and make observations to elicit the results you want.

INFORMATION

Facts, figures, observations, guidelines, and similar data can't be more current than when they're gleaned directly from a person doing vital research or making vital decisions on a topic in your projected book, whether it's fiction about a cancer clinic or fact about the stars. Our *Do-It-Yourself Custom Van Book*'s final chapter, only a few hundred words long, attempts to predict the future appearance of American vans. For authoritative input, we spoke with van designers at all the big-three van makers, and we told our readers that the predictions are based on what they told us. Without that first-hand backup, our chapter would be just the idle musings of two word-spinners. (Illustration 8.1 reproduces all the copy in that chapter.)

Ill. 8.1

Here Comes Supervan!

Faster than a speeding Oldsmobile! More powerful than a Mack truck! Able to leap over tall sand dunes without leaving the ground! It's supervan! Four-wheel drive, four on the floor, short turning radius, traction like a Caterpillar, and metal the strength of a tank. Beauty like a Rolls Royce Silver Shadow.

Inside, accommodations for six in king-size beds, two bathrooms and showers and hot water, room to do a handstand, and so quiet the driver goes stir-crazy if the hi-fi ever gets turned off. That's the stuff us van fanatics dream about.

Fortunately, that's also the stuff Detroit engineers and designers sketch for their bosses to see. We know; we talked with them; we borrowed some of their sketches; we picked up the excitement they have for this relatively young thing called the van.

It started as an underpowered, ugly delivery truck. But because dreamers adopted it as their own, Detroit built it the way we wanted. The manufacturers are plugging into our dreams, and the dreams are heading for the assembly lines. Vans soon are going to roll off them higher, wider, and still more handsome than they are now. They'll be streamlined like the Super Chief, but they won't waste a cube of space on their good looks.

We didn't stop at Detroit. We picked the brains of anybody who'd talk—van customizers, van magazine editors and publishers, van shop owners, van fans with Star Trek minds, van-minded kids ogling the van shop windows. And you know what? For every futuristic idea that some van designer thinks he has cooked up, some van dreamer has already worked up a rolling van using that idea!

Tomorrow's van is here, on some of these pages full of sketches—ours, designers', van shop folks' . . . Blending the hood of one, the suave, svelte interior of another, the powerhouse of another, the windows of another—tomorrow's van is here somewhere.

We're betting on another van for a nearby tomorrow, one that most of the dreamers have overlooked so far. We've seen it already; it's on sale at your local truck dealer . . . now. It's the step van. Tall, wide, long, and boxy, it's now the ugliest looking duck on the lot. But the step van—$7\frac{1}{2}$ feet wide inside, 12 feet long behind the driver's seat—has room enough for 6-footers to stand tall inside, room for king-size bunkbeds, room for a shower, a water heater, and two weeks' supply of goodies in a refrigerator. And you can get it with four-wheel drive and desert-style boots on the wheels and four wheels in the rear to even out the ride.

Sure the step van looks ugly today. Our smaller van, nowadays a swan, was once an ugly duckling too. As more and more van fans adopt the bulky, boxy step van for their personal nirvanas on six wheels, Detroit will have to clean them up, polish them up, outfit them the way we want.

When *that* van's day has come, watch for *The Do-It-Yourself Custom Step Van Book*. For now, 10-4, Good Buddy. Catch you on the flip. These few pages of merriment and craft, telling and questioning, pictures and prose have sure been fun! We'll wave on the way by, because our van's got only two pedals—when we step on the brake we stop, and when we step on the gas we fly!

ANECDOTES

Exciting writing is built on exciting real-life experiences, so the good interviewer is always listening for them. More, a really sharp interviewer listens for clues to remembered experiences that lie in waiting and then suggests that the source "Give me an example" or "Tell me about a time when that actually happened." In fiction, experiences often make up the fabric of our scenes; in nonfiction we write them as anecdotes. We'll talk more about them in our next chapter.

DESCRIPTION

Your sources don't sit in colorless vacuums. Readers need to see them in real-life settings. If you're researching a book about the interviewees, you may want to point out the special surroundings that reflect their personalities. If you're writing about technology, it may help readers visualize your points if you tell them what the equipment and labs look like. Notice our description of the step van in Ill. 8.1. To write that, we couldn't just look at a picture of a step van; we had to see the actual van, inside and out.

If description of your source or his surroundings is important, you'll probably have to interview in person instead of by phone or mail.

AMBIENCE

Is the person you're interviewing just doing her job, or does she feel like a pioneer? Does the office look like that of a corporation that's really earning $27 billion a year? Ambience is the *subjective* description of all the clues and hunches that color an author's viewpoint. It, too, can best be noticed during an in-person interview. Instead of picking up unconscious "feelings" you can't substantiate, go into each interview consciously prepared to jot down clues to ambience. Your writing will have more texture and more depth.

In Ill. 8.1, notice that, with one word, we transmitted to readers the *excitement* we sensed as we were interviewing van designers.

QUOTES

Novice researchers believe that the primary purpose of interviews is to gather quotes for verbatim use. Actually, that's the *least* important purpose. Beginning authors often use too *many* direct quotes. For discussion of how quotes should be used in writing your manuscript, see Chapter 9.

LEADS TO ADDITIONAL RESOURCES
One expert usually knows the other experts in his field. During interviews, whether in person or otherwise, make it a habit to find out whom your interviewee can suggest for additional help. Make it a rule to ask, as well, whether you can use the first source's name in contacting the second. It's a valuable way to sneak past red tape and reluctant secretaries.

Referral works with others besides experts. When Judi was researching *Stopping Out,* she found that each stop-out she spoke with had invariably met several other stop-outs or potential stop-outs. Through referral, she got most of the anecdotes for her book.

8·3 Gathering Information by Letter

For *Stopping Out,* Judi also needed to know the attitudes of law and medical school admissions committee members toward applicants who'd taken time out from college. She wrote to committee leaders at 47 representative schools, describing the purpose of her project and listing the four specific questions to which she needed answers. She enclosed a stamped, self-addressed envelope with each letter and was rewarded with 21 responses—including several good quotes she could use verbatim in the book.

Results received by mail sometimes arrive slowly (or not at all) and are rarely directly quotable, but for lengthy projects it's often the preferred way. Jack Harrison Pollack, former Senate committee investigator and author of best sellers such as *Earl Warren: The Judge Who Changed America* and *Dr. Sam: An American Tragedy,* tries to reduce his by-mail research requests to a form letter. But to *every* copy, he appends a short handwritten note like the one that went along with the form for his Earl Warren book: "My apologies for this form letter. I'm trying to meet a deadline." People these days understand deadlines, and Jack had no trouble eliciting replies. "Even Haldeman and Ehrlichman wrote from jail," he told us. "Supreme court judges, college professors, presidents' wives, all answered promptly."

To be successful at researching by mail, always:

Address the letter to a real, live person.
Keep it typed, businesslike, and short—no more than one page.
Tell why you need the information.
Tell how the information is to be used. (Is it background? Are you asking permission to quote it?)

Ask *specific* questions. If there's more than one, number the questions. Don't expect more than a few words for each answer—though you may be pleasantly surprised.

Refer to your deadline. However, allow at least a week after the letter is received for reply.

Enclose a stamped, self-addressed envelope.

8·4 Gathering Information by Telephone

Most beginning authors have little trouble phoning for information, but they hesitate to make long-distance phone calls. For a book that will have nationwide readership, it's important to have a nationwide sampling of primary sources in order to show that conditions are universally applicable or, conversely, that they change from place to place.

The easiest way to get information from distant sources is by telephone. It's less expensive than most people realize, especially with the new competitive long-distance services. An eight-minute phone call to Anchorage, Alaska, from our Wisconsin home was about $5 when we last checked, and an eight-minute call to Washington, D.C., less than $3 during business hours. (It's a good deal cheaper in the evening.) We figure that eight minutes on the phone is roughly equivalent to twenty minutes or more face-to-face. We take light notes and use tape recorders for backup, and because of that there's little dead phone time.

The techniques we use in phone interviewing are roughly comparable to those used in-person in almost every detail. Often, we write or phone first to arrange an interview time when our source won't be interrupted. When we fix the time, we also summarize the topic of the interview. That way, the source can assemble pertinent facts and figures and prepare the observations she'd like to make. When Don and Joan German researched their bank marketing books, they mailed detailed questionnaires to bank executives. But having learned from experience how few questionnaires bankers return, they appended covering letters saying that they'd call on such-and-such-a-date to take the information over the phone.

With just an electronic connection between you and your resources, you won't be able to see their office settings, faces, or clothes. But you can pick up cues from the voice—whether they're hedging or responding straightforwardly, whether they're pleased or feel put on the spot. Humor, anger, sarcasm, cynicism, wistfulness—

all transmit well over telephone lines, giving you the chance to gather insights as well as factual information in minimal time.

8·5 Interviewing Face-to-Face

For beginners, face-to-face interviews are the hardest kind. Too many try to emulate television interviewers like Dick Cavett and Mike Wallace, unaware that what they're seeing is most often a carefully edited version or a reinterview of a person who has already had a preliminary interview with the TV personality's researcher.

Unlike Wallace's questions, yours are not prescreened and annotated with likely responses. Unlike Cavett's subjects, yours are not there to chat and entertain. In order to keep them from wandering off the track, ducking the issues, or giving superficial responses, you've got to take charge. To help you, we've condensed some of our techniques into eleven easy-to-remember commandments. Adapted to your style and personality, they keep you in control of your interviews.

DEFINE THE PURPOSE OF YOUR INTERVIEW

You have to know in advance concretely why the interview is taking place, or you'll end up with a conversation. It helps if you run through the six kinds of data that interviews offer (see section 8.2) and decide what you're looking for. Usually it helps to let your subject know in advance what you want from him. Most people want to help. In leisure, they prepare charts or find papers that make their points better than words can. They remember anecdotes that last-minute questioning won't call to mind. They pull together their muddled thoughts.

Even if you're doing a tough investigative book and are tracking down shady characters, it's wise to assume that when you find them, they'll know pretty well what you're looking for.

Draw up a list of questions that need answering. Use it as a guide, not a bible. Make sure to get complete answers to each question, but be prepared to ask other questions suggested in the course of your interview.

DO YOUR BACKGROUND RESEARCH

If you've done your preliminary research as suggested in Chapter 7, you know something about the topic and the person before the interview begins, including her title and the spelling of her name. (You can get it from the secretary). Your prepared questions will then display intelligence instead of ignorance, and you'll elicit more thoughtful, less simplistic answers.

If your subjects have written books or articles, be familiar with them. Mention that you've read their work; it may make for an easier interview. Don't ask questions that duplicate what's been answered in their books—or if you do it deliberately, let them know you've seen the answer they've given to a similar question.

If you're researching a technical topic, become passingly familiar with the field's vocabulary before the interview. Nothing freezes an interviewee quicker than to finish a five-minute detailed discourse, only to have you ask a question that shows you didn't understand a word.

GET OFF TO A GOOD BEGINNING

Review your background notes and questions in advance. List questions in the order in which they can be most logically answered. Get to the interview on time. We try to arrive five minutes early; it shows that we're there on business, not for a social call. Look and feel like you're ready. Dress appropriately and, when in doubt, conservatively. Take two pens so that when the first one quits, the other one is ready. Take a pad, not scraps of loose paper.

Begin the interview in a cordial yet businesslike manner. We know that a lot of old pros suggest you start like a peddler, with talk about sports or the weather, but we believe it relaxes a nervous subject (and novice interviewer) more to get right to what you're there for rather than to meander through five minutes of aimless chatter and then make an abrupt switch to the *real* business.

GET TO THE POINT

Don't be vague. Don't let your subjects be vague either. If their answers aren't to the point, ask for more specific information. Be sure *you* stay on the point: few things make a busy subject more nervous than an interviewer who beats around the bush or can't keep to the topic at hand.

Don't ask complex, multifaceted questions. Most people think—and speak—one thought at a time.

BE SENSITIVE ABOUT RAPPORT WITH YOUR SUBJECT

Tune in to your subjects' needs. Don't take out a cigarette or a stick of gum unless they smoke or chew first. They may hate smokers or gum chewers, and then where are you? On the other hand, if you're offered a cup of coffee or a cigarette, it may be a clue that a break is needed.

It's okay to acknowledge that you know you're putting some strain on the subjects. But don't ever think that you must apologize. If you've done your job right, they've known in advance what you were after and have agreed to see you about it, even if reluctantly. If the strain is due to information you're bringing out (or struggling to bring out), it isn't your fault.

If the strain is due to your ineptness or impoliteness, that *is* your fault.

SAVE SENSITIVE OR EMBARRASSING QUESTIONS FOR LATE IN THE INTERVIEW

There are two major reasons for adopting this stance. The first is very practical: if you get booted out for asking impertinent questions, at least you've managed to get *some* information, and someone's refusal to talk about certain things may make a dramatic point in your book. Second, during the early part of the interview you can assess whether the subject is giving candid answers—something you'll have to know during the tougher give-and-take.

However, don't consciously shift gears for tough questions, or in other ways signal that you're on the touchy stuff. Just carry on normally into these topics. The more matter-of-fact you are, the more matter-of-factly the subject will answer.

Don't save difficult questions for too late. If you do, your subject might simply do a quick, "Oh, I'd love to answer that, but our time is up."

Don't feel you have to be a nice guy and avoid controversial, embarrassing, nosy, or probing questions. If they're needed in your pursuit of information, it's your duty to ask them and unprofessional not to. Keep your fact-finding responsibility as an author in mind and you'll be surprised at how easily even impertinent questions get answered.

Terry Brunner, executive director of the Better Government Association, a citizen watchdog organization in Chicago, says that his technique when dealing with a hostile subject is to accuse him of a dozen different foul deeds. "Sometimes he'll deny one or two but not even attempt to deny the others." Devices like that enabled Terry to help convict Mafia members and corrupt police officers. If your book calls for you to interview shady characters, you might give Terry's way a try. But for most interviews, honest, straightforward, tireless questioning—whether it's "Where were you born?" or "Why did you disappear with the document?"—pay off most consistently.

VERIFY WHAT THE SUBJECT IS TELLING YOU

Everyone who's read Woodward and Bernstein's *All the President's Men* knows that investigative authors must check the accuracy of everything they're told. Every interviewer ought to also at least spot-check that he's *hearing* the subject accurately and verify that the subject is *telling* the truth. Section 7.4 detailed the five checks for accuracy in researched material; you can use the same checks for evaluating first-hand information. In addition, you can make *internal* checks, if you think quickly enough, by simply asking several well-spaced similar questions that should bring forth identical information—and *external* checks by asking questions that you already know the answer to, probably through background research. If you get the answer you expect, then probably your subject is telling the truth and you're hearing it right. If the answer sounds wrong, you'll have to find out if you heard it wrong or it was told wrong. Or both—or neither.

LISTEN TO WHAT YOUR SUBJECT IS SAYING

If you work only from a prepared list of questions, you may miss some very valuable information. If you are lucky enough to interview a subject who plunges into new ground, or you're skillful enough to lead the conversation there, follow up with some more questions in that direction, or take up some other pastime. We'll never forget the transcript of an interview one writer sent us (in our days as editors) in which controversial basketball great Kareem Abdul-Jabbar ended an answer about his youth by saying, "But that wasn't the worst of my problems then." The writer's next words were, "What about your eating habits now?" At that instant, Jabbar had been set to reveal something special, perhaps even that "exclusive" every author dreams of. He may never be in just that expansive mood again.

SAY AS LITTLE AS POSSIBLE

A subject can't give information while your own voice is in gear. A good interviewer is a great listener. This simple, self-evident fact is overlooked by countless authors who monopolize their interview time.

On many occasions we've actually used silence as a device. We've just sat quietly, not asking another question, waiting to see what the subject would add spontaneously. Often it's a surprising elaboration on the last question we asked. That's because, not knowing how much we knew or didn't know, the subject felt we could evaluate the answer better than we actually could and, eager to stay clear of trouble, tried to explain the response more fully.

END WITH AN OPEN-ENDED QUESTION
"Is there something I didn't ask that you thought I ought to?" and "Have we covered everything now?" are two of our favorite endings.

EASE OFF BEFORE LEAVING
If you feel obliged to chat, *this* is the time for it. First of all, valuable information often changes hands when the interview seems to be over. The subjects give answers they were hesitant to reveal before your pen was put away. Or they nervously pull out the file they slipped into a drawer so you wouldn't see it on the desk. Or they start to return the urgent phone call they wouldn't take while you were listening attentively. Or, getting back to work, they put on the glasses they usually wear.

Second, it's good to part on a cordial note, especially since you'll want to leave the door open for a follow-up phone call in case you missed a few important points, think of other questions, or need clarification of points already made.

8·6 The Great Tape Recorder Question

The hardware of our profession is much less important than the skills we hone. Still, one question beginners always ask us is whether they ought to use tape recorders for live interviews. Our response is, never use a tape recorder unless you're convinced it's the best way to accomplish your goals. We've interviewed hundreds of people during our careers and have used tape recorders no more than a few dozen times. In fact, it's been more than three years since a recorder has gone along on one of our in-person interviews.

In deciding whether to record, keep in mind that there are at least six kinds of input to go after in almost every interview. Only two of them—quotes and anecdotes—can be captured on tape. Even then, you can't capture a quote's context, only its words. Ambience is tough to tape. So are scene descriptions, unless you add them afterwards. You can tape facts, figures, and leads, but for easy access to the data you'll have to wait until your tape is transcribed.

Technical errors are rife: batteries go dead, cords pull loose, background sirens cover just the most important phrases. We're sure you can supply your own horror stories. Also, technical problems aside, when you're considering the use of a recorder, there are plenty of practical questions to answer:

WILL THE SUBJECT BE AT EASE?
In this era of electronic journalism, most people are perfectly comfortable with tape recorders. Many authors we know simply turn theirs on at the start of interviews without even asking permission. Others consider permission a professional courtesy that writers ought to extend to their subjects. You'll have to base your decision on your instincts.

WILL YOU BE AT EASE?
If you're forever fiddling with the machine, you'll end up nervous—and so will your subject. Since the recorder can capture only a small part of what you probably hope to find out during an interview, you may miss out on ambience and description while worrying about technology.

WILL YOUR MIND WANDER?
Some writers are less alert to answers when confident that the recorder is taking down all the words. They miss important afterthoughts that might clue them into asking unprepared questions.

WILL TRANSCRIBING THE TAPE BE A TERRIBLE CHORE?
Once the interview is recorded, the best-selling (or independently wealthy) author can have it typed by someone else. Most of us have to transcribe it ourselves—and can that kill time! A few writers work with the tapes, not the transcriptions, to pick up nuances that get lost in the transcribing. Those writers have good memories they know they can trust. In any case, if you interview a subject who rambles, or if you're prone to invite rambling, relying on a tape recorder ensures a monumental job before you can get to the actual writing. And if you've got a mumbler for a subject, you may also find yourself with a tape that's nearly worthless.

ARE YOU PRONE TO EDIT INSTEAD OF WRITE?
Many books based on interviews read as if they were edited from tapes instead of written. That's because they were! The creative input, the interpretation by the author, just isn't there. If you find yourself

cutting and pasting transcripts and inserting transitions that merely edit them into order, you should seriously consider working from notes instead of recordings.

AFRAID YOU CAN'T TRUST YOUR MEMORY?
Several years ago Frank had a standing magazine assignment: if he ever managed to interview the at-times reclusive Professor Marshall McLuhan, he would be paid well for an article entitled "Marshall McLuhan, What're You Doing Now?" On a trip to Toronto, he finally managed to wangle an hour with the media guru. McLuhan specified right up front: no recorders. Not even any note-taking permitted. After chatting with the wizard for an hour, Frank had to hop a cab to the airport and then a plane back to New York. But all the while, his feverish pen was recreating the interview from memory. By the time the 727 touched down, his first draft was finished, crammed with fresh, accurate, witty McLuhanisms.

Playboy interviewers have to use tape recorders; no assignment is given without that understanding. Still, the famous *Playboy* quote in which then President-to-be Jimmy Carter admitted to having lusted in his heart was written from memory. Carter didn't make that remark until after the machine was packed away and the *Playboy* entourage was on its way out the door.

Given a chance (and a bit of on-the-job training), your memory can probably serve you better than you think. That plus your eyes, your pen, and your pad are all the tools you'll need to handle most interviews successfully. If, despite all our advice, you do use a recorder, here are some technical tips based on many authors' sad experiences:

Be sure you know how to work the recorder
Be sure the recorder is working and the batteries are fresh
Be sure you have enough tape to last the entire interview, even if it takes twice as long as expected
Set up some foolproof gimmick for knowing when the tape has run out (unless your recorder features a built-in signal)
Set the recorder's microphone as close to your subject as practical, to minimize voice-muddling room noise and echo

Even if you've taken every precaution, you still might want to cross your fingers—and take backup notes. During the most important taped interview of your life, your recorder is sure to give you trouble. We can't help but remember the young California writer we assigned to interview Alex Haley, who was practically a neighbor of his. Murphy's

Law prevailed, of course. His second reel of tape turned out blank. Having relied entirely on his recorder, all the young writer could do was drop an S.O.S. into Haley's mailbox and pray. His prayers were answered when Alex phoned to say, "Come on over, and this time use my recorder." The famous author of *Roots* admitted sympathetically that he'd had some recorder failures himself in his career.

Your subject might not be as simpatico as Alex Haley.

Chapter Nine

Three Ways to Write Exciting Nonfiction

PROLIFIC BONNIE REMSBERG, WHO'S WON AWARDS for her magazine articles and Emmys for her TV scripts, was once asked, "What's the best thing about writing?"

Her reply: "Having written."

Many of us share Bonnie's feelings. To go even further, many of us agree that the worst thing about writing is getting started on that first draft. We procrastinate by researching and researching until we're drowning in enough knowledge to write seven books. Or we put off the time by making involved schedules that detail our projected turnout. Or we copy our notes onto other note cards, in what we like to think is more logical order. Or we find a million priority items that need attention. There are as many wrinkles on the fabric of procrastination as there are talented writers to think them up.

Nevertheless, there comes a time when you have to face the first blank page. Once you've done several books, you recognize that time as an urge to get to work—to sit at the typewriter and start pounding out words or, if you're a longhand first-drafter, to get out your pad and pen. If this is your first or second book, you'd better not wait for the urge to prod you or terror may take over and you may *never* begin. The best way for you to get writing is to collect your outline and notes and plunge in. Start at what seems the most logical point, and keep writing at a steady pace, in the same location and for the same length of time each day, until you get to the end of Chapter One. Take a break for pleasure—an evening or a day or so—and then do the same with Chapter Two. Try to avoid lengthy interruptions; the momentum of chapter after chapter gives half the energy authors need to finish.

Don't go back and rewrite until you're done. By then you'll have the perspective to do a good editing job. Until then, many of the piecemeal changes you make may only have to be made again.

There are two opposing traps for the beginning *nonfiction* author who is attacking the first draft. The first trap is overwriting—filling the page with so many facts, figures, and examples that the points get buried. The second is writing too thinly—presenting generalized statements without enough explanation or support. Overwriting can best be corrected during the editing phase, so if you overwrite, don't worry about it for now. But if your writing tends to be thin, you *must* deal with that in your first draft. The very best way to avoid underwriting is to make full use of the nonfiction writer's three basic techniques.

9·1   The Three Basic Nonfiction Techniques

To put flesh on the skeleton of a chapter outline, the nonfiction author has only three basic techniques to choose from: exposition, quotation, and narration. These techniques are also used in writing articles, reports, and even fiction. Let's define them from the author's point of view:

> When an author *believes* something and reports his belief to readers along with the unattributed facts and figures to prove it, that's *exposition.*
>
> When an author *hears* (or reads in print) something worth repeating and repeats it for his own readers, attributing it with or without quotation marks, that's *quotation.*
>
> When an author *sees* something happen and reports it just as it happened, or reports what someone else has seen, also in story fashion, that's *narration.* (In nonfiction, narratives are generally called *anecdotes.*)

You must also understand each technique from the *reader's* point of view.

> When readers encounter *exposition*—your own conclusions, based on your own knowledge—they may be skeptical unless you're a currently renowned expert in the field you're writing about, or unless you're such a fine writer you spellbind them into forgetting their skepticism. It's a good idea to limit exposition to information that readers have no trouble believing, or use it to unify and reinforce passages that rely on the other two techniques.
>
> When readers see exposition coming, they expect to be bored. That's largely because so much exposition is written in a boring way. It's a challenge to make facts and generalizations come alive for readers. Your skill as a weaver of words is most tested here.
>
> When a reader sees *quotation*—from someone else who agrees with what you have to say—your own believability increases. We wish we could say that the increase is in direct proportion to the amount of genuine

expertise your quoted source has attained, but often it just depends on the length or prestige of his pedigree.

When a reader finds in your chapters *narration* of real-life instances of what you're talking about, your credibility increases dramatically. Perhaps it's because anecdotes generate strong visual images, and seeing is believing. In fact, the more vivid your anecdote, the more the reader believes both it and the point it makes.

The liveliest writing intermingles techniques whenever possible, inserting a quote within exposition or anecdote, or pausing within an anecdote for some exposition. Authors of nonfiction discover quickly the useful magic in the number 3: if they offer the reader three examples that fortify a generalization, whether presented as quote, anecdote, or expository fact, no further proof is generally needed. They keep that magic in mind, along with their overall goal: to present convincing evidence in a mix that's a pleasure to read.

9·2 Anecdotes

Everybody loves a good story. Who can pass up a chance to hear juicy gossip about the next-door neighbors? And what's more exciting than a bit of innocent eavesdropping? Some of the most successful recent nonfiction has depended heavily on anecdotes, the little narratives within our factual writing: Gay Talese's *Thy Neighbor's Wife,* Norman Cousins' *Anatomy of an Illness as Perceived by the Patient,* Tom Wolfe's *The Right Stuff.* Except for the fact that they have actually happened to real people, they have all the elements of fiction. (Ironically, many novels are thinly disguised narrations of real occurrences—and many nonfiction writers fictionalize names, places, and other story elements to protect their sources or to heighten the points they are trying to make. So even in this regard, there's often little difference between an anecdote and a scene in fiction.)

Many of our students start out confused about how to use anecdotes and how to recognize them, so we'll begin with a working definition:

An anecdote is a complete story in miniature.

It has a beginning and an ending.

It takes place in a particular setting, and the scene is usually delineated.

It shows a real person or people.

It shows something happening to the people—or shows them making something happen.

It shows time passing or people moving about.

It is nearly always told in the past tense, unlike the rest of the chapter, which is often in the present or sometimes the future tense.

Effectively used, the anecdote *takes the place of* exposition, the laying out of your facts. It not only whets reader interest by spinning a yarn about interesting people in interesting settings doing interesting things, but it conveys some of the information readers need to understand the thrust of your chapter. The point it makes should not be summarized before or afterwards. If you feel the point isn't clear enough, fix the anecdote. (That's where creative retouching of details sometimes come in.)

Anecdotes can be about other people, or about yourself. Hal Higdon, who has written twenty books and several hundred magazine articles over the years, is not only a winning marathon runner, but a master of the anecdote. In his book *On the Run from Dogs and People,* he tells them about others and about himself. Here's an example of the former:

> I suspect that if you have to ask, why run marathons? you're better off not running them. Leave the sport to us addicts, addicts like the runner who staggered into the locker room after finishing in the District of Columbia 25-kilometer championships one year. The race had been conducted despite a blinding snowstorm, which made it impossible to see more than five yards ahead. The runner sat on a bench next to Ed O'Connell, a government employee. For several minutes both competitors were too cold to talk. Finally the other runner turned to O'Connell and chattered through half-frozen lips: "Did you see those crazy people out there trying to drive in that weather?"

Let's examine the above anecdote, which begins with the words *like the runner who.* What is everything before that? It's exposition: a generalization that real runners are "addicts." What is a running addict like? Higdon could have told you with lots of specific details in more exposition: an addict runs in blizzards, he keeps on despite discomfort so intense he can't talk, and so on. Instead, he told a little story about just two runners, and let that make his points.

Check this anecdote against our definition of the elements of an anecdote. Notice that it contains every element.

Here's another passage from Higdon's book. He first makes a generalization, then bolsters it with three specific examples; then, to make even more specific the last of his three examples, he tells an anecdote about himself.

> Scientists are always studying marathoners, both from a psychological and physiological standpoint. Quite frequently we are requested to weigh in before and after our races, give urine specimens, and otherwise submit ourselves to indignities usually inflicted only upon pregnant women. After finishing the Kosice Marathon in Czechoslovakia one year, I was recovering while sitting on a bench under the stadium, when an attractive young girl in a white smock approached and took me by the hand. She couldn't speak English, but motioned me to follow. How nice, I thought, anticipating that she would offer refreshments or guidance to a hot bath.
>
> Instead, she led me into a medical room, sat me down in a chair, tied a rubber cord around one arm, and approached with a long needle. "This isn't fair," I cried. "You should be giving blood, not taking." She simply smiled and jabbed.

Notice that the point is actually made just before the little dialogue, but without the dialogue, the story wouldn't have had an end.

Higdon's book shows anecdotes within quotes, as well as quotes within anecdotes. It shows lengthy anecdotes as well as brief ones. It's a fine book to study for anyone who wants to improve anecdotal techniques. As you study these or other anecdotes that you find in your nonfiction reading, keep in mind, too, what they are *not*:

> Anecdotes are *not* spliced into exposition simply to offer readers diversion. Each anecdote must carry its weight by making a pertinent point.
>
> Anecdotes do *not* merely duplicate information already given through exposition or quotes. They add new details, new observations.
>
> Anecdotes are *not* passages in which the author repeats information told to him or repeats someone's *summary* of an event. Unless there's setting and action, it's merely quotation.

Because this last concept is tricky for beginners to grasp, we'll give an example—also from Higdon's book—of a passage that, despite its entertaining quality, is not anecdote but quotation:

> Arthur Lydiard has a test he uses on anyone who approaches him uncertain what event to run. "I take a flashlight and shine it in one of

his ears," explains Lydiard. "If I see light coming out the other side, he's a marathoner."

We know several authors who, while researching, put each anecdote they find on a single 3×5 card. To organize a chapter, they group their note cards into a logical layout. To write the first draft, they just fill in the transitions and generalizations. That's how vital anecdotes are to many kinds of books.

Obviously, a large part of your research should include a search for anecdotes. How should you go about this? One way is through interviews, to which we devoted much of Chapter 8. When you ask people to provide anecdotes, they may not understand what you're talking about. But instead, if you say, "Give me examples," you'll get the same thing from their own experience or from others they know.

The ring of truth in an anecdote is achieved by getting all the vivid details and making the reader see them too. If your anecdote reveals material that's quite personal or embarrassing, neither editors nor readers expect your confidants' full names. Nancy Friday used only first names—and changed even those—in her *Men in Love*. In her foreword she explains her reasons, and readers never doubt the authenticity of her male fantasizers. Other authors don't spell out the name changes or the reasons why they write just Janice or Janice D.; they assume their motives are obvious.

The only time you weaken an anecdote by not quoting a person's full name is when the strength of your anecdote rests on some public recognition or reputation important to the reader. Still, if your only choice is between using an anecdote with the participants disguised, or discarding a good anecdote, by all means drop the name and not the story. (Until you've built a reputation for yourself, editors may insist on being told your sources' full names and addresses for verification. But they should promise not to reveal the identities.)

If you don't need a full name, what's to keep you from making up a harmless anecdote that illustrates the point? That's a question our students ask repeatedly. And we answer repeatedly, "Try it!" You'll find that making up a believable setting, history, experience, and voice of a fictitious character is much harder to pull off than getting on the phone and soliciting a true anecdote. Ask any novelist. The fictions you create are never as farfetched as the truth! In faking an anecdote about a man who studied books to trim his waistline, would you think of going into intimate detail about how the books improved his sex life too? In making up an anecdote to prove the earthiness of a prominent southern mayor, would you tell how he'd gotten a girl in trouble in his younger days? These and other stranger-than-fiction anecdotes rewarded our for-real research efforts.

Calling it New Journalism, some writers have openly (and sometimes not so openly) invented settings, people, and situations. As expected, the people they've described sound like stick figures; the anecdotes fall flat. The *true* New Journalists use real people involved in real happenings. Sometimes these writers set their subjects in their natural milieus even though the interview may have taken place somewhere else. It works best when, during the interview, the successful author—old or "new"—has solicited enough facts to reconstruct the subject's natural habitat on paper. We don't consider that invention at all.

Another technique that some might consider invention is the amalgamation of several incomplete or unexciting anecdotes. When we were writing our *Eat Anything Exercise Diet,* in order to make one interesting and pointed anecdote about bingers, we made a composite of several bingers we'd known, taking the colorful personality of one, the ingenious binging technique of another, the setting of a third. Our amalgamation came out so real that when our book was syndicated in the hometown newspaper of still another friend, she phoned to tell us she recognized herself in our anecdote.

Manipulating anecdotes in any way is controversial. Some editors consider it taboo. Our philosophy on controversial techniques is, simply, when in doubt discuss it with the editor in advance. Then, in print, tell the reader what you've done the way Nancy Friday did.

9·3 Direct and Indirect Quotes

Quotation marks are among the most misused symbols in written English. They're second only to exclamation points, which are misused for exactly the same reason. When a novice author finishes a sentence that he hoped would generate excitement, and suspects he's failed, he hits the ! key on his typewriter in hopes it'll do the job. When he suspects that an idea falls flat in his own words, he looks for someone else's mouth to put it in on the false assumption that the quote marks provide interest of their own.

There's no magic inherent in either exclamation points or quotes. They do not cause excitement in themselves. They do not improve boring, hackneyed writing. Exclamation points indicate strong, personal emotion, which should be carefully hidden in most nonfiction books. Quotation marks indicate *only* that the words between them have been borrowed.

One reason some people think quotes are a magic device for lifting an idea out of the mud is that an anecdote often quotes the words of people involved in the action. (Look at the way Higdon's good anecdotes use quotes.) But it is not the quoted dialogue in anecdotes that makes them work; it is the action.

If there is no action—if nothing is happening but the transfer of information, experience, or opinion—and if the words involved in the transfer have been borrowed from someone else, the information is not an anecdote but a quotation. When we borrow our informant's exact words, we put quotation marks around them to show that they are secondhand.

DIRECT QUOTES
Just as you must learn to choose among possible anecdotes, you must learn to choose *only* the direct quotations that make your chapters exciting. Improperly used quotations say as much about your writing as improper table manners say about your upbringing. They may say, for instance, that you lack confidence to draw conclusions on your own, that you lean on others to draw them for you. They may lead readers (and editors) to conclude that you lack the originality to cast your own sentences, paint your own prose pictures, turn your own phrases. If you're quoting currently fashionable intellectuals or obscure men and women of letters, they may smack suspiciously of name-dropping or of padding a poorly prepared outline.

There are three major areas in which direct quotations should be used in a book.

1. FOR TONE OF VOICE
When the source's use of language is particularly picturesque, and sharing it with your readers will add to your point, use the direct quote. *Both* criteria must be present. Picturesque language alone is not enough. In *Maybe You Should Write a Book,* longtime editor and publisher Ralph Daigh uses a quote in this way:

> A talented, experienced editor, W. C. Lengel, then editor in chief of Crest and Gold Medal, summed up this situation: "Buying an unpublished book for reprint is like playing poker in the dark—without a deck of cards."

2. FOR AUTHORITY

When it is important for written information, especially interpretive information, to come from an obviously authoritative voice, use the direct quote. Remember that this works only if your reader knows the voice is authoritative. You'll have to make her credentials clear unless they're as well known to your readers as James Michener's are to you. Imagine how much less effective this Michener quote would have been had Daigh paraphrased it:

> "*Hawaii* went very slowly and needed constant revision. Since the final version contained about 500,000 words, and since I wrote it all many times, I had to type, in my painstaking fashion, about 3,000,000 words."

3. FOR PROTECTION

When you want to insert an opinion or point of view that the reader may quibble with, use the direct quote. This is particularly useful if the opinion is not a popular one or shows the opposite viewpoint from your own. When readers see the quotation mark, they get a clear and quick signal that *your* viewpoint has paused and *another,* perhaps contradictory, viewpoint has temporarily taken over. Daigh relies on that effect to share with his readers what he thinks is Mario Puzo's unorthodox acceptance of, as Daigh puts it, "only $25,000 for screen rights to *The Godfather,* and thus locking up the greatest bargain in movie history." He tells this fact as exposition and, directly after it, quotes Puzo:

> "That twenty-five grand was the whole world to me, then," Mario said. "It was not only the most money I had ever had in one lump, but it was practically the first time I was ever out of debt. Paramount took a chance on me and it paid off for them. They don't owe me a thing."

INDIRECT QUOTES

Some authors, having encountered a useful direct quote in their reading, will splice it into their writing in exactly the same way they would if they'd spoken directly to the expert. Here is an example of that from *Diets '80: Rating the Diets,* in which Theodore Berland quotes from our *Eat Anything Exercise Diet* as if the words have been told to him by our co-author, Dr. Frank Konishi:

> Says Frank Konishi, professor of nutrition at Southern Illinois University, Carbondale: "The energy we burn in moving our muscles around—in *exercising* them—that's the important ingredient in keeping our weight where it ought to be."

Then a little footnote number alerts the interested reader that she can turn to notes at the back of Berland's book, and she discovers there that the quotation came from our volume, not a personal interview. Since this controversial technique can mislead readers, it ought to be discussed with your editor before you use it.

However, in addition to *direct* quotes, the kind we put within quotation marks, writers can also *paraphrase,* which amounts to quoting indirectly. If the person we want to quote is long-winded or unclear, we can throw away the quotation marks, rewrite his clumsy constructions, but give him credit for his ideas. That way, we can rest on his expertise without burdening our readers with his wordiness. This is true whether our source is a person we've met or someone whose writing we've read.

Here's an example of paraphrase, taken from Judi's book *Stopping Out:*

> Dressel and Thompson, in the book *Independent Study,* point out that although such study is the intended goal of all higher education, nothing in traditional college courses teaches a student how to undertake such a project. They suggest that the ideal path to *your* independent study should include, in the following order. . . .

and the paraphrase goes on for about 100 words more. Though you're sharply limited by copyright law in the amount of words you can quote directly from another source, the limits of *fair use* that apply to indirect quotations are broader. (For further discussion, see Chapter 16.)

CREATIVE QUOTATION

Even a direct quote is not always what it seems, despite the definition that has been advanced by English teachers. At the risk of their enmity we'll share with you the way most working writers we know use quotations when taking them from *interviews with live sources:*

A well-written passage is placed within quotation marks to indicate that the information or opinion contained therein has come directly from the attributed source—but *not* that it necessarily duplicates each and every specific word that the source used.

This understanding is so important to working authors that we'll risk boring you by expanding on it:

An accurate quote is not necessarily simply the words the writer heard a person say, but may include words the person would say if he were asked to retell his ideas within the context of that part of the book in which the quote is going to be written.

To illustrate how important this point is, we put to our classes the following puzzle:

Let's suppose John Dean was told that President Nixon was about to bug his inner office, and two writers heard Dean's reaction. One sent in the story this way: ". . . Dean said approvingly, 'I'd like to see him do it.' " The other wrote, ". . . Dean challenged, 'I'd like to see him do it.' " Which reporter was quoting Dean correctly?

Obviously, it is more important to reflect what your source *meant* to say than to quote his exact words. A good writer makes the *sense* of his interviewee's words accurate, but not necessarily the *exact language* of those words. It is dishonest to quote precisely if you know that it gives a false impression of what the person really meant.

This definition of direct quote meets head-on a situation that almost every experienced writer faces time and time again: You interview a person with one idea firmly in mind and then, after more research, the theme or point of view shifts slightly so that the interviewee's responses are no longer precisely in context. If you quote the person's exact *words,* you may find you're no longer representing his exact *ideas.*

This working definition also simplifies the interviewer's job, because in most situations a pro's note-taking gets the gist but not all the words of a person's thought. If, in reviewing notes, an experienced author wants to quote that thought directly, he often bridges the gap with words the interviewee would have said in the appropriate time and place.

Only once in our decades of writing has a subject later claimed, "I didn't say that." In that particular case, we had transferred his *exact* words from our notes to our manuscript. People recall their own precise words as rarely as interviewers remember them. It's their exact *ideas* that you'd better get right.

Academics troubled by our pragmatic definition of *direct quote,* which forces writers to think at least as much as their interview subjects, will find little comfort in the next refinement we'll detail: A quote may be the words a subject wishes he had said.

Very few people speak in a style that reads as if it expresses precise or exciting thoughts. Most tend to be tentative, internally contradictory, ungrammatical, and either overly choppy or overly long-winded. One of the easiest ways to make your interviewee appear illiterate is to quote his exact spoken words.

Sometimes a writer does want to make the point that the interviewee's speech patterns are illiterate, picturesque, or disjointed. Then he copies the words exactly, and quotes them without cosmetic improvement. But in most cases it is the essence of a thought, not the manner in which it is delivered, that's important. When the good writer cleans up mistakes in grammar and word usage, the interviewee is always grateful for the courtesy. In fact, people who are interviewed frequently *expect* writers to make them sound educated and may be indignant at anybody who seems to ridicule them by printing their exact off-the-cuff words.

What if you interview someone who has trouble saying what she really means? The ideas may all be present, but the presentation so poor you can't extract a good quote even by cleaning up the fuzzy language. In a case like that, the experienced interviewer listens for quotable ideas. When we hear one that's good, but not said well enough to make exciting reading, we prompt the interviewee with: "Do you mean to say . . . ?" and then, on the spot, rephrase the material so it can be used in our book. If the interviewee says, "Yes," then we feel we have received permission to write the quote the way *we* said it and attribute our restatement to the source of the idea.

Were the working definition of the quote not so vital to tenderfoot authors, we might not have dwelled on it so frankly. By revealing what is not commonly shared with the public, we're inviting caustic comments from critics of the press and from folks who were taught in journalism school (and may be teaching it there now) that true integrity of the press calls for copying down words exactly, their meaning be damned. We want to stress, especially for those people, that we cannot condone writers who invent quotations from whole cloth, who put words into unwilling mouths, or who in any substantive manner alter the true meaning of what a person has to say. Ethics aside, such perversions invite libel suits, and justly so. But the opposite is equally unethical—and equally libelous—as shown by our John Dean anecdote at the beginning of this section, in which at least one hypothetical writer was misrepresenting what he heard while reporting the words precisely.

9·4 Exposition

In addition to quotes and anecdotes, the only technique available to nonfiction authors is exposition: the presentation of your thoughts with the data that back them up. The thoughts are offered in *generalizations* of fact and opinion. The backups are all the *specifics*—the dates and statistics, the definitions and concrete examples—that prove the generalizations without the need to call on other people's experiences (anecdotes) or authority (direct and indirect quotes).

Most of our students come to us knowing all the fundamentals of expository writing except how to make it colorful. It's the only nonfiction writing they've been taught in college and high school. All those "compare and contrast" essays have prepared them to find facts and figures and to pepper their papers with lots of convincing examples. For those who need brush-up review in the art of exposition, or those who need special help in making their words vivid and their sentences lively, we recommend our basic textbook, *Good Writing.* Mostly, we find ourselves trying to steer students away from lengthy exposition unrelieved by anecdotes or by lively, pertinent quotes.

Some books, especially how-tos based on your own experience, don't lend themselves readily to anecdotes and quotes. Others, in which the author relies for credibility on her own reputation or authority, can get away with mostly unattributed specifics. They become entirely, or nearly entirely, exposition. Alvin Toffler's *The Third Wave* is written like this, but a glance at the back of the book shows doubting Thomases that many unattributed statements are in fact carefully documented.

Keep in mind that your expository writing can—and *should*—be as vivid as your quotes and anecdotes. One easy way to keep readers interested, when you've got long unrelieved exposition, is to speak directly to them. Examples are evident throughout this book. To keep her exposition lively, Nancy Friday used the technique this way in *Men in Love:* "There was always an imaginary reader in mind— probably me—and I had to make what I was saying emotionally clear to the reader, so there was no way he or she could fail to think about it."

Toffler's writing in *The Third Wave* is an example of how a vivid, explicit, rhythmic style of expository writing carries the reader along:

> An information bomb is exploding in our midst, showering us with a shrapnel of images and drastically changing the way each of us perceives

and acts upon our private world. In shifting from a Second Wave to a Third Wave info-sphere, we are transforming our own psyches.

Each of us creates in his skull a mind-model of reality—a warehouse of images. Some of these are visual, others auditory, even tactile. Some are only "percepts"—traces of information about our environment, like a glimpse of blue sky seen from the corner of the eye. Others are "linkages" that define relationships, like the two words "mother" and "child." Some are simple, others complex and conceptual, like the idea that "inflation is caused by rising wages." Together, such images add up to our picture of the world—locating us in time, space, and the network of personal relationships around us.

Notice the strong image of an exploding bomb carried through the first sentence in this excerpt. Observe that the vivid word *skull* is chosen rather than the more pedestrian word *head* at the beginning of the second paragraph. See how Toffler uses definition and example to make his words "percepts" and "linkages" come alive, and how he specifies the exact picture of the world he has in mind: the picture that puts us where we belong in it. Such vivid exposition is difficult to achieve, but it's worth striving for.

Once you master this technique, and the other two techniques of nonfiction writing, you'll discover that it becomes almost a reflex action to mix them pleasingly in chapter after chapter. Although the best thing about writing will always be, as Bonnie Remsberg says, "Having written," getting to that point—while always a challenge—will cease to be a terror.

Chapter Ten

Five Ways to
Write a First Novel

S OMERSET MAUGHAM WAS GUEST-LECTURING TO A
class in English literature, so the story goes, and a student asked
the inevitable puzzler, "How do you write a novel?"

Maugham answered, "There are three rules." Every pencil poised
at the ready. "Unfortunately, no one knows what they are."

Even without such a prestigious disclaimer, we wouldn't presume
in one chapter to try to teach you how to write a novel. There are *books*
on that subject—and most people who follow them assiduously still
produce nothing publishable. Even more than the craft of writing
nonfiction, the art of fiction writing has to be absorbed through the
pores like venom from a noxious weed—to leave you scratching at a
typewriter for the rest of your life.

The best we can do for you is describe the processes that various
novelist friends have gone through to get their first novels written and
sold. You can probably pick up hints from each. You might even
identify closely with one of the five in particular, since each of our
colleagues went at the grind from a different perspective.

10·1 Born to Write Novels

When Kentuckian Margaret George was all of seven years old, she
wrote her first novel—a melodramatic saga of a horse. She expanded on
it, illustrated it, and at the age of ten, persuaded her father to ship it
off to an editor at Grosset & Dunlap. It didn't have just a title page and
chapter headings, but a dedication page, a table of contents, and a
copyright notice. The editor didn't buy her novel, but did send a
warm, personal rejection slip that urged Margaret to keep writing and
send another manuscript after she put some years on.

Most ten-year-old writers grow up to write teenage love letters.
Margaret's intention to publish never wavered. When she was sixteen,
her first work appeared in print, an article in *Teens Today* about why
some older girls date younger boys. Two years before that, she'd

completed the first draft of her first full-length adult novel, *Island*. Not only that, but she recognized—at fourteen—that it was just a first draft, badly in need of polishing. Teen responsibilities kept getting in the way but, "When I was twenty, I just had to finish it, so I took the whole summer between years in college, went back to Paducah, and did nothing, absolutely nothing, but work on that book." Since finishing that second draft, she's done three or four more versions of *Island*, a romance set on a desert island peopled by noble savages and three shipwrecked young Americans: a macho but dumb male, a not-so-macho but bright male, and a beautiful but brainless bikini-clad blonde with a good heart. By fourteen, Margaret knew the elements of the commercial novel. Well she might, having already read hundreds of them. In fact, she recalls, "I started writing because I wanted to put my own endings onto the stories I was reading. Pretty soon I was writing new stories, beginning to end."

In her mind, that's still the way she works: "I just have an innate need to dramatize the nondramatic. To be honest, I do it with all my life, not just my writing. It's like spending your whole life in the movies."

Margaret never shoved *Island* into a box and mailed it to one publisher after another, the strategy of so many budding novelists. She stuck the manuscripts of her many drafts into a closet and went on with the rest of her multifaceted life, becoming a career woman, wife, and mother. "Then in 1971 I saw BBC's *The Six Wives of Henry VIII*, and I got interested in Henry himself. I did some research and found that nobody had ever written *his* point of view. I wanted to exonerate poor Henry." She paused. "Also, that genre was popular then." Since then, Henry and Margaret have become such intimates that a friend described her husband's role thus: "Paul lives in the here and now while you, you're in the then and maybe."

While living a year in Sweden, Margaret wrote a rough 100 pages of her planned fictionalized autobiography of Henry VIII. Back in the states, a friend at *Voice of America* read and liked it. (Most friends, you will find, like most of what you show them.) This friend encouraged Margaret to send her 100 pages to his local literary agent and, surprising herself, she did. That was in 1974. "He didn't like it," she recalls. "I didn't either. However, he did like the idea and said he'd like to see me work it up into better shape."

But how to figure out the form of that better shape? Margaret felt she had to do it alone. "I'd once taken a creative writing course at Stamford, and it had seemed dedicated to stomping on writers. I'd gotten nothing out of it except the later satisfaction of seeing the instructor's own novel on a cheapy remainder table in a bookstore. In general, I think creative writing classes are a waste."

By trial and error, she finally found the right form for her novel, did a new 245-page version of Henry VIII's early years, and asked us—who had recently become her friends—to have a look at it. We assured her she was right on the mark, and in 1979 Margaret mailed the incomplete manuscript to the agent who'd encouraged her back in 1974. He liked it and showed it immediately to an editor at St. Martin's Press, who was so impressed that, almost by return mail, Margaret George received a contract with a $15,000 advance to write Henry VIII's belated autobiography.

Could she have gotten there faster? "Yes, if I'd spent more time writing. You progress through writing without outside help. You perfect your own style. The process of writing teaches you to write. No course can do that." She adds, "But you can learn what to write *about*. For my next book I'm going to choose a story that can be published and reject noncommercial ideas.

"Most writers think that publishing is a great charity like the National Endowment for the Arts. Writers have to learn that it isn't. Once I learned that, although it didn't influence my writing style, it did give me a thicker skin."

10·2 She Worked Her Way Up

Jill Ross Klevin is one of the fastest typists we've ever seen. She can turn out well over 100 words a minute, 100 pages a day. But initially, her speed actually got in her way.

At the urging of a friend, Jill first attended a magazine-writing class Judi was teaching. Jill, an active, athletic Long Island housewife and mother, had already supplemented her income with a number of porn stories. She could knock out one a day—not bad, she felt, for the $500 apiece the publisher paid. Sometimes she'd get work writing ad copy, financial reports, educational materials, anything in English. "But it wasn't literature in any shape or form," Jill remarks. What she wanted was to write something that took effort and gave emotional rewards.

Jill was tuned in on children and their constant hassle with the adult world. She was aware that her own two growing children had confusions and questions that were met with honesty by few of the children's novels they were reading. Jill wished more young-adult novelists would deal with the theme of the young person who is different from the rest. She devised a plot based on some incidents in her own life, and tentatively began her first young adult novel.

As she started work, several insights surfaced to help her along. Most obvious was the fact that she knew how to tell a good story. Up to that point, all of her writing (porn included) had contributed to her instinctive but well-formed ability to lay down a good plot. Her alertness, sensitivity, and years of apprenticeship helped her draw brilliantly defined characters like Abby, narrator of her first novel, *The Summer of the Sky-Blue Bikini:* "I haven't changed, physically speaking, since I turned ten, which gives you a pretty good idea of where I'm at in the body department." Or Abby's buxom but nonetheless dissatisfied sister Mel, self-described: "You know what? Fat's *obscene!* When you're fat you're practically *deformed!*" It's obvious from the preceding snatches that along the way Jill had developed a fine ear for dialogue.

Only two things stood in her way. The first was her shiny IBM Model A, which roared and soared like a race car every time Jill sat in front of it. She was accustomed to grinding out words so quickly that even her unusually sharp instincts didn't have time to take charge of the plot, dialogue, and characters. We threatened to make Jill use one of our beat-up portable manuals. Her fingers slowed, and her talent took over.

The second thing that got in Jill's way (and gets in the way of so many others) was doubt. Like Margaret George, Jill Ross Klevin liked to make up dreams. But unlike Margaret, who plotted her whole career from the beginning, Jill didn't believe her talent was exceptional. We told her to stop worrying and just write, that she was on the verge of completing a publishable novel. But because we were her friends, our advice was suspect. So we steered her to an agent, who not only seconded our faith but sold Jill's first novel two months later. Now finally she believes in herself too. In fact, the last time we heard from her, Jill was finishing the last novel in a three-book contract and tackling a new challenge: her first serious adult novel. She's ready to move on again.

10·3 Read and Write

"First of all, decide what you want to write, what genre you want to write it in, and read that genre," Bernhard J. Hurwood advises new novelists. He's had over two dozen thrillers published under his own name and several pseudonyms—but, he recalls, "First I read all of Ian

Fleming's James Bond stories and all of the super-mysteries like them."

Bern came to novel writing from film editing and then movie reviewing, both of which honed his keen sense for a good story. His fictionalized autobiography of Edgar Allan Poe, *My Savage Muse,* is a recent—"and demanding"—step out of the genre he's been grinding out for years. Bern recalls, "I got my first contract to write a series of four quick-and-dirty sex novels based on just a couple of really dynamite plots I'd dreamed up. The editor was stuck. He needed those four books in six weeks, so he took a chance on me because of my film background." It took Bern seven days to crank out the first 120-page novel from his outline, "And each of the others took about that long too." After that, Bern did nine more in quick succession for the pleased editor. "I actually developed a spy series. The Man from T.O.M.C.A.T.—Tactical Operations Master Counter-espionage Assault Team. For each of the T.O.M.C.A.T. books, I'd work up a 30-page outline for the editor's okay. The finished manuscripts were supposed to be 240 pages each, and I kept pretty close to that. My first drafts, then and now, come so easily I almost never make any changes. If I do try to make changes, I find it often sounds worse."

Bernie, whose mind is quick and sharp and always plotting something, would have you believe that the toughest part of learning to write novels boils down to, "How do you keep from constantly saying, 'he said' 'she said'?" To solve that snag, he says, "I studied my thesaurus until I came up with over 300 variations. In fact, it worked so well that for a while I was selling printed copies of my list for three dollars."

Pushed a bit, Bern admits, "I once did take this short story writing class taught by Adela Rogers St. Johns. She told us she swiped ideas for constructing stories from Dickens. Since I was about the only one in class who turned in anything, we became pretty close. In fact, I still count her as my mentor, although I prefer swiping ideas from Robert Louis Stevenson."

Bernie clarified his larceny: "I still read him a lot. He really knows how to tell a story, and he tells it the way I like to. He's got very complicated plots, he ends every chapter with a cliff-hanger, his villains are always colorful and bizarre, yet there's something lovable about 'em. That's what I attempt in my novels." On the other hand, Stevenson is noted for an overwhelmingly male cast of characters and, for today's reader, what good is a spy without his trusty *femme fatale?* "Besides," says Bernie, "they're more interesting than the men," proving that he follows his model only so far.

While we were gathering details for this chapter, Bernie remarked that he had 100 pages left to write of a book due the next week, and then was off to put in an appearance at a convention of fantasy-book buffs on his way to England to research yet another project. "I'll share one final tip with your readers," he said. "Never let your editor know the ending to your novel until he's bought it."

10·4 Collaborate

"Moving from nonfiction into fiction is like going from carpentry into metaphysics," says Tania Grossinger. When she decided to write her first novel, she had already been a publicist for such clients as Stein & Day Publishers and had written such successful nonfiction books as *Growing Up at Grossinger's, The Book of Gadgets,* and *The Great Gadget Catalog.*

"It was during work on my *Growing Up at Grossinger's* that I got this idea for a novel," Tania recalls. "It was just so great that I didn't want to risk blowing it. You know, I *thought* I could write one, or at the very least learn quickly enough. But what if I couldn't? There was always that nagging feeling whenever I thought about it."

So Tania did what most established pros do when they're in a professional quandary: she talked to another seasoned pro, in this case her good and trusty agent. "She liked the book's idea too." In fact, she sold it to St. Martin's Press, which offered a comfortable advance. "I figure I was being paid to learn how to write a novel."

Tania decided on a unique learning tool: a collaborator. "I'm a fatalist. The day I started to look for likely collaborators, Andrew Neiderman called me to ask for the name of the agent I liked so much. I knew Andrew from my days at Stein & Day. I'd done some publicity on his novel *Sisters.* I felt the two of us could work together. So I put the idea to Andrew and he went for it."

The actual writing of the novel that became *Weekend* took less than five months. "That's because we worked at it, I mean really *worked.* I didn't even know the names of Andrew's kids until after we finished the manuscript. We'd get together, plot out a couple of chapters in advance, then he'd go back to his home in the Catskills and do the first drafts and I'd take it through five or six revisions."

Ever the closet realist, Tania muses, "Somebody else could have done it better. Somebody else worse. But not like mine. Such joy!" She took charge of her own book's publicity, of course, but immediately began to plot her next novel, too—this time solo. Her lessons-by-collaboration taught her she *can* write a novel on her own.

10·5 Fiction, Nonfiction, It's All the Same

Murray Teigh Bloom is an elder statesman to magazine and nonfiction book authors, especially among members of the American Society of Journalists and Authors, where he has headed the sensitive Editor–Writer Relations Committee for a decade. To his colleagues, Murray lectures, formally and informally, "Every ten years you ought to take a flyer, try something different, get into some project that you've always wanted to do. It can pay off financially, but it doesn't have to. At the very least, the break from your routine will leave you refreshed, inspired, and you won't feel like you're in that rut so many writers get into after enough years in this business."

For Murray, one such break resulted in his writing the play *Leonora*. Although it hasn't been commercially produced yet, eight different producers have taken options on it, paying a total sum that has rewarded Murray handsomely for his writing time. Now the ninth optioner appears ready to actually produce it on Broadway.

When he wasn't taking once-a-decade breaks, Murray developed a reputation as the author of deeply researched, well-crafted nonfiction articles for magazines such as *Reader's Digest,* and as the creator of books like *Money of Their Own* (1957), *The Man Who Stole Portugal* (1966), *Rogues to Riches* (1972), and *Lawyers, Clients and Ethics* (1974). His muckraking 1969 *The Trouble with Lawyers* clung to the best-seller list. A proficient craftsman, an excellent researcher, a savvy marketer, he had learned to tell a good story, too, but his stories had all been nonfiction.

Then, while researching a project, he stumbled on the fact that from 1880 to 1930 Jewish underworld gangs managed to grab a small piece of the international prostitution racket, against the bloody opposition of British, French, Italian, Chinese, Japanese, and Rumanian gangs. What particularly fascinated Murray was that only in the Jewish communities was there forceful and consistent opposition to the white-slavers among them. He thought that the battle between the opposing forces would make an intriguing nonfiction book. "But editors were afraid the subject would raise too many hackles. So I sat down with my agent and told him what I had in mind: turning the idea into a novel. He told me, 'Give me 40 pages of the novel and a synopsis and we'll see what happens.' So I gave him what he asked for."

Murray's agent went to the marketplace with the idea. "The most excitement came from Tom Congdon, who was then at Doubleday. He wanted to work with this book the way he'd worked with Peter

Benchley on *Jaws,* one chapter at a time with as many as five rewrites. That would take too long!" Murray took that once-a-decade flyer he talks about. He decided to finish the novel and sell it that way. At first he approached the writing cautiously. "I worked on it between articles. But it was obvious that would take forever. By the end of June 1975 I'd finished only half the book. So I decided it was time to work on it fulltime." By the end of August, Murray delivered ten copies of *The Thirteenth Man* to his agent, who submitted them to ten likely publishers. Several made offers to buy, and Macmillan won the bid. The gamble had paid off.

"Before the book was published, I sold movie rights. It was a fluke. I was playing tennis with a friend who had been a United Artists executive but left to go independent. While we were waiting for a court, I chatted, 'Oh, by the way, I just finished a book.' Of course he wanted to know what it was about, and the next week he phoned to say, 'I want it.'

"Nineteen out of twenty film options don't work out, but this did," Murray says. Shortly after his first novel was published, his first motion picture was released, renamed *Last Embrace.* "Like Hitchcock," Murray likes to say, he even had a walk-on part in the film.

How did Murray train his nonfiction typewriter to turn out a novel? He didn't, he says. He feels there isn't any difference between writing convincing nonfiction and writing credible fiction. "It isn't a sense of 'fiction' that helps, it's a sense of people and places, voices, strange places to be pulled out of your head. These are *your* characters, *your* scenes. This is a nonfiction writer's treasury." In classic nonfiction style, he first filled in the broadest strokes of his story. "I wanted to do it in the here-and-now instead of setting it into history. And I wanted it to be a diary of the main character, so I had to do it in the first person, even though most people advise first novelists to stick to the third person. Then I started on a framework.

"The thing I needed most was a motive. Of course, revenge was the obvious one. So I started researching in psychological studies about revenge. Pretty soon I started on Biblical references and discovered 'the avenger of the blood,' Deuteronomy 19:12. Once I saw this, I knew I had my theme. It was exactly the same as if I were researching nonfiction." The novel's theme had moved from the brothel syndicate itself to the solution of the murders of twelve descendents of syndicate members. The thirteenth intended victim happens to be a CIA agent—coincidentally, a fine narrator.

As in so many nonfiction articles and books by experienced

authors, many characters and scenes came from Murray's mental treasury. Even the CIA agent was based on memory. Murray cryptically explains, "I had friends who knew that occupation very well."

But, what about the actual writing?

"In fiction, technical aspects are not important. You have to trust your subconscious. Until the last day, I didn't know how it would end. It helps to have a good ear; without that, writing a novel can be rough. And there is an advantage to coming to a novel with some reputation as a nonfiction writer. It won't sell your novel, but it gives you an element of trust."

Murray's next book was *The Brotherhood of Money,* about the public and private makers of the world's currencies. His research, his mental storehouse of scenes and characters, and his typewriter make it as fast-paced as *The Thirteenth Man,* but it's shelved in the nonfiction section of your local bookstore. He still sees himself as a writer of nonfiction, and suggests: "Every nonfiction writer should do a novel, if for no other reason but to improve his nonfiction technique."

Chapter Eleven

How to Edit and Prepare Your Final Manuscript

MORE THAN ANYTHING ELSE, THE ONE THING that causes writer's block is the notion (fostered by schoolteachers who revere the published word) that fine writing flows like magic from the pens of a few special people blessed with the gift of effortless creativity. Thus misguided, hopeful writers collect their thoughts and poise over their typewriters. Then, unless the words flow, they think something is wrong with *them* instead of their misinformed teachers. No wonder they freeze up and can't write a word.

There *are* a few blessed writers whose first drafts are practically in publishable form. But James A. Michener writes his novels "over and over again, up to six or seven times." Taylor Caldwell told interviewer Ralph Daigh that "after writing about twenty pages, I go over them and over them and over them, cutting and changing words to bring out the meaning more clearly." Norman Vincent Peale writes his first drafts in longhand and, "After I've written two or three thousand words, I go through the penciled copy and correct it and mark it up. . . . Then, when I can't read it any more myself, because it is so marked up, I have it typed. Then I go over the typed copy."

Each of the three has a different method of revising, but for all three accomplished and prolific authors, the first draft is barely the beginning: the setting down of the chapter line. Most authors find that writing well is not just a matter of cleaning up a first draft's spelling and punctuation errors for a neat final copy. It's in the editing that the real act of writing takes place.

Let's examine all that revision entails. Along the way, we'll suggest the writing methods we've developed that make the procedure easier for us. Until you find your own best way of working, you might want to try our way.

11·1 Prepare Your First Draft With Revision In Mind

You can usually tell experienced writers by the look of their first drafts. If they've stopped along the way to erase or to rewrite a page so it has no typos, they're probably beginners. If some words are misspelled, some sentences are mispunctuated, and there's lots of crossing out scattered through the pages, they're probably serious writers who've been at the game awhile.

In writing your first draft, the best use you can make of your time is to concentrate on putting down all your ideas with enough fleshing-out to make them convincing, inserting all the details that make your scenes move and your characters breathe. Do it with as few stops and starts as possible. Don't bother to type footnotes, but do key research material to the manuscript as you go along, whether you're writing fact or that type of fiction facetiously called faction. That way, you won't waste a lot of time later on tracking down the sources of various pieces of information. Sometimes we type sources' names and page numbers in our margins; other times we type sketchy clues in parentheses at the ends of passages that rely on research notes. Only if we'll need footnotes for the final draft do we type all these details.

We're not always as careful as we'd like to be, and sometimes we forget to transcribe all the data we'll need. In one chapter of our last book, the college composition text called *Good Writing,* we introduced the fact that subordinate clauses are not usually subordinate in idea. As we typed that, we decided we'd better back up our statement with an illustration from someone else's prose. On the spot, we found one in our pile of magazines. We copied the author of the selection, the page number, and the magazine it came from—only we forgot to write the title or issue date. When we needed the full reference for the final draft's back-of-the-chapter footnotes, it cost us a day of hunting at home— and then, since we discovered we must have thrown out the magazine, it took another day at the library to find the reference again.

When we type our first drafts, we don't worry about correct spelling, punctuation, or grammar. We don't hunt for the right word or phrase either. If what we've written is just an approximation of what we really want to say, we type a parenthetical question mark after the word, phrase, or sentence to remind us to take more time with it later. The emphasis is to have on paper, when we're done, the entire grand scheme of our outline, along with all the details we think we need, in what seems at the time to be the most logical order. In short, we mull over ideas, not their execution.

We recommend that you use a typewriter for your first draft. Some writers, like Norman Vincent Peale, do well starting out in longhand. But since the typewritten page is what must be turned in, the way your words look on that page counts a great deal. It's much harder, too, to estimate the pacing of a story if you write it first in pen. When typewritten, a paragraph that takes up several pages in longhand often reduces to less than a page—and a typewritten page becomes approximately half a printed book page, as a general rule. It pays to take the time now to learn to think at the typewriter.

It's important to double-space your typed (or scribbled) first draft so you'll have room between the lines to make revisions. If you leave wide margins (a professional inch-and-a-half at the left and an inch each at the right side, top, and bottom), you'll be able to use them to insert notes to yourself and longer corrections that don't fit between the lines. The few pages that you can save now by typing from edge to edge will be lost on your next draft when you have to tear up and start again due to confusing insertions. If you need to conserve funds (and we know few authors who don't), recycle your first-draft pages by using their blank reverses for the next book. (To avoid confusion, run a diagonal line through each old page before you turn it over.)

Number your pages in case a wind or a careless cat tosses them about. Instead of consecutive numbering, we use the 11/5 system for first drafts: for example, this is the fifth page in this draft of Chapter 11, so we've put 11/5 at the upper left corner. This way, not only do we know at a glance the approximate length of each chapter, but we can easily switch chapters around if we want to.

After finishing your first draft of a chapter, put it aside for a while so you can get some psychological distance before rereading it. At this point, though, don't let anyone else read it. Keep this draft for your eyes only. That way, you can put down *anything* without feeling self-conscious. Besides, there's probably a lot of work to be done before it's ready to be shown.

11·2 Become Your Own Best Editor

Pat Strachan, a top editor at Farrar, Straus & Giroux, told interviewer Nancy Evans for *Publishers Weekly:* "There are two levels of what the writer is trying to do: (1) what he's trying to do in the book as a whole and how he may have gotten off the track; and (2) what he's trying to do sentence by sentence." Editing must attack both levels. That's why a thorough editing of a manuscript page may take two or three times as long as drafting that page in the first place.

A number of writers edit each chapter as they go along, but sometimes that requires duplication of effort. As an idea or story line develops, it often brings changes in concept that require the author to go back and make revisions along the way. It's usually best to save all your editing for after you've written the entire first draft.

Some people can do all their editing, both for organization and for execution, with one careful reading of each page. Others find they have to edit the manuscript in two stages, either with two first-to-last-page readings or by chopping it into chapter-sized bits. Here's a brief description of the way we edit manuscripts.

THE BOOK

First we consider the book as a whole, asking the following questions. (Whether an answer is "right" or "wrong" sometimes depends on the book's purpose.)

1. *Content:* Does it fulfill its promise to the reader? Does it do what the proposal or story outline said it would, and if it doesn't, is that for good reason? Have you carried through the message or thrust cohesively from beginning to end?

2. *Organization:* Is the book organized logically, or do some chapters or scenes need moving around? Is the organization the most effective one emotionally?

3. *Execution:* Does the book seem weighty enough? If fiction, do the characters and action come alive? If fact, does the case seem well supported; is there enough information supplied to be worth the price of a book? When reading fiction, William Morrow's editorial director, James Landis, keeps his eye out for inconsistencies in character, as well as for climaxes that come too soon or too late.

4. *Style:* Is the tone of the book consistent? Or is it dead serious in some chapters and satirical in others? Is it wordy, repetitive, pretentious? Is it too chatty and loose?

CHAPTER BY CHAPTER

Next we edit consecutively, chapter by chapter. (Again, "right" and "wrong" in some cases depend on the book's purpose.)

1. *Content:* Does the chapter have a unifying theme? What is it? Does it have a lead and an ending? If so, do they stick to the theme? In fiction, does the content advance the movement of the story? Is the plot too intricate, or not intricate enough?

2. *Organization:* Does all of the body of the chapter pertain to the theme, or does some of it belong elsewhere? Jeanette Hopkins, a leading Harper & Row editor, looks for "a pervasive, consistent thread of argument that the reader can resist or welcome or question along the way." That thread should follow through the action in fiction as clearly as it does through a nonfiction argument.

Does the chapter follow your original outline? Do you proceed in logical order? Can you find a more logical order? Are all the points in your outline covered? Do you now see gaps in argument or logic or story line that should be filled? Is the viewpoint clear and consistent? If fiction, is there enough suspense?

3. *Execution:* Does every sentence say what you mean it to say? If nonfiction, is your approach varied, with full use of exposition, quotes, and anecdotes? Do you support generalizations enough with specifics to make your points believable? Have you chosen the best supports for the generalizations, or is better evidence still in your research notes? Have you verified your facts? Have you given credit where credit is due? Are all your numbers copied correctly? When you've used quotes, have you chosen only the best parts to quote and paraphrased the rest interestingly? If you've used a primary source, have you indicated that and identified the basis of your source's expertise? If it's a secondary source, have you also credited the place where you got the information? Does the quote or paraphrase say what its source really meant to say? Does every anecdote make a point—and does that point belong in the chapter? Is the anecdote complete?

If fiction, is your approach varied, with full use of exposition, dialogue, and scenes? Is there a main scene and a small climax? Have you chosen the best action, setting, and characters to make your points? Have you used only dialogue that either advances action, shows character, or in some other way adds to the reader's enjoyment of the story? Is characterization vivid, interesting, and consistent?

Pat Strachan suggests, "I think an inexperienced writer's main faults are overwriting and overexplaining. There tends to be a very didactic strain in them. An accomplished writer really doesn't underestimate his audience. I'm very merciless about overexplaining, whether it be using too many adverbs or being unnecessarily graphic. I think it puts the reader off. One needn't say how a character said something; one need only say that they said it. It's a matter of showing rather than telling." That's good advice for nonfiction as well as fiction.

4. *Style:* Is your tone appropriate all the way through the chapter? Crackerjack editor James Landis likes to ask, "What's it like to read? Does the writing work as an exciting reading experience?" Jeanette Hopkins looks for "vividness, simplicity, and strength" of language. These qualities in your writing, she believes, will interest and engage the reader. We couldn't agree more.

Good editing, as we've said, takes time. Finding the right word may take half an hour. Here, a good thesaurus is an indispensable time-cutter. Ours is dog-eared and never far from reach.

When you're studying your words, watch out for sexist language. In fiction, it is perfectly acceptable for characters to use appropriate sexist language. But when it comes to nonfiction, book publishers are in the forefront of the move to remove sexist words from written English. Many publishers have devised rules of thumb for their writers. Ask your editor if she has guidelines for you. If not, try the ones we use:

a) We avoid the unrelieved use of *he*. We also avoid *he and she* and the equally distracting *he/she* that pepper some books. We randomly vary our *he* and *she,* our *him* and *her* as we go along.

b) We also avoid such awkward constructions as *mailperson* and *chairperson,* preferring to use *letter carrier* and *chair.* Since nearly every word has its near-synonym, we've rarely failed to find a graceful substitute for any word that could offend a segment of society. Instead of writing, "Volunteers will man the booths," we check our thesaurus and find that volunteers can *run* the booths, or *operate* them, or *handle* them, or *supervise* them, or *manage* them. Often, problems with sexist terminology can be avoided simply by changing the sentence's construction. For example, "Joan will be the spokesperson" can be changed to "Joan will speak for the group."

When you edit for style, be sure to examine more than just words. Look at words in their sentences, sentences in their paragraphs, and paragraphs in the context of what goes before and after. And once you make changes, be flexible in your thinking. You may decide, on reconsideration in context, that the original words were the best way to present your statement after all. If you edit, as some do, by rewriting the page instead of marking the draft, you'll have to hunt through the previous draft if you want to pick up discarded words.

We find our edited first drafts so full of valuable clues to our thoughts, we never discard them until we're sure the final manuscript is at the printer's. We suggest you hold onto your first drafts at least that long, too.

After you edit your first draft, if it's heavily marked up you may need to type—and edit—a second and perhaps a third draft before you do your final. But do remember to stop short of absolute perfection. The fact is, perfection is never reached. Past a certain point—a different point for every individual—the flow of the message starts to grow stale and artificial. Whether it's fiction or nonfiction, a line editor is waiting at your publisher's office to pick up any small problems that are still left.

Fiction is even more difficult to edit well than nonfiction. Getting enough distance from your story and characters is truly a challenge. If you've landed a really good editor at your publisher's, his help may be invaluable. But senior editor Marian S. Wood of Holt, Rinehart & Winston cautioned Nancy Evans, "There's nothing flatter than an editor's prose," and Follett's Elaine Goldberg told us, "Editors can't write. That's why they're editors." They can only "find the confused places," according to Random House's Anne Freedgood, who edited Mary Gordon's *Final Payments*. They can point out where changes should be made, and suggest direction. *You* have to be the final word-maker.

It's easier to learn good editing skills on someone else's manuscripts. You can be much more objective than you ever can with your own words. We've found that, in order to explain to other people how to correct their sticking-points, we've had to formulate intellectual understanding out of what had till then been mere instinct. Because most beginners never realize how much editing working writers do, we've reproduced, just the way we typed it, several pages of this book's first draft. (See Ill. 11.1.) Study the editing changes and see if you can figure out why each change was made. Then see if you can find another author with whom you can exchange material for editing, or try editing some of the writing you did so long ago that there's no emotional attachment left.

11·3 Writing the Final Draft

Some pros never type their own final drafts. They farm out the work to paid typists or unpaid lovers. We think they're missing a lot. In typing the final draft, we get our first objective feel for the flow of the book. We make the small but significant changes that smooth the rough spots, cohere the style, correct the spelling, grammar, and punctuation. If there's anything left that's illogical or flimsy, we generally catch it then.

Most of the mechanics of typing a book manuscript are universal, whether it's fiction or nonfiction. We'll enumerate the major conventions. Your publisher may have additions or substitutions to our list; ask if there's a style sheet or style manual or any special preference for manuscript style.

The best use you can make of your time in writing your first draft is to concentrate on putting down all your ideas with enough fleshing-out to make them convincing, or inserting all the details that make your scenes move and your characters breathe. Do it with as few stops and starts as possible. Don't bother with typing footnotes, but do key your research material to your manuscript as you go along, whether you're writing fact or that type of fiction called facetiously faction. Then you won't waste a lot of time later on tracking down the sources of various pieces of information. Sometimes we type source names and page numbers in our margins; other times we type sketchy clues in parentheses at the ends of passages that rely on research notes.

We're not always as careful as we'd like to be, and sometimes we forget to transcribe all the data. In one chapter of our last book, the college composition text called GOOD WRITING, we introduced the fact that subordinate clauses are not subordinate in idea. As we typed that we decided it needed for evidence an actual illustration from someone else's writing, and on the spot we found it in our pile of magazines. We copied the author and title of the selection, and the magazine it came from—only we forgot to write the page number and issue of the magazine, and when we needed the full reference later for back-of-the-chapter footnotes typed into the final draft, it took us a day of hunting at home and then, since we discovered we must have thrown the magazine out another day at the library to find the reference again.

When we type our first draft, we don't worry about cor—

rect spelling, punctuation, or grammar. We don't hunt for the right word or phrase either. If ~~we feel we may forget that~~ what we've written is just an approximation of what we really want to say, we type a parenthetical question mark after the word, ~~or~~ phrase, or sentence to remind us to take more time with it later. ~~on~~. The emphasis is to ~~get out material down logically into correct logical order~~ have on paper, when we're done, the entire grand scheme of our outline, along with all the details we think we need, in what seems at the time to be the most logical order. In short, We mull over ideas, not their execution. ~~That's what editing~~

We recommend that you use a typewriter for your first draft. ~~We know~~ some writers, ~~who,~~ like Norman Vincent Peale., ~~who~~ do well starting out in longhand. But since the typewritten page is what must be turned ~~into~~ in ~~to an editor~~. ~~it's~~ the way your words look on the page ~~that~~ counts a great deal.ᐱA paragraph that takes up several pages in longhand, reduces ~~itself~~ to ~~much~~ less than a page typewritten—and a typewritten page to approximately half a printed book page ~~or so~~ as a general rule. It's much harder, ~~therefore,~~ to estimate the pacing of a story if your write it first in pen. It pays to take the time ~~now, as a beginner~~, to learn to think at the typewriter. ~~Usually the transition takes no longer than switching from a manual typewriter to an electric.~~ It's important to ~~If you~~ type (or ~~hand-write~~ scribble) your first draft double- spaced, ~~or even triple- spaced,~~ so you'll have

1. Use only 8½ × 11 inch white unlined bond paper, preferably in 20-pound weight. Steer clear of patterned or gaudily watermarked paper, and of easy-erase paper.

2. Use only black ribbons that are still dark. (Save your old ribbons for first drafts and odd-colored ribbons for love notes.) Clean your typewriter when the e, o, or d starts to fill with lint.

3. Pica type is preferred to elite, but not enough for you to scrap your elite machine. Don't use fancy italic or script type, not even for passages that you'd like to see printed in italics or script. (If you want italics, <u>underline.</u> If you want extra-black type—called bold type by typesetters—underline with a wavy line. If you want script, put a circle around the words to be set in script, and write *script* in the left-hand margin. As a rule, try to avoid both bold type and script, since they add cost to the typesetting job.

4. Set margins of 1½ to 2 inches at the left and 1 inch at the right (about 20 and 75 on your pica carriage). On every page but the first page of each chapter, leave margins of about 1½ inches at the top and 1 inch at the bottom, so you get about 26 lines per manuscript page. (Setting all your margins as we suggest will give you an average of about 250 words per page; it's a quick way to figure on approximate word count.)

5. Type on only one side of the paper.

6. Double space *everything,* including long quotations.

7. Make a carbon or photocopy and keep it separate from your original manuscript. A talented nonfiction writer we know was meticulous about keeping his carbon separate when he wrote his first novel. But when he was done and ready to mail it to his publisher, he left both manuscript and copy atop his typewriter for one night. That was the night a burglar broke in, taking not only typewriter but both manuscript copies. "Heaven only knows why," he told us. He never had the heart to start that novel again, or any other.

   Some publishing contracts call for submission of two copies of the manuscript. In that case, make another copy. Don't ever send your last remaining copy. Editors have been known to lose manuscripts, and the mails are to be trusted even less.

8. Indent five spaces for paragraphs as well as for the entire text of long quotations (without quotation marks).

9. Indicate dashes with two hyphens (--) and no spacing. (If you put space in, the copy editor has to close it up.) Don't hyphenate a word from one line to the next. The copy editor will only have to

go through and mark these words for the typesetter to set without the hyphens.

10. Footnote only if you want the footnotes included in the book. More and more, book designers are putting footnotes at the ends of chapters or in an appendix, rather than at the foot of a page. Decide with your editor on a style, and type the manuscript that way.

11. Your first page is a title page. On it, at the approximate center from top to bottom and side to side, put the book's title and your byline the way you want it to appear on the book's cover. (Unless your name is valuable for publicity, your editor probably won't care what name you use, whether it's yours or a pseudonym. But beware: eager publicists may already be promoting the book under the name you signed on the contract.)

12. Your second page is the dedication page, if you want to dedicate your book to anyone. Just type what you want to say. (If you have no dedication, omit this page.)

13. Your third page (and perhaps your fourth and fifth too) is the table of contents, if your book has one. Type it just the way you want it to appear, with or without subheads, summaries, or whatever. For the editor's convenience (and ours), we type in appropriate manuscript page numbers for chapter beginnings, even though the copy editor will remove them.

14. For every page but the title page, put at the left-hand margin, way up at top, your name or your book's title or bits of both—whatever key words will signify that this is your manuscript when an editor drops it on the floor. Be sure to keep the same words throughout. We like to put the page number right after the key words. (This page, for example, is: author's handbook. . . . 230.) Some people like to put the page number at the right-hand margin.

15. For every chapter beginning, put the chapter number or title or both halfway down the page and begin your first paragraph several line-spaces below that. (This gives the book's designer plenty of room to write instructions for the typesetter.)

16. Use your left-hand margins for suggestions to the editor and designer: *ITALS* for long passages you want in italics (for words or phrases, an underline is preferred); *f/n* to point out where there's reference to a footnote within the manuscript; *ill. 4/2* to show where there's reference to an illustration; *c.e.: stet underline* to tell the copy editor to keep the underline you've typed in instead of changing it to an italicized word; and whatever other messages you may have. We write ourselves a note, *ck,* when there's something in

the manuscript we still want to check. We key our subheads *SUB A* or *SUB B* in the margin. We write *SIC ERROR* when we want the copy editor to leave in an error we've made on purpose. You may devise other designators that apply to your particular book.

17. For correcting final drafts while they're being typed, invest in correction fluid or correction paper. The neater your page, the less the copy editor will be inclined to make his own stylistic changes.

18. Make last-minute corrections on your final draft neatly in black ink. If there are more than a few corrections on a page, or if there's a long insertion, retype the page. If you need to insert a page, number it 101A and type: *(101A follows)* on the bottom of page 101; that way you won't have to renumber 320 pages. We find that we save time and turn in neat manuscripts if we liberally use correction fluid, correction paper, scissors, and tape, and then make two photocopies to send to the publisher, keeping the original as our "carbon." The photocopies don't pick up any shadow from the tape, correction fluid, or paper, and they look impressively clean. The practice also serves two additional purposes. First, we don't need to type a carbon. (For those of you who like to keep two copies of unfinished manuscripts around, having just an original may be more nerve-wracking than you care to endure.) Second, we always have that crisp original to make another copy if the publisher loses the two we sent or if (as has already happened) a book club wants to see a clean manuscript after the copy editor has already messed up one of our submissions and the other is hiding under some editor's pile.

19. For photos and illustrations, follow the guidelines in Chapter 12.

At this point in your preparations, it is tempting to ask friends to read the final draft. But that's a dangerous practice. They may react well—but that could be simply out of politeness. They may react badly—but that could be because they always wanted to write a novel different from yours. We find that amateurs have trouble reading typewritten pages with the same objectivity and enthusiasm they bring to a printed book. In any case, the only opinion that really counts is your editor's. So right after step 19, we suggest you proceed to:

20. Find a large enough envelope or box, put in your pages—unbound, unstapled, and unpaper-clipped—and mail by registered or insured mail directly to your editor. (If it's been a long time since you've spoken, a covering letter is appropriate. No return postage

is necessary if you've written under contract.) Then celebrate while you can. It's a long time before pub date, and that time may very well be taken up with editors' revisions and queries and autobiographical questionnaires and all the other small and large details that help turn a manuscript into a book.

Chapter Twelve

How and When to Prepare Illustrations

M OST AUTHORS WOULD LIKE TO SEE THEIR BOOKS
come out with catchy sketches introducing every chapter and full-page, full-color photos illustrating every point—but not the publishers who have to pay for them. Artists' and photographers' fees are only part of the problem. Reproduction can be just as costly. Publishers, therefore, tend to shy away from illustrations, except for craft and children's books.

So when it comes to illustrations, the first step is to convince the publisher that they're needed. Will they tell the story better than your words? Are they required to clarify step-by-step instructions? Will readers really want to see the cave entrance before they decide whether to visit it in their imaginations? Our do-it-yourself books all have illustrations—some by us, some by other pros hired by the publisher. Our *Stopping Out, Eat Anything Exercise Diet,* and books on writing have no artwork because they don't need any.

After *you* decide that illustrations are essential, ensure your editor's agreement. Your book proposal should touch on the subject. Your contract should formalize the approximate number and precise kind to be included, and should designate who's to supply them. The contract should also spell out exactly who is to have final approval. Unless you have some clout in that area, your editor (or usually his art director) will insist on the authority for ultimate acceptance or rejection. For Frank's *Children's Toys You Can Build Yourself,* the contract dealt with illustrations in two separate places. Clause 8 of the printed contract reads:

> 8. The AUTHOR will supply with the manuscript a preface or foreword, if any; table of contents; and when requested by the PUBLISHER all photographs, drawings, artwork, charts, index, diagrams, forms and illustrations; if the AUTHOR shall fail to do so, the PUBLISHER shall have the right to supply said photographs, drawings, artwork, charts, index, diagrams, forms and illustrations and charge the cost thereof against any sums that may accrue to the AUTHOR under the terms of this agreement.

Into that nebulous clause, after the first mention of the word *illustrations,* the publisher inserted the following limitation we had agreed on: *Approximately 150 line drawings and two or three dozen black and white photographs.*

Then another clause was typed at the end of the 19 printed clauses of the contract:

> 20. The AUTHOR hereby agrees that a sum not to exceed $2,600 for the redrawing of his artwork by an artist acceptable to the PUBLISHER may be charged against his royalty account; provided, however, that should said sum be less than $2,600, the difference shall be advanced to the AUTHOR upon receipt by the PUBLISHER of finished copies of the Work.

The art director did opt to hire an art studio to ink Frank's pencil sketches, and blew more than the $2,600 for that. But the publisher had to pick up the difference.

Once you and your editor agree on the content and terms for illustrations, the final step is to test the waters. If you're supplying the artwork yourself—as you may decide to do after you read this chapter—it's a mistake to complete all the photos and sketches before sending some in for approval. Along with several representative illustrations, send your editor a covering letter; spell out that these are a sampling and that if he okays your general approach and technique, you plan to start doing the rest of them by such-and-such-date. Be sure he replies in writing. Editors come and go quickly, and you don't want to hand in the final batch of artwork only to discover that the nice guy who telephoned his okay has left for Tibet and his successor doesn't like what you've done at all. (Six of our editors have moved on in the last six years, including the one who first signed up this book.)

We urge you to proceed cautiously with illustrations: what even the experienced writer considers "professional" drawing or photography is often far removed from what art and photography experts call professional quality. We've seen far too many heartaches because of that and urge you to be sure you know what you're doing before you do too much of it.

12·1 How to Take Your Own Photos

These days it's hard for people to make bad snapshots, what with InstaMatics, sonar focusing, automatic flash units and the like. But it's a big leap from a snapshot to a photograph that's sharp enough, exposed well enough, and composed effectively enough to illustrate a book. It's most helpful to read some good books on the subject. But we can offer some preliminary checks to help you determine if your eye and your equipment are up to the standards of book publishing.

First, take a number of photographs of a subject that you hope to have in your book; if you can shoot one of the actual illustrations, so much the better. Get proofs made and single out the best shot. Have an 11 × 14 inch print made of it—in black and white if your book illustrations will be done that way, in color if your editor has okayed the use of color. This preliminary procedure won't be cheap, but you can't expect to create cheaply a set of professionally useful photos.

Take your sample 11 × 14 print to someone who really knows photography: the photography head at a local newspaper, a photography instructor, a professional photographer, or anyone else you can trust to give you a *professional* evaluation. You'll want to learn whether your camera lens is sharp enough, your hand steady enough, your lighting suitable, your exposure right on the mark, your composition adequate. If you pass this preliminary test, then you're ready to try out your work on your editor.

Shoot a dozen different views, exposures, and compositions for each of half a dozen illustrations that you plan to include in your book. If you're working in black and white, have proofs made and, after marking the best shot of each, get an 8 × 10 inch print of it. If you've taken color film, pick out the best transparency for each of the half dozen scenes and send this small collection of slides for your publisher's approval. If they're close but not right on target, the editor or the art director may be able to help you find the mark.

Some of the most common problems that writers encounter when they attempt to illustrate their books photographically can be corrected before you send your first trial shots.

CONTENT AND COMPOSITION

These are both so subjective, you'd better work them out carefully in advance with your editor or art director. The psychological impact of illustrations is more important than you may realize. Herbert Wise, publisher of Quick Fox books and creator of a series called Living Quarters, points out that the series titles *Made with Oak* and *Living Places* sold over 90,000 copies each, while their companion book *Good Lives* just poked along. The difference? The houses shown in *Good Lives* had people in them whereas the other volumes in the series showed only inanimate structures. Wise agreed with a *Publishers Weekly* editor's conclusion: "Perhaps dream-book buyers don't want their dream houses occupied by real people."

If you're using photos to show arts or crafts described in the text, composition should be kept as simple as possible: a view of the finished or in-process item from its most useful view. Flat art such as a painting is generally reproduced without frames and with no view of a wall behind it. Nature scenes for nature buffs who like their nature unpeopled should be simple, dramatic views of startlingly lit natural wonders.

However, when you move into subjects where personality is important—yours or the reader's—some hint of humanity is probably a worthwhile addition to your photos. For Frank's heavily illustrated *How to Fix Damn Near Everything,* he made sure to show a hand firmly gripping every tool whenever possible. In addition, in taking before-and-after shots, he graced each successful *after* shot with a smiling face unless it crowded the composition. His reason for including people—especially women, children, and lightly muscled men—was to make each fix-it task seem as do-able as possible. Because even the idea of fixing a toaster scares most of us, these photos' message to the reader was, "Look at all the kinds of people who've succeeded at similar tasks."

Photos are rarely used these days simply to pretty up a book. They must usually add substantial information that can't be given as well in words. They're a challenge, but the rewards are great. Frank's *Children's Toys You Can Build Yourself* became more than just another craft book when he added photos of children playing with the toys he'd made. It developed into a personal statement of his love for children.

CAMERA

The camera doesn't have to be fancy, but Polaroids and InstaMatics are out. Unless your camera costs $200 or more new, it probably cannot handle this job.

Whenever we're cornered into recommending a modestly priced all-around workhorse for book illustrations, we tell people to buy one of the inexpensive Nikon bodies with a 55 mm. macro lens. But along with the camera, buy a dozen rolls of film and shoot them all, one by one, studying the results of each roll carefully. Learn what the camera can do for you, and how to make it do what you want, before you attempt to take a photo for publication.

FILM

Don't get sucked into the camera magazine buff's trap of using every exotic new film that's put on the market. For black and white, Kodak's old Tri-X is a fine all-around tool. For color, forget about color-print films like Kodacolor and Ektacolor; they haven't yet won professional acceptance in publishing. The finest color film for most uses is Kodachrome. It has quite a slow speed, but most of the very high-speed color films are unsuited to most book reproduction except in the hands of seasoned pros.

LIGHT

Ordinary sunlight by itself is rarely a suitable light source for portraits or close-ups of gadgets, art, or handiwork—it's best reserved for scenics like mountains, trees, rivers, and such.

An amateur generally slips just one flash unit right into that handy little shoe attached to the top of the camera. With rare exceptions, one flash unit is never enough. Even that first unit should never be fired while sitting atop your camera. If this surprises you, carefully study some lighting manuals.

PROCESSING

You can do your own, assuming your standards are professional. You can be sure your corner drugstore's processing isn't. For black and white, hunt for a store equipped to send your film to a high-quality lab that does custom work. If none can, locate the name of a custom lab in the advertising pages of a photography magazine. For color, always spend the extra bit of money to have Eastman Kodak do the processing.

PRINTS

The standard of the industry is the 8 × 10 black-and-white print. It can have either a glossy surface—traditional for single-weight prints—or what's known as semimatte, for double-weights and for prints that require even small amounts of retouching. You may save some money by using smaller prints, but you risk having a hypercritical art director toss the whole project back as being unprintable.

Make sure to mark every print with the title of your book and a caption. Don't ever scribble this data on the back with a ball-point pen, since the pen point can emboss right through a single-weight print. If you must write by hand, use a blue felt-tipped marker. But there's a better way.

Type all your captions on 8½ × 11 paper in triplicate. Keep each bottom copy for your files. Send each top copy to your editor along with the stack of prints: he'll be able to edit your captions on those sheets and send them directly to a typesetter. Cut up the third set and fasten each caption to the back of its matching print with rubber cement or cellophane tape. The art department will use these captions for guidance as they lay out your book.

When typing captions, number the prints and matching captions consecutively. The numbers should also match all references to illustrations in the text of your book. Also show, alongside each caption, the page number it belongs with in your manuscript; and in the margin of your manuscript, on that page, type the illustration number so that the editor, art department, and everybody else along the way will be able to match text and pictures easily. We designate our illustrations with both chapter numbers and consecutive numbers. Thus, if this chapter had an illustration right here, "Ill. 12/1" would be marked both on the caption sheet and its carbons, and right here in the margin of our manuscript. We would probably also type (See Ill. 12/1.) at the appropriate place in this paragraph.

SLIDES

For color, industry standards call for submitting *only* original slides, not duplicates or prints. Deliver the slides slipped inside 8½ × 11 plastic protectors. With 35 mm. slides, you can get twenty to a protector sheet. Write the title of your book as well as an illustration number on each slide. You won't be able to tape a caption to each individual slide, but organize your typing so you can tape one duplicate caption sheet to each appropriate sheet of slides.

Whenever you submit original color slides to a publisher, send them by registered mail and declare a high enough value to let you replace them. Many photo agencies charge $500 to $1,000 per slide, but if you've taken the slides yourself it's extremely unlikely that you could collect that much if they were lost.

12·2 How to Illustrate Your Book With Drawings

It's true that thousands of people have chuckled over author James Thurber's amateur sketches which were accepted in more innocent times by relaxed publishers. But you can't count on any of today's art directors indulging your primitive artwork. As with photos, what most of us regard as nice art often falls a country mile short of professional standards. We can't warn you strongly enough of the importance of getting agreement on both the quality and the economics of your artwork before signing the contract.

For starters, here are just a few of the taboos you'll find in publishing houses that you won't find in fine art schools:

textured paper or canvas
pencil drawings
any drawing fluid except darkest India ink
perspectives that vary between sets of drawings
washes

If you have the basic talent to turn out workable sketches for your book, your editor can arrange for the art director to fill you in on the company's mechanical requirements. Even then, he may have you do only comprehensive pencil sketches, and then use an outside artist or in-house staff for a professional inking job.

If you haven't enough art experience or skill to tackle your own sketches, you may want to look for a local artist. If you live anywhere but in one of the largest cities, you may be surprised at how inexpensively you can hire a member of a commercial art studio if you promise prominent mention somewhere in the book. Another way to locate an artist is through an art school.

For a children's book, the editor usually "marries" the author to one of the many talented illustrators the publisher knows. Often, the two collaborators never meet face to face. So if you've written a terrific children's book, but can't supply the art, don't be concerned, though if you can sketch or photograph some rough, even amateurish guidelines for illustrations, you'll help stretch the editor's imagination.

12·3 Where to Find Somebody Else's Photos and Drawings

There are libraries full of professionally taken photos and handsomely drawn art. Some of them command high fees, but vast collections are available for free, or almost.

One of the largest collections of historically valuable photographs is in the Library of Congress: Matthew Brady's classic images of the Civil War era; photos of Greeley's expedition to the Arctic in the 1880's; portraits of the braves who helped create Custer's Last Stand; and on and on. Most of the collection is card-catalogued, and expert librarians stand ready to help you find what you need. There are even published guides, so you can select photos by mail or over the phone.

Elsewhere in Washington, other government agencies maintain huge picture collections which they'll share for use in your books. The Department of Agriculture, for example, can provide you with scenes of farms, logging, reforestation, forest fires, national parks, schoolchildren eating hot lunches, and people building low-cost houses.

Government agencies don't limit their pictorial assistance to photographs. Many have prepared comprehensive sets of drawings to illustrate various publications, and the drawings in the public domain are free to be used. Don't forget state government agencies or the various United Nations offices either. Most UN personnel are researchers and office staff; their jobs are to be of help. Be wary, however; too many others may have already dipped into the same illustration pool. The excellent line drawings from the comprehensive tool manuals printed by the U.S. Navy during World War II have illustrated at least a dozen inexpensive how-to-do-it books we've leafed through, so when we prepared our own books, we tracked down less-familiar sources for our free illustrations.

Public relations agencies can be invaluable sources of illustrations. When preparing our book on customizing vans, we notified every public relations officer we could think of who had any interest in promoting vans, vanning, or vanners. Some we contacted directly, others we located by placing a free notice in a weekly newsletter that alerts public relations personnel to placement possibilities (*PR Party Lines,* 35 Sutton Place, New York, NY 10022). We were inundated with catalogs, brochures, P.R. releases, and several hundred photographs. We chose the best to supplement the ones we had already taken ourselves. Despite a very cramped budget, we ended up with a highly illustrated book. The procedure worked so well that when asked to do a book on snowmobiles, we didn't even plan to take our own photos. The various public relations agencies and corporate P. R. advisors cheerfully provided us with more than enough snowmobile shots, most of publishable quality.

Colleges have active and generally useful press information departments that maintain picture files and, like other P.R. agencies, can often be counted on to take photographs specifically for your project if its subject or purpose interests them. Again, your publisher may not accept the quality of the photos, so don't guarantee publication.

Chapter 7 provided guidelines for locating the agencies that can help you obtain free illustrations. If you are willing to pay for photographs, there are additional sources. Picture agencies stock millions of slides and black-and-white prints, all carefully categorized. Most of them are leery of dealing with individuals, but if your editor assures them that he guarantees payment, these agencies will help you select photos on nearly any subject. Both United Press International (UPI) and the Associated Press (AP) store news photos dating back almost to the invention of the camera. Black Star agency is the place to go for depictions of all the great social movements and causes (unemployment in the 1950's, civil rights in the 1960's, peace in the 1970's, ecology in the 1980's). The Bettmann Archive is an immense repository of historic photos, drawings, engravings, cartoons, and other art forms. Both *Writer's Market* and *Literary Market Place* annotate their lists of picture agencies so you can judge who has what you're looking for.

You can contact ASMP—The Society of Photographers in Communications (60 East 42 Street, New York, N.Y. 10017) for a directory of members who span the world. This is especially useful if you're searching for photos in a particular part of the globe. Each member's specialties are listed too, in case you decide to hire an ASMP photographer to shoot illustrations for you. (If you do that, try either to clear the photographer with your editor or to specify in your agreement for photos that payment depends on acceptance by your publisher. Better still, have the publisher–photographer's contract separate from your own.)

Another possibility is *PhotoLetter,* published by Rohn Engh (address: Osceola, WI 54020). If you list in this publication your requirements and, if you like, the rates you can pay, they will be read by Rohn's mailing list of hundreds of subscribing professionals all over the country. You'll receive packets of photos from which to single out the ones that best illustrate your book. (If you haven't mentioned price, negotiate on your preferred choices before returning the rest.) Sometimes the mail brings so large a choice, and so excellent a selection, the decision is tough. But what a wonderful book it makes!

The Birth of
Your Book

Chapter Thirteen

What to Expect from Your Editor (and When)

FINALLY! YOU'VE TYPED THE ENTIRE MANUSCRIPT, proofread it fastidiously, keyed all your illustrations to the appropriate pages, packaged the entire precious cargo, and entrusted it to the U.S. Postal Service. Your job is done, you think; can you relax?

Hardly! Only the first part of the work on your book is really finished. Let's hope your editor actively involves you in one decision after another. If not, and you sit back and let your book's manufacture and sale pass you by, once you see the finished book and then your royalty statements you may regret not having insisted on checking every detail.

Nobody knows your book as well as you. That's why you should look discreetly over editors' shoulders to ensure that your manuscript is faithfully translated into print. All too often, the title, blurb, art, and even the text of a book get distorted beyond belief—not generally out of ignorance or malice, but out of pure haste. So we devote this chapter to describing the editorial steps that take place after you turn in your manuscript, and suggest how you can keep your eyes on them.

13·1 Editing

Your editor will probably be the first to read your completed manuscript. Until he does, you're not likely to get the final payment of your guaranteed advance, since that's contractually contingent upon your turning in a satisfactory book. But don't wait at the phone to hear whether he likes it, or you'll wait anywhere from weeks to months. Since the day your editor excitedly signed up your book idea, he's probably taken on several dozen other book ideas he's liked at least as much, and maybe a dozen previously signed-up manuscripts have arrived at his office, like yours, ready to be published. His energies and loyalties to you are divided. In addition to all those demands on your editor, he wrestles with the fact that his office competes with Ringling Brothers for noise and razzmatazz. Tom Congdon, publisher of Thomas

Congdon Books, distributed by E. P. Dutton, shared with an Authors Guild audience a bit of the flavor of the typical editor's workday: "Editors by and large never do in the office the two things you think an editor does. We never read in the office and we never edit there. The office is for telephone calls and for visits. And it's for making the lunch appointments and then recovering from the lunches. It's for running down the hall and saying, 'My God, you printed page 211 upside down.'"

If your editor is like most, he'll take your manuscript home —eventually—and read it there. If he's the get-involved type, he'll read it with a blue Bic ball-point pen in hand doing what's known in the trade as *line editing*. That includes making marginal notes about possible factual errors, fixing obviously clumsy language, suggesting deletions of paragraphs he considers extraneous, drawing lines through every one of the eighteen cute phrases you so cleverly coined; in short, doing everything possible to strengthen the content of your epic. Tom Congdon figures he can line-edit about ten or twelve pages an hour. Divide a 300-page manuscript by ten pages an hour and you'll see why your editor may unconsciously forget to shove your manuscript into his briefcase as he rushes to catch the Friday evening 5:18.

But it's not very gratifying to finish your job on time only to wait months for a reading. Indeed, editors don't expect that you'll sit by patiently. They assume that you'll persistently nudge them into editing still one more book.

We begin our nudging about a week *before* we mail the completed manuscript. One of us calls the editor to say, "Hey, we're putting on the finishing touches right now, and you can expect to get it in the mail by next weekend."

Inevitably the editor rises to the bait: "How is it?" she asks.

"Boy, it's even better than we expected," we inevitably respond. "During our research we discovered . . ." and then we share half a dozen genuinely sensational oddities we've dug up since our book proposal was written. Our excitement comes easily, now that months of mind-deadening work are approaching a halt. We're hoping to rewhet the editor's edge of excitement. When we ship off the manuscript, it's via the fastest way possible so that her reinterest has no chance to dull while some Pony Express rider sits on our package.

The mails (and mailrooms) being what they are, we wait a week or two after mailing the manuscript and phone again just to inquire whether the precious cargo has arrived. While on the phone, we may ask discreetly how soon we're likely to get the check, since we're hoping to take a much-needed vacation after working so hard so continuously. We point out that we'll be happy to schedule our rest so that we're back in the office by the time the edited manuscript is returned for our approval. While we appear to be just touching base, we're also letting our editor know that we intend to stay fully involved in every stage of its manufacture. Both points are almost as crucial as securing that final check as promptly as possible.

If the editor has found what she thinks are substantial problems, you may be asked to rewrite part or all of the book. You don't have to, of course—but then, the publisher doesn't have to publish it or pay you the final installment of your advance, either. Before you do anything, we suggest you discuss all the book's problems with your editor; in many cases, there are simple solutions to what seem to be vast difficulties.

At times, editors are just out-and-out wrong. If you're absolutely sure that yours is far off base and discussion doesn't help, you can go over the editor's head. But the odds of success are skewed against you, so you'd better be prepared not only to document your point of view but to argue it persuasively and, above all, diplomatically. If you win, your book will probably be assigned to another editor. If you lose, it may not be published at all, at least not by this publisher.

Most stories about editor–writer conflicts have become so legendary that it's tough to separate fact from fiction. We can recall firsthand, however, how furious we were when the original editor of one of Frank's earliest books took a heavy felt-tipped marker and crossed out almost every active verb, putting sentence after sentence into the passive voice. In that case, Frank did fight—and his active verbs won. A senior editor of the publishing house took over the book. The passively inclined culprit went back to the sales department—not entirely because of Frank's pique, we're sure.

Most books win approval without major conflicts between author and editor. In fact, if the editor's adverse comments are few and minor, they may be discussed on the phone. You may not even hear of them until after the next step, copy editing.

13·2 Copy Editing

Right after God handed Moses the Ten Commandments, She told him to train six copy editors to ensure that the written word would be kept sacred. Unfortunately, God has never thought to increase the number of qualified copy editors beyond the original six. If you're fortunate enough to get one of them in the manuscript lottery, you'll be in heaven. We know; it once happened to us.

The ideal copy editor studies your every word to make sure of correct spelling, grammar, and usage. He also keeps your style consistent from beginning to end so you don't have, for example, "six copy editors" on page 145 and "6 copy-editors" on page 418. Many publishing houses have style manuals, and the copy editor conforms your usage to the house style unless you voice strenuous and well-reasoned objections.

Simple corrections are made directly on the manuscript. When the copy editor feels he's caught a slip in logic or out-and-out factual error, he discreetly inquires on a colored slip of paper pasted to one margin (variously dubbed a flag, an ear, or a slip, and often colored pink) whether you mean something other than what you said. Good copy editors fill in your lapses wherever possible, leaving final approval for the changes up to you. If they can't find the missing information, they simply ask you, on the colored flag, to do your homework.

Many publishers seem bent on keeping copy-edited manuscripts out of their authors' hands. If you care what your book says, and how you appear to say it, you'd better let your editor know early that you expect to review the copy-edited manuscript. For Judi's first book, *Stopping Out,* she made that clear to her editor. Nevertheless, when too much time seemed to have passed, she phoned to inquire about it. "Oh, we just got it back this morning," she was told, "and it must go out tomorrow to the typesetter, so there's no time for you to see it at all."

Luckily, Judi lived near her publisher and insisted on going into the office that afternoon to read the manuscript—a good thing, because it had been heavily edited into the copy editor's writing style. There were many places where the meaning had been changed to something factually wrong. Working feverishly to get important changes made, Judi managed to make her way through the manuscript by five o'clock. If she had been more experienced—particularly if that had not been her first book—she would have insisted on a delay in typesetting to permit reediting. But beginners are so afraid of battling with their publishers that they often give in when they should fight.

On the other hand, many neophytes' first reaction to their copy-edited manuscripts is to rage on every alteration. We urge you to give your copy editor a chance. Read through enough pages to judge whether the changes have been for the better: you are human, after all. Read all the slips carefully: often, lots of thought has gone into writing them. Answer all the questions they pose, unless they're stylistic questions directed to your editor.

If, after careful reading and long thought, you're convinced that your copy editor doesn't know a preposition from a prone position, tell your editor. Next you may have to go through the manuscript patiently, consult respected grammar books and other authoritative resources, and document each and every *stet* you write across a change. You'll need to be as consistent about your language and ideas as a good copy editor should be in his alterations, and as rational and well-reasoned as possible. No doubt the copy editor did catch some of your oversights; do leave these alone. If you go out on a limb to show that the copy editor knows nothing, you may lose all your credibility.

When you've completed an arduous reediting task, ship off the manuscript with a covering letter that points out just a handful of the worst examples. Assure your editor, if you can, that you've done a thorough reediting job but that you'd welcome having it shipped off to yet another copy editor. Be firm in insisting that the original miscreant is not to lay hands on your work again.

Handled properly, editors respond favorably to authors' efforts at achieving properly edited manuscripts. We've found that to be true, and colleagues have told us it's been true for them. Incompetent copy editing is frustrating and infuriating, but it's one of those incongruities that are entrenched in the publishing business.

13·3 Typesetting

After the copy editor's work has been completed and okayed, the publisher's production department will decide on type faces for your book as well as its subheads, chapter headings, captions, title page, and whatever else there is. Only if yours is a very unusual project will you ever get consulted in that stage of manufacturing.

After the type is set, however, you should receive a set of galleys. That's an unwieldy pile of extra-long pages full of type. Properly divided into standard page-sized nuggets, this is the type from which your book will be printed. Use the galleys to check for mistakes in the typesetter's handiwork. Many publishers seem to think they can handle this job all by themselves, so more and more authors are complaining that they never see galleys. Let your editor know that you expect to see them. Find out early when they're scheduled to be ready and don't let anybody "forget" to put your set into the mail.

Read the galleys carefully for errors—yours, editor's, typesetter's, anybody's. We suggest that, at this stage, you make no further additions or substitutions to the book. If you do make many changes in the galleys, you'll be charged for extra typesetting, and the book may be delayed.

Typesetters' errors cost you nothing to fix, so in the margin alongside each one of them mark PE for *printer's error*. Alongside every one of the changes you decide to make, you're supposed to mark AA for *author's addition*. (If you haven't seen copy-edited manuscript, mark EE for errors the editor made.) You're bound to spot a few awkward phrases or inconsistencies that have crept past everyone, so go ahead and fix them. For any change, the entire line has to be reset, so fix anything else in the same line that looks bad. Most contracts specify that you'll be billed only for the cost of your changes over and above 10 percent of the cost of the entire typesetting job. (To keep costs down, try to substitute corrections that fill the same amount of space on a line. Otherwise, changing one word may require resetting an entire paragraph.)

13·4 Layout and Design

For most books, after the type has been set, the production department oversees its slicing into page-sized *proofs,* numbers the pages, and assembles the project for the printing press. A very neat manuscript is often set directly into page proofs. Correcting a page proof is more expensive than correcting a galley, so if you expect to have complicated late changes, be sure you notify the editor.

In the case of an illustrated book, the production department designs a layout before sending for page proofs, to fit together type, captions, and art as harmoniously and economically as possible. In that instance, you'll probably be given a chance to look over the layout to make sure that illustrations are close to the appropriate written matter and that each caption is pasted under its correct photo or artwork.

At this point, if you did not personally provide the art for your book, or at least supervise whoever did it, you'd better be prepared for some vigorous back-and-forthing with your editor. You're on safest ground if you've alerted the editor before now that you want to okay the art. Dodi Schultz's *Home and Family Medical Emergencies* advises readers to wear long pants while hiking—but the book's artist drew happy hikers all attired in shorts. You have to know Dodi personally to

What to Expect from Your Editor (and When)

appreciate the storm she must have raised with her publisher when she caught the artist's error. Dodi tells us, "The editor had it fixed right away." Other authors have been burned, especially those who aren't as assertive as Dodi.

Children's book author Osmond Molarsky told a group of Authors Guild members about his books' artwork: "With a dozen books in print, I have learned virtually to count on gross errors of fact in illustrations, distortion in the characterization of key characters, and the elaborate depiction of minor episodes where key situations are ignored." Molarsky cited, as examples, a baseball umpire wearing a referee's whistle; an ultra-feminine girl shown as a blustering tomboy; a middle-aged, heavyset football great shown as a slight, scholarly man in his late twenties; the entire cast of a lighthearted book appearing as advanced cases of melancholia. Molarsky reported that he'd tried to rely on his editors' verbal assurances that he'd be able to inspect the illustrations, "but almost invariably by the time I receive the sketches, the work has been finished and gone to press." So if you value the integrity of your book, and haven't been able to work in a contract clause that gives you final okay over the artwork, this stage of production may seriously test your powers of negotiation and persuasion.

13·5 Page Proofs and Bound Galleys

The artists, designers, typesetters, and editors have all had their next-to-last crack at your book. The art is all in place. The type has been distributed neatly onto pages. The pages are numbered, the title page is ready, the table of contents is set, and only the final proofreading remains—along with the index, if your book requires one. Although indexing seems like a frightening chore to those who've never put one together, it's a straightforward job that shouldn't take more than a few evenings of simple effort.

A-Z

Use a loose-leaf notebook or a pad of paper with strong enough glue at the top to withstand hundreds of flips back and forth. Label the pages A through Z. Then, begin to read the page proofs carefully and, as soon as you come across the first word or phrase you want indexed, write it on the appropriate page of your notebook along with its page number in the book. Move on until you locate the next key entry; jot it down and continue. By the time you've finished, you'll have an index, complete except that the entries for each letter must be alphabetized. Often, you can do that as you type it up.

If you prefer, your editor will send the page proofs out to a free-lance indexer, and the fee (usually a few hundred dollars) will be charged against your royalties. But we like to see writers prepare their own indexes, for two reasons. First, nobody knows the material better than you, who should therefore best be able to identify the key words to be indexed. Second, publishers more and more are trying to keep page proofs out of authors' hands because any errors they spot at that stage of production are costly to fix. But if you insist on preparing your own index, then the publisher has no alternative but to send you a set of page proofs to work from. (If the publisher had sent us page proofs of *Eat Anything Exercise Diet,* we would have caught the misspelling of Frank's name on its title page—and insisted on correction.)

The next stage of book production is usually to compile sets of bound galleys, which are little more than photocopies of the page proofs bound into book format. Usually, the book's actual cover is still unprinted at this stage, so a simple colored-paper cover has to do. Bound galleys are relatively expensive, so publishers mete them out like gold bars, seldom to their authors. The bulk are shipped to *Publishers Weekly, Library Journal, The New York Times,* and other important book reviewers. Bound galleys may also go to newspaper syndicates, major magazines, and other big-budget subsidiary rights buyers. While they're being sent off to the VIP's, the printer is at work on the real thing—your book.

Chapter Fourteen

How to Help Sell Your Own Book

W ITH YOUR BOOK FINALLY IN PRINT, YOU DRIVE hours to the windy city to do the crack-of-dawn *A.M. Chicago* show live, only to find that the books you're trying to push are still in a Hoboken, New Jersey, warehouse and won't be shipped for another three weeks. Or you sit in your editor's New York office as she jovially tells the story about how all of a sudden every West Coast bookstore has been magically swamped with requests for your book, only there isn't a copy to be had out there and you can't laugh because you personally notified her two months earlier that the biggest papers in Los Angeles, San Francisco, and Seattle were about to carry five-part syndication of the book so wouldn't she make sure that enough copies were shipped to West Coast stores. Or you wake up in your office proudly tacking onto your wall dozens of favorable reviews of your book and promotional mentions in prestigious publications, as the letter carrier brings a royalty statement that shows your publisher hasn't gotten any copies into the bookstores.

These are not the Edgar Allan Poe nightmares born of an opium trip. All three of them have actually happened to us. Our friends have told worse true tales. In fact, every time you find two authors in the same room, the odds are better than 50–50 they're swapping horror stories about the latest sales atrocities their publishers have committed.

More and more authors are concluding that publishers generally don't know how to sell books, or that if they do, they hide it very well. So if we want our books to sell, if we want magazines to buy first serial and second serial rights, if we want newspaper syndicates to run excerpts from our books—we figure *we* had better sell them. An author will have to kiss a lot of toads before she finds that prince of a publisher who will promote her book even half as much as she's entitled to. So don peddler's clothes over your artist's smock.

Not everything that helps to sell a book involves hustling, pitching, and wooing. You can often help just by coming up with selected lists and clever ideas. But in order to be of assistance, you have to understand more about the whys and wherefores of book promotion than most publishers volunteer to tell you.

14·1 Start Your Campaign Early

Selling your book starts before you even sign the contract. During negotiations, you can test how much promotional effort your editor has in mind. Ask for a clause spelling out how much money the publisher will commit to publicizing your book. You could be shocked: the editor might agree to it. More than likely you'll be turned down, but to ease the blow, your editor just might quote a projected publicity figure or two.

Ask him to follow up by sending you a letter with those figures. Again, you'll probably be turned down. But at each frustrating stage of negotiations, you'll be clarifying in your own mind what to expect from your publisher—and with luck, you might start your editor thinking promotionally.

It's better by far to have an editor who promises nothing and delivers exactly that, because you know from the beginning that the whole job is up to you. If you're lulled into believing an editor who promises a million-dollar radio, TV, magazine, newspaper, and Good Humor truck publicity tour, you might delay your own publicity campaign until it's too late for maximum impact. Promises are meant sincerely at the time. But the truth is, editors get excited about nearly every book they sign, and it's not often *their* decision which books get what piece of that year's promotional funds.

Part of your prepublication planning has to be an assessment of your publisher's promotional and subsidiary rights departments. (The two work hand in hand, as a rule, at getting sales and exposure for your book.) The typical promotion or publicity department consists of one modestly paid and two underpaid staff members, usually female, who must not only think up the entire publicity campaign for ten or twenty books every month, but mail review copies, forward author mail, and perform other menial chores. They form their first opinion of you by reading the Author's Questionnaire.

Typically, you receive this form shortly after the publisher returns your signed contract. It asks about your family, education, career, memberships, awards, previous publications—everything short of whether you sleep in pajamas. Trivial as it seems, fill it in carefully. Think of it as a tool to stir up enthusiasm and anticipation for your book, to convince the publicity department that you're an undiscovered dynamo, and to show them how you and your work can best be publicized. For instance, if you're a member of six different fraternities that publish newsletters that plug members' books; if you number among your professional colleagues several Nobel laureates who might be willing to write plugs for the dust jacket; if you syndicate a column that's a hit in 27 major cities; if you're a second cousin of the Dionne quintuplets; every one of these facts thickens your book's potential slice of the promotional budget.

If you've sized up the publicity department as typically underpaid and overworked, begin now to make the best use of your budget slice. Along with your questionnaire, send all the lists *they* won't prepare because they don't have time. Send lists of all the organizations that have an interest in your subject. Send lists of professionals in the field your book is about who know you and just might help you promote it. Send lists of magazine, newspaper, journal, and newsletter editors who know you or have run articles by or about you. Send lists of radio and TV producers, personalities, reporters, and secretaries who know you or have worked with you and might line up a mention or an interview. Send lists of people cited in your book, pro or con, who might be interested in seeing you sell more copies. Send lists of publications that might be interested enough in your subject to plug the book or buy reprint rights to portions of it.

Make all your lists as complete as possible. Look up addresses and phone numbers, because a busy promotion director might use the lack of them as an excuse to ignore your lists. If you know of a directory or mailing list of pertinent individuals or organizations, describe it and tell how the publisher can get a copy. (Better yet, offer to lend them yours or to send a photocopy.) Don't just list publications or radio and TV stations; if you have a contact—anyone who knows your name— give that too.

And keep carbons of all these lists, because if the promotion department forgets they exist—as well it might—you ought to follow through yourself. (Sections 14.4 and 14.5 will show you how.)

If you feel reasonably capable of speaking before audiences or on radio and TV, say so. And even if it's not requested, include a recent black-and-white head shot—a flattering one—so the promotion director knows not only how you'll look on TV, but that you're professional enough to realize the importance of appearance.

If you give your keenest attention to the Author's Questionnaire and the materials you send back with it, you can reasonably expect the promotion director to remember your name. Not too long after you've returned the Questionnaire, you should launch the second stage of your personal promotion campaign.

14·2 Prepublication Planning

If your book is hard cover or trade paperback, the first several months of its sale are crucial. (For mass market paperbacks, the first couple of weeks, sometimes the first few *days,* can seal a book's fate.) While the book is still being printed, the sales force will be using whatever promotional literature it has (from posters and flyers down to just a line in the season's catalog) to collect advance orders. Hopefully, the shipping department will fill these orders prior to your official publication date, and bookstore clerks will put them onto bookstore shelves. Then will come the book's real test: will there be returns or reorders? Remember, most unsold books are returnable to publishers for 100 percent credit. There's great temptation for booksellers to dump a book that isn't moving quickly. If the book starts dribbling back to the publisher's warehouse, the promotion department's excitement over advance orders (no matter how sizable) fast turns to nervousness. On the other hand, if reorders start flooding in, excitement may pick up. Therefore, before your book is printed, bound, and in a warehouse waiting to be shipped, you'd better begin to ensure that bookstore customers will buy it.

After you've turned in the manuscript (or after the revisions, if your editor asks for them), one of your very first goals should be to arrange a face-to-face meeting with both your editor and your publisher's promotion director. The ideal time to have that meeting is when the galleys are ready. It gives you a chance to size up how much effort the publisher already plans to put into publicizing and selling your book, while the publicity crew gets a chance to size you up and—if they're ambitious—also get some out-of-house reaction to the book. If a face-to-face confab isn't practical, have a three-way telephone talk.

When your meeting takes place, you'll probably hear a lot of superficial generalities about plans for promotion and sale. Watch for subtle signs that tell whether your book is regarded as a "list leader" or as just one more title to move out as quickly and cheaply as possible. Here are some of the indicators:

HAS THE PUBLICITY DIRECTOR ACTUALLY READ YOUR BOOK?
You'd be surprised how seldom a publisher's employees more than glance at what they're supposed to sell. Ask a few questions or make a few specific comments that only someone familiar with your book can answer correctly. If the publicity director hasn't read it, you can probably expect the standard cursory P.R. effort: a buncha review copies

to standard list 22, a coupla releases to the guy's hometown paper and college alumni bulletin, and if anybody calls about the book, give 'em his home address.

HAS THE PUBLICITY DIRECTOR ACTUALLY STUDIED YOUR AUTHOR'S QUESTIONNAIRE?

You can test with questions or comments based on information you put into it. If she fails the test, it's the old P.R. 1, 2, 3 for you.

DOES THE PUBLICITY DIRECTOR HAVE SPECIFIC PLANS TO FOLLOW SOME OF THE LEADS AND SUGGESTIONS YOU'VE SUPPLIED?

If so, she'll volunteer specific comments or questions. Offer to draft the mailing pieces for each group on your lists, or to at least offer helpful comments on her drafts. You can point out that your expertise in the field of the book will help. (Actually, your ruse is intended to stretch your book's budget to cover these mailings, and every hour she spends on a letter is charged against the budget.)

DOES THE P.R. DIRECTOR WANT YOU TO HELP PUBLICIZE THE BOOK?

If she hopes to ship you on an expense-paid city-to-city promotional tour to do newspaper interviews and autographings and TV appearances, she'll generally ask right out about your schedule and limitations. These days, such a tour can cost a publisher $1,000 per city by the time the bills are all in for phone calls, plane fares, taxis, hotels, meals, publicity-release mailings, book submissions to potential publicity sources, and more. No P.R. director will line up two weeks of high-cost touring unless she thinks you can make back more than twice the cost in sales. Through experience, she knows that very few authors can do that.

But there are many other ways to actively promote the sale of your book. Most publicity directors welcome your interest and appropriate efforts. If you're not sure what's appropriate, you're far from alone. Tania Grossinger told us, "Most book authors don't know how to promote." Tania was director of promotions for Stein & Day until she quit to devote most of her time to writing her own books and the rest to free-lance book promotion campaigns for publisher and author clients. "It's important," she insisted, "to get your editor and your P.R. person on your side when it comes to book promotion. To do that, you have to prove you know what you're talking about. You have to know your own book. You'd be surprised how many authors really don't understand, or don't remember, what's in their own writing."

Tania reinforced our contention that, although book promotion campaigns don't start until about two months before publication, you have to lay the groundwork much earlier. She counseled, "Forward your ideas to the promotions director by mail, *not* by phone. She really is busy, and it takes more time to take a phone call than to look at a letter." She also suggested that you keep in mind the other books that your publisher is bringing out on the same list. "Help promote them, too, if you can." A friend of Tania's was writing an article that could include information from another book by Tania's publisher. Tania put the friend and the publisher's publicist in touch, and they were both grateful. "Always remember that you're in business to sell books. Don't be a pain in the ass, but try to get it done." If pressure on the promotion department sells lots of copies of your book, the publisher will want your next book even if you're a bit of a pest. If it doesn't, you probably won't want that publisher for your next book, anyway.

Until now, we've concentrated your efforts on the promotion director. But actually, throughout the entire procedure of planning the publicity campaign and promoting the book's sale, the editor is your book's captain for your publisher. A strong editor can usually force a strong promotional campaign onto an otherwise reluctant publicity department, if you provide enough ammunition. And at sales conferences, an imaginative editor can make the most of his allotted minute's parade past the publisher's sales troops, and drum up enough excitement that in their subsequent visits to bookstore owners your book will be touted harder than the other 24 that have just been pitched. This is most important, for no matter how much publicity you or the company's P.R. force garner, it can't sell books that aren't on bookstore shelves. (For textbooks, the mechanics of selling are a bit different: the individual professor or district purchase committee that selects them receives the brunt of the sales force effort. But the mechanics of inspiring the promotion department and the sales force are the same.)

What happens if your editor doesn't excite the sales force? Then, as publisher Thomas Congdon told a special meeting of the Authors Guild, "There is a lamentable thing called a skip. It is a book that the salesmen don't even mention when they go into the bookstore because it doesn't have anything going for it: there aren't any wonderful quotes, nothing has happened at the book clubs or at the reprinters'. The editor hasn't made the people in the house want to read that book. That book is as good as dead long, long, long before it's published." How can you avoid writing a skip? Congdon says, "One of the best things you can do is to help your editor. Think along with him."

But think assertively. All along the manufacturing process we outlined in the previous chapter, drop notes to your editor whenever any kind of sales or promotion ideas occur to you. For example, we had an idea for a unique premium that Franklin Watts could offer for sizable orders of our textbook. We let our editor know about it as soon as we thought it up and he passed on his enthusiasm to everyone connected with the book.

One important job that you can do well is the solicitation of blurbs—those brief accolades that should go onto dust jackets and covers and into ads and catalog displays. They may sound trite to you, but if a browser finds a short rave recommendation from someone whose name he recognizes or whose credentials he respects, he will be more inclined to plunk down money for your book. In truth, these blurbs have the same psychological effect when they roll in on editors, who often use them to psych up the sales force, publicity department, and important company decision-makers.

Editors and publicity people sometimes solicit testimonials from celebrities or experts whose names they think can help the sale of your book. But you can't count on them. And even if they're trying, you—as the author—are more effective at garnering laudatory blurbs that sound as if their authors read your book.

First list a dozen or more people in your field whose names, titles, or credentials might impress your potential readers. Pay special attention to acquaintances, colleagues, friends, anybody you've ever done a favor for. Prepare a personal note to each person on your list saying how much you'd appreciate a short comment that you can use on the cover or in promotion, and ask your editor to send your notes along with copies of the manuscript or galleys. We make the procedure as painless as possible, always offering to take collect phone calls if the potential blurb-writer is more comfortable talking than writing. But we also couch our notes in terms that tell the recipient we're depending on a response, whether it's positive or negative. (We've found that even our worst critics have had fewer negative comments than positive ones and have been happy to let us excerpt.)

14·3 How to Promote Your Book With Subsidiary Rights Sales

Every time your book is mentioned in any way, in any length, in any medium, you stand to sell more copies. In fact, Charles Silberman, author of best sellers such as *Crisis in Black and White* and *Crisis in the*

Classroom, told an audience of fellow writers that he believes "word of mouth, ultimately, is what sells a book. Unfortunately, you cannot get word of mouth unless you first publicize a book to get enough people to buy it who can talk about it and let word-of-mouth buying take over." Silberman feels that one of the most effective ways to build up word of mouth quickly is through book clubs. "They're so important, less for the income they bring in than for the way they get thousands of copies into people's hands quickly."

When we sold portions of our *Eat Anything Exercise Diet* to *Woman's Day* and the *National Star,* our editor at William Morrow was delighted even though we got 100 percent of the money for these first-serial sales. Since the two publications reach over 20 million readers, it meant tremendous exposure for the book. Unfortunately, her delight was never transmitted to the sales force, who never got the books into the stores to be bought. Although ours was another frustrating example of publishing's Neanderthal ways, in general it's safe to say that the subsidiary rights income derived from book clubs, newspaper syndicates, and magazines is of secondary importance. More valuable is the impression these sales can have on everyone connected with selling your book, if it's pointed out to them that there's a presold market out there.

Subsidiary rights buyers are accustomed to dealing almost exclusively with publishers' subsidiary rights departments and with literary agents. But on our own, we have contacted and sold rights to book clubs, newspaper syndicates, magazines, tabloids, and newspaper supplements. (If yours is a scholarly book, there may still be a sub rights market for it. A book club was interested in buying our textbook. As editors of a national magazine, we bought book excerpts from publishers that included the University of Oklahoma Press and Louisiana State University Press.) When we deal with prospective sub rights customers, we try to initiate contact on the telephone because that's our style; many writers feel more comfortable working by mail. In either case, start out with a brief pitch to the appropriate person at the club or publication. If he wants to know more, he'll ask. Volunteer to mail a copy of your book, galleys, manuscript, whatever form you have available at the time.

It's seldom a good idea to mail your book to anyone cold. Most sub rights markets are swamped with unsolicited books. They do get read, but the ones that come to an editor who's expressed interest get read quicker and with greater care. You'll find an extensive compilation of book clubs in *Literary Market Place,* along with names of key personnel, addresses, and phone numbers. *LMP* also lists magazines that buy first and second serial rights, but here the selection is quite abbreviated. *Magazine Industry Market Place* and *Writer's Market* are more valuable in reaching greater numbers of more specialized magazines.

Selling subsidiary rights is similar to negotiating book contracts. The buyer usually has a licensing fee in mind when she says, "We'd like to reprint part of your book in our magazine." Ask if that's the best fee she can offer or use any technique you've found helpful at this stage of a sale. However, unless you have a hot book or a hell-fire sales pitch, you may not sway the buyer much—on money. You *can* count on considerable leverage on matters such as whether or not you can sell similar rights to similar markets. Of the handful of magazines that pay many thousands of dollars for a reprint, most expect exclusivity and generally they get it. But that applies just to the portion they're buying. The less money that's offered, generally, the easier it is to bargain for nonexclusivity. But unless a promise of exclusivity cuts into other exposure outlets, it seldom pays to turn down a subsidiary rights sale of almost any size as long as it provides publicity for your book.

When the subsidiary rights sale is to a newspaper, payment is usually on publication. Magazines, as a rule, send checks within a month after they settle on terms. Book clubs and newspaper syndicates are accustomed to paying guarantees or advances at the time you sign the contract, and additional fees hinged to how many copies are sold if it's a book club, or how much income your reprint or condensation earns the syndicate.

To milk maximum publicity value out of your sub rights sales, insist on page proofs or paste-ups of all reprints and of all ads produced for your book by book clubs. These materials make it easier for you to parlay early exposure into subsequent reprint sales and into even greater promotional exposure. We're sure that the fact that we could flash *National Star* and *Woman's Day* reprints to the Los Angeles Times Syndicate helped us sell them syndication rights to our diet and exercise book.

14·4 How to Get Radio and TV Exposure

So you want to go on the "Today" show to plug your book because you've heard that an appearance can sell thousands of copies? So does almost every other author. But the "Today" show each year features only 250 of all the books it's bombarded with, and schedules most of its author guests six to nine months in advance. Its producers make their preliminary selection from advance copies of publishers' catalogs; by nature, they concentrate on the highlighted books—the ones to which the publishers have already committed top dollar.

Other nationally known talk shows, like the "Tonight" show, "Donahue," and "Dick Cavett," are equally unlikely to roll out the mat unless their audiences already know your name. Of course there's always the slim chance you can intrigue them into taking a flyer on your entertainment value, so if you're a gambler, spend a few dollars to send the book and a catchy, short covering letter that oozes personality while singling out a few lively angles.

Fortunately, lots of smaller TV and radio shows sell books by the thousands, sometimes by the tens of thousands. Well-stocked libraries have directories of national, regional, and local outlets that welcome authors or that cover special interests, some of which are likely to encompass the topic of your book. *LMP* lists many, *Working Press of the Nation* lists many more, and there are lots of useful directories like them. The better you study these guides to find out the subjects that interest each show, the more effectively you'll use your money and time.

It doesn't pay to actually mail books en masse to TV and radio show producers, since they're likely to be read less carefully than well-drafted personal letters. The second best approach is to send them a short, catchy press release including an offer to mail a copy of the book to interested producers. Don't limit your mailing to talk shows that like authors. If a show covers the subject of your book—for example, if it's a health program or a cooking hints show—explore how you or your information can add to the program. (The fact that you expect a mention of your book's title, author, and cover price is understood without your having to spell it out.) Even news shows are willing to mention books if you stress the newsworthiness of what you've written.

Don't expect harried producers to search out kernels of knowledge in your letters. We'll show you in section 14.6 how to prepare an eye-catching mail-piece.

Always follow up letters and press releases by phoning a week or so later. If you don't expect to phone, don't bother sending the release. Especially for radio and TV, the phone call is almost indispensable. No producer can tell from a piece of paper whether its author can chitchat entertainingly into a mike. Your release will be filed in the trash unless the book's subject grabs at the pulse-beat of a staff member. (It *can* happen. Patricia McCann's producer phoned to ask Judi to be on that WOR New York radio show when she read our letter about *Stopping Out*. It had arrived just a week after Patricia's daughter announced she was dropping out of college for a while. Judi's reassurance was just what Patricia wanted to hear—and she heard it for half an hour on one of the East Coast's most popular daytime programs.

Your phone call may not get through to the show's producer to whom you addressed your envelope, but you'll probably reach a top assistant, usually the one who books the show's guests. Likely as not, she hasn't seen your letter or release, but when you mention it, she'll usually give you a few minutes to pitch your book and sell your personality. Sound as silver-tongued and honey-voiced as you can, and watch your slang; a censurable word now will make her back off fast.

Using the procedure we just outlined, we managed to talk Frank onto New York's local WOR afternoon "Sherrye Henry Show." Prentice-Hall's New York salesman used news of that appearance to get book displays into the windows of two major Fifth Avenue bookstores, and he reports that for days afterwards, *How to Fix Damn Near Everything* sold out all over town as fast as he could get fresh stock to the stores.

Next we parlayed that appearance into others by writing up a lively publicity release about how successful the "Sherrye Henry Show" had been. For an example, we told how Sherrye was so enraptured with the notion that a housewife could actually fix a grouchy refrigerator, she proposed to Frank on the air. Once other producers had this proof that Frank could handle a live show, they were more receptive to asking him onto their own programs. Just as book editors feel more comfortable working with published authors, radio and TV producers feel safest inviting experienced talk-show guests.

Fortunately, hundreds of radio talk shows around the country are equipped to interview you via the telephone. Art Finley at KGO in San Francisco had Frank on an hour-long "live" evening show in which Frank lounged in his bathrobe at home in Madison, Wisconsin, while answering fix-it questions (with frequent mention of his book) that were phoned into the studio by Art's faithful listeners and transmitted directly to Frank over the phone wire.

You may have to be persistent to get your book noticed by producers. A letter, phone call, press release, reprints of magazine or newspaper stories, another call, more letters, more releases, more copies of more reprints and more phone calls . . . do as much as you can afford, depending on the show's importance in generating sales.

Finally the producer will either give in or tell you why he can't. Either way, he'll remember your name. Next time you write a book, he may treat you like an old friend.

14·5   How to Promote Your Book in Print

The procedure for getting your book free exposure in newspapers, magazines, newsletters, and journals is little different from the approach outlined in section 14.4, except in the form of your mailing.

Most authors forget that print media editors hate to give out free publicity, so they usually throw away releases. However, they love to *receive free editorial copy.* If the *article* you send an editor fits adroitly into his pages, it won't matter that you've shamelessly plugged your book midway through it. He might even pay you for it. (A great many book authors have already sold magazine articles. If you haven't yet, you might want to invest in our *Magazine Writer's Handbook.*)

We can't think of a more obvious example than the efforts we've put into selling Frank's *Children's Toys You Can Build Yourself.* Every year, when editors start to think of Christmastime issues, we excerpt a few of the book's toy projects into article length, gather collections of photos and sketches, and ship off the packages to editors of selected newspaper Sunday magazine sections. Every year several editors run the articles and pay us for them, and none has ever crossed out the ending—a strong plug for the book. Every year, Prentice-Hall's sales force notices a sales peak in cities that have run our annual opus.

Don't limit your sights; many magazines have columns or features far afield from what their names imply. Judi's *Stopping Out* got a magnificent plug in *Better Homes and Gardens,* whose monthly articles on education topics poll consistently high in reader interest. How did we arrange for the article with education editor Dan Kaercher? We must confess we didn't. The subject was another author's suggestion, and the book a serendipitous discovery of hers.

Each publicity effort can snowball considerably. It took many mailings and more than a dozen phone calls to entice the Los Angeles Times Syndicate to offer its members a five-part serialization of our *Eat Anything Exercise Diet.* One paper that carried the feature was the San Francisco *Chronicle.* A New Orleans radio show host who read the Frisco paper (don't ask how come) decided to do a noontime on-the-air telephone interview with us. As a result of that, several southern papers ran news and feature articles about our book. One of those fell into the hands of a reporter for the *National Examiner* in Montreal, and she interviewed us extensively by phone for yet another article.

Again, we see the thin line between sub rights sales and promotion. The moral is that every little bit of effort counts.

14·6 How to Sell Your Book in a Press Release

Here's the challenge: you have 25 words in which to capture the producer's or editor's attention while he's finishing a cup of coffee or nodding over an overly long phone call. If that works, then you've got 500 words to sell him on all of the following:

> that you've got something new and exciting to say
> that you can articulate it inoffensively yet excitingly
> that you and your book are not a hoax

If he's a print editor—of a newspaper, newsletter, or journal that's interested in you or your subject—your 500 words must do all of the above and, in addition, contain the complete short article you want in print, just about ready to hand to the typesetter. Even seasoned P.R. pros on-staff at major publishing houses have to go through many drafts before creating a release that they feel stands a chance to work. Small wonder, then, that authors suffer trauma about writing their own releases.

We can't offer a cure for publicity trauma, nor teach you all about promotion in one chapter, but we can share hints that have worked for us and for friends who promote their own books.

TAILOR YOUR RELEASES TO SPECIFIC OUTLETS
One release is seldom effective in several media. For TV and radio show producers, stick to one terse page that highlights several important and catchy points in your book that can be bantered about for maybe six minutes of air time. For the feature editors of newspapers, try for a two-page release that can be run as is, summing up the book's general topic (which often takes no more than half of a compound sentence) and offering pithy information on several salient, specific points. In addition, work in a direct but not too obvious teaser that makes readers want to buy your book.

For our *Do-It-Yourself Custom Van Book* we prepared a short feature describing our adventures taking three little boys from New York to California and back in our specially equipped van. The only mention of our book was a line telling that all the van's special features, and directions for building them, could be found in its pages. The release made dozens of newspapers across the country, complete with the photo we'd sent along.

LET SOMEBODY ELSE DO YOUR BRAGGING

Most people imagine that self-promoters are charlatans, so before you can get your message across, you have to establish credibility. Media people are particularly skeptical of puffery in self-written releases. They're afraid that you may not be able to deliver what you promise. But if even a little-known expert in your field is willing to say your book is a gem, work that in near the top of your release.

PARE YOUR PHRASES

You can't knock off a press release the way you write to your mother. Rewrite, edit, and reedit your one or two pages until you've packed in as much information, promise, and personal credentials as you can squeeze in.

PARLAY YOUR SUCCESSES

Every time you find favorable mention of your book in print, clip it out, type boldly across the top "REPRINTED FROM THE JOURNAL OF AEROBIC SUN BATHERS. FOR MORE INFORMATION AND INTERVIEWS WITH THE AUTHOR, CONTACT. . . ." You can mail these unescorted to the list of media contacts you've picked out of the directories, or you can send along short, punchy covering letters. We reprint our press clips on colored paper and attach them to follow-up mailings.

If you've already been on a TV or radio show, no doubt the host had a few kind words for you and your book. Make sure to have the show recorded so you can use her flattering comments in future releases. But use media people's comments with discretion. You won't want a Kansas City producer to think that your one-shot Des Moines appearance was part of a big national tour that he missed out on. Since nobody in the media likes to be scooped, make the Kansas City producer feel he's the next stop in your national promotional efforts.

KEEP ACCURATE LISTS OF YOUR PRESS CONTACTS

Every time you speak to somebody as a follow-up to a release or letter you've sent, make note of her name, spelled accurately, especially if she's been helpful or encouraging. Then mail your subsequent efforts directly to her, and if you include a covering letter, be sure you work in the fact that you've conversed.

ASK FOR HELP

If you're stuck figuring the best tactic to take during some stage of your self-promotional efforts, many of the media pros around town will gladly lend a hand. We've had good luck calling a producer at a show we were eager to crack and asking, "Maybe you could give us some advice." With luck, the promotion director or an assistant at your own publisher's might even spend some time helping you.

14·7 How to Manage a TV or Radio Show Appearance

The best way to manage an appearance on the air is to take charge of it. Except for the big national programs that have large staffs, you can't count on a show host's being prepared. All too often, she won't have read your book, she'd forget your name if it weren't printed on a card in front of her, and she scarcely knows the topic you've come to discuss.

Pros plan ahead by sending both the producer and the host— since studios are matched in efficiency only by the Postal Service—a half-page summary of the book and its salient points, plus a list of ten to twenty questions together with highly abbreviated but dramatic answers. Be sure you choose *good* questions; some should sound really challenging. The whole package should fit onto two pages.

You wouldn't believe the number of shows on which we've been asked our own prepared questions. But of course, we don't count on that. We reread the book before we go on the show, and we urge you to read yours. It's a long time since you wrote it, and it's amazing how much you've forgotten. Mark important statistics or quotations by stapling colored slips of paper to the appropriate pages. Key the slips if you have to, or use different shades of paper. And for TV, keep the book right on your lap. Believe it or not, you'll look authoritative if you answer questions by referring to pages in your book. More important, while you're holding up the book to read your answer (hold it high), the TV camera will have to focus not only on you but on the book's cover. Every time that cover is shown, it adds to sales. We watched, fascinated, as Terry Davidson was being interviewed in our living room during a promotional tour for her book *Conjugal Crime*. Terry had trained herself to sit ever so comfortably in such a way that the cover of her book was quietly on camera every minute that she was, and the host never noticed at all.

The host may ask dumb or embarrassing questions. Remember, nowhere is it written that you must answer what's asked. Choose a good answer—to a good hypothetical question, not the one on the host's lips. When you get really good at this, you'll be able to tell the audience exactly what you think will make them rush to buy your book, while at the same time earning a reputation for making media hosts look good.

On talk shows, practice does make perfect. If you have no deep-seated neuroses, you can learn to be a suave and witty media guest simply by doing it often enough. Many colleges and college extensions offer short courses that can help. Some companies run hands-on seminars that teach executives and others how to act in an interview. Charles Silberman's publisher paid for a one-day program "that ran me through three mock talk shows, one press conference where they brought in a half-dozen other people, an impromptu speech, a speech from text. All was videotaped and played back. I learned a great deal about using the medium." Silberman told us that he could have learned as much through trial and error but that the formal training "gave me a one- to two-week start on the talk-show circuit."

Silberman's course cost $500. He advises, "If the publisher won't pay for it, it's an investment well worth making."

14·8 Book Promotion Is a Lifelong Job

Every time we run into Annie Moldafsky, Chicago author of *Welcome to the Real World* and *The Good Buy Book,* she shares her latest discovery about how to promote books effectively. Every time our Chicago chapter of the American Society of Journalists and Authors has a meeting, promotional chitchat flies. You see, we're all born-again authors who've seen the light: that if we want our books to reach the reading public (and our incomes to reach our expectations), we must ensure our books as much promotion as our budgets and schedules can stand.

Annie never visits out of town friends or business associates without writing or phoning ahead to schedule interviews with newspaper reporters and program hosts. While she's in town, she visits the major bookstores. If they have her book on the shelves, she thanks the manager for caring enough to stock the very best. If not, she lets the manager know who she is, what she's written, and why he ought to order it. (She even carries brochures with her name, titles, prices, publishers, and ISBN numbers for easy ordering.) Annie reports, "Usually as I'm on my way out the door, the manager is starting to write up an order."

There's no book whose sale cannot be enhanced by promotion. Nonfiction is easiest to place nowadays, followed by novels based on factual research or tied in with issues currently on the public's mind.

For other novels, often the author's personal experiences can be hyped—especially the romantic experience of being a first novelist. There's nothing to stop you from arranging your own expense-paid tour. While we were taking our boys on that coast-to-coast van trip mentioned earlier, Judi arranged *Stopping Out* interviews for a network radio show in San Francisco, two newspapers in Minneapolis–St. Paul, and other media at points between.

4

The Business of Writing

Chapter Fifteen

Is Self-Publication for You?

RECENTLY, ALL KINDS OF WRITERS HAVE SEEMED hypnotically drawn toward self-publication as an escape from the bind they believe their books are in. Many neophytes, tired of collecting rejection letters instead of royalty checks, see self-publication as a way of pulling a fast one on the shortsighted, narrow-minded editors who would have turned down James Joyce. And most seasoned pros, tired of overworking, bowing, hassling and being hassled to scrape together next month's rent, see self-publication as an easy way to pocket *all* the profits instead of only one dollar out of every ten.

Reduced to simplest terms, self-publication means that you, the author, are your own publisher. But there's nothing simple about self-publication.

Publishers themselves seem to be explicit models for self-publication. Many well-known publishing houses are little more than two-desk operations that have managed to stay afloat for years by pinching nickels, secretaries, and authors. Some of them have little more than letterhead, checking account, and office space. They borrow money, buy manuscripts, and hire free-lance copy editors, outside typesetters, free-lance book designers, outside printers, outside binders, outside advertising and public relations counsel, free-lance jacket blurb copywriters, free-lance cover designers, and an outside sales force. They even hire service corporations to warehouse and ship books. No wonder writers are tempted to expend a little time coordinating the specialists themselves in exchange for keeping all the money that comes in.

But let's see if it's really as easy as it looks.

15·1 The Two Kinds of Vanity Publishing

The term *vanity publishing* is often used in discussions about self-publication. We want to clarify its meaning—first in its classic sense and then as it applies to some self-publication we've seen.

First of all, it means *subsidy* publishing, an ancient practice. A company, usually containing "Publisher" in its name, floods business, academic, and artsy publications with carefully written ads and deluges purchased lists of hopeful writers with alluring brochures. The ads and brochures would have you believe that, finally, here's a publisher that's hungry for manuscripts and that really cares about new authors. Books in all stages of readiness pour into these companies like ants to spilled honey. The unwary authors get sweet-talked into paying thousands of dollars to see them in print, often believing that their cash is a subsidy or co-investment. In return, they anticipate 40 percent royalties. But like ants on honey, they get stuck. You don't need a pencil to calculate 40 percent of zero. With rare, very rare, exception that's the kind of income they can realistically expect.

Many vanity-published books look respectable. Your mother and children will be proud of you. And if you're like our friend Ed, a professor at a small eastern college, your vanity-published book might help you on your publish-or-perish treadmill. But reviewers won't review a book with a vanity imprint; no major media outlet will publicize it; no self-respecting distributor will take on its sale. In short, unless you yourself handle every stage of promotion and sales following its actual manufacture, don't count on even your friends to buy the book.

If your goals really are linked to what you'd have to realistically call vanity, then a subsidy publisher might be the right place for you. But go there expecting just the pleasure of seeing your name in print, not the reward of having your bank account cushioned or your fame spread. And go there with a lawyer, because many vanity publishers' tactics are so slippery that several have drawn the complaints of consumer protection agencies.

That's the first kind of vanity publishing. The second kind starts with the same frustrated author who can't find a publisher. Sometimes he has a novel like the one a disgruntled student of ours called a *belle lettre;* he sent it to three publishers, decided they didn't know a blooming genius, and published the book himself. We don't know all the details, since he stopped coming to class as soon as we started saying that writers must act as if they're in business. We can't judge the book, since he wouldn't let us read it. We know only that he talked several bookstores in town into putting it on the shelves for several months, and a copy or two actually sold. The rest were sent back to him when the space was needed for other books. We haven't seen or heard from him since.

Often, the book is a good nonfiction idea with an identifiable market, but it's been circulated to only a handful of companies—and that's not enough. (If we gave up that easily, Frank's most profitable

book, *How to Fix Damn Near Everything,* would still be collecting dust.)
Believing, perhaps correctly, that the publishers don't know a money-
maker when they see one, its author decides to gamble on its potential
and publish it herself. Some gambles do pay off. Rod McKuen made a
killing by publishing his own first poetry efforts, and Washington
Irving's psuedonymous pseudo-*History of New York* took off thanks to
his wry publicity stunts. The trend-setting *Whole Earth Catalog* might
never have surfaced if Stewart Brand hadn't self-published it (with a lot
of help from his friends). On the other hand, self-publisher Thomas
Paine never earned a shilling on *Common Sense* after paying his printer.

There's now a number of books advocating self-publishing, and
most point out that half of all commercially published books make no
profit. (They fail to add any self-publishing statistics; we'd guess
they're even gloomier.) Ironically, some of these books aren't self-
published themselves. They read like the pop-psych books of the '70s
and would have you believe that self-publication is as easy as painting
your house. Actually, it's more like getting the whole house designed,
built, and landscaped. It requires not just manual labor, but a lot of
knowledge about a number of jobs. The unwary who read these
self-styled primers may rush into just another form of vanity publishing, requiring even larger outlays of time as well as cash. And the
books we've seen turned out by the subsidy presses are more attractive
products than many self-publishers' first efforts.

15·2 The Business of Self-Publication

If we define success in self-publication as the sale of enough books to
enhance your reputation as an author or to profitably recoup your
investment of time and money, almost the only people who've
succeeded have been those who've known something about publishing
to begin with and were also crackerjacks at business. These people
could make a living selling used cars, aspirins, or encyclopedias, and
they unromantically considered a book a manufactured product.

Any book's success in reaching an audience depends as much on
marketing skills as on editorial expertise. Don't make the mistakes that
have killed so many self-published books: assuming that any writer can
write a good ad, that any writer can write a good press release, and that
anybody who loves books can sell books.

Most successful self-publishers have either been entrepreneurs
long enough to understand the business side of publishing, and have
only to hire out the editorial and writing jobs, *or* are successful writers

familiar with editing and production and willing to do menial work or spend the capital to get it done. If your dream is to self-publish, honestly decide whether you fit into either category. That's the first decision. Next, choose your goal: your name proudly displayed on a bound volume, or a self-publishing business, and if the latter, full-time or part-time business. Whether vanity or business, your rewards will depend on how thoroughly you learn every step of the book publishing process.

We won't insult you or the publishing business by trying to teach any of it in a chapter. There's more to know than even one long book can tell. If you need information about any aspect of publishing, we strongly suggest you consult the books written for publishing professionals. Also consider investing in some of the seminars designed for book professionals, such as the "Learn to Sell Books Profitably" seminar sponsored by the Association of American Publishers (1 Park Avenue, New York, NY 10016), and the courses offered at major colleges in various parts of the United States. Most of these are announced well in advance in the pages of *Publishers Weekly*.

15·3   A Self-Publisher's Checklist

To help you assess whether you know enough about publishing or about business to jump into a self-publication venture, we've reduced its components to an abbreviated checklist. As you read, remember that you'll have to either do each step yourself, or contract out to people who have the tools and machinery.

SUPPLYING CAPITAL

It's unrealistic to start a book publishing venture unless you already have or can raise enough money to cover the entire process. As you'll see, there's more involved than just writing and printing, the two things that come immediately to most authors' minds.

Some self-publication financing arrangements we've heard of are as creative as the books involved. One man formed a corporation and, instead of collecting praise from friends and relatives, sold them stock. Several have taken second mortgages on their homes. When Susan Jeffers and Ellen Carr self-published their brief book *How to Find a Job,* they both held onto full-time jobs that covered both their $5,000 out-of-pocket investment and the year of moonlighting it took them to conceive, write, and publish.

We've seen recommendations by self-publishing prophets that you take out a bank vacation loan to cover publication. One problem with short-term installment loans is that you must start repaying almost as soon as you get the cash. You may not start collecting money on self-publication for a year or more after your initial outlay. You'd better know, before you spend it, where the repayment money's going to come from.

Banks love to lend money to businesses, old or new, that have sound underpinnings, and a business loan doesn't ever have to be repaid as long as you keep making interest payments and keep showing your banker that you're running a sound business venture. If you're really in business to publish, and if you're going at it in a businesslike way, approach your bank for a business loan. If your banker doesn't think your venture is worth a loan, respect his opinion. Ask his objection and see if he can steer you to people who can help you overcome it. Bankers are valuable allies; they'd like to see you succeed.

If you're in self-publication for vanity, forget about trying to get a business loan. Only do know the size of your investment before you begin, particularly if your book won't recoup your outlay.

MARKET RESEARCH

Your book had better be about something that enough people want to read—and therefore buy—if it's to turn a profit for you. It's not enough to know that there's a potential audience of a million readers out there. You must find them and sell them. That's why most successful self-publishers first zeroed in on topics with localized or highly select audiences. Merle E. Dowd has concentrated on regional markets in the Northwest, where he lives, for self-published books like his *Seattle Guidebook.* Chicago's Jerold Kellman started off with *A Writer's Guide to Chicago-Area Publishers,* and California's Fran Halpern with *A Writer's Guide to West Coast Publishing:* both aimed at filling specific holes in specific markets.

Jan Venolia had for years made a career of free-lance editing for corporations near her Woodland Hills, California, home. She recalls, "People would always ask if there wasn't some book they could buy to use when I wasn't around. I didn't know of any, so I wrote and self-published *Write Right!* My first sales effort was a mailing to corporate librarians and, amazingly, it paid off."

It isn't enough just to conjecture about your potential audience. You must pinpoint it concretely enough to be able to reach it economically the way Jan Venolia did. If you can't, forget about self-publishing for anything but vanity. (This is why few, if any, novelists have ever succeeded at self-publishing.) Talk to everybody who might know something about your market, about how to zero in on it, and about the best way to convince customers to buy from you. Unless your book directly competes with theirs, most successful self-publishers are a ready source of information. Other people who think in terms of targeting markets for products are advertising account executives, independent sales representatives, and media space reps. They may not know anything about your particular market, but they may be able to offer shortcuts for pinpointing it.

A MANUSCRIPT

If you're going into self-publication to escape the rigors, incongruities, rituals, and discipline of preparing a manuscript acceptable to a trade publisher, your chances of making a go of it as a business are diminished. If you're hoping to end up in the black, be prepared to accept that the reading public knows quality when it sees it and is more inclined to spend money on a quality book than on something substandard. Don't be fooled by all the bad books you find in bookstores; most of them do not make back their cost. The poor ones that do sell well are generally the result of very expensive ad campaigns.

EDITING

A good editor is more important to a writer than even a loving mother. Peter Benchley's *Jaws* and Jacqueline Susann's *Valley of the Dolls* were helped by fine editors, and novelists from William Faulkner and Thomas Wolfe down to James A. Michener have depended on them. But nonfiction writers need a seasoned professional independent viewpoint, too. The reason we've become personally confident in our writing ability is that we put in years of tutelage under tough editors who wouldn't accept half-baked ideas, cutesy constructions, or ungrammatical English.

Evaluate yourself critically. Can you honestly assure yourself that you've had enough experience as a word-crafter that your book will look carefully edited? (If every word in Chapter 11 is old-hat to you, we'd say you've passed the test.) This is especially important if you hope to depend on reviews for sales or promotion. (Though *The New York Times* and *Publishers Weekly* don't review self-published books, many newspapers and journals will *if* they have special interest in your topic.) Even some reviewers of nonliterary books are sensitive to the literary merits of what they're reading and reviewing.

The best advice we can give is not to do both writing and editing. Frankly, too many self-published books we've seen could have benefited from an editor's blue pencil. Consider hiring an editor. *Literary Market Place* is a good place to look. (If you'd rather edit and hire a writer, call Dial-A-Writer, a service of the American Society of Journalists and Authors, 1501 Broadway, Suite 1907, New York, NY 10036).

LEGAL ADVICE

It's foolhardy to plunge into business without knowing the laws that govern you. You can research them on your own, of course, if you want a fool for a client—to borrow a well-worn phrase. If you've never been in business before, it's worth the cost of legal consultation to find out what your state laws say about incorporating, running an unincorporated business, collecting sales tax, unemployment, covering workers under worker's compensation, Social Security, using your home as your place of business, and on and on.

Then, what about your liability for what you write? Two nationally prominent publishers were each forced to pull cookbooks off the market because, federal agencies said, they offered potentially dangerous advice. Could a small mistake that creeps into your book put you out of business, or worse?

DESIGN

If your book is more than straightforward type—if it has charts, illustrations, or fancy layouts—you must design it before you can get a meaningful estimate from typesetter and printer. You have to figure out what material will go onto which page, and how many pages you will have, and in some cases you must create an actual dummy. If you have a bit of the artist's flair, you might be able to handle book design on your own or with some help from a book on the subject. Otherwise you may have to employ a free-lance artist or book designer.

TYPESETTING

Many local printers set type. Sometimes you can get a good price by going that route. But don't overlook the way most companies go about manufacturing books: having type set by one specialist and printing done by another. Offset printing has made it possible for many self-publishers to set their own type on specialized electric typewriters, but offset printing is often more expensive than a letterpress job. You must compare costs on a book by book basis.

Jan Venolia went the letterpress route on her *Write Right!* but she was lucky enough to have a neighbor in the printing business who taught her how to use his Linotype machine and let her run it during off-hours. If you disregard the time she spent pecking away at the old Mergenthaler, she got her type set almost for nothing. But you can't disregard it; every businessperson can tell you the monetary value of her time.

ILLUSTRATIONS

Reproducing illustrations can be very expensive. Jan wanted to pattern her self-published book after Richard Bolles' *What Color Is Your Parachute?* "I really liked the looks of all of its graphics and loose layout. When I priced it out, I was shocked at the cost." Jan did without the graphics.

PASTE-UPS OR DUMMYS

Once your type is set and your illustrations, if any, are prepared, you have to assemble the bits and pieces into book pages. For letterpress, you'll probably cut apart the type proofs and paste them onto dummy sheets supplied by your printer. For offset, you might choose to make only a rough dummy and then work with the actual type, pasting it carefully onto forms that will be photographed to make printing plates.

Either way you go at it, this job is time-consuming. It must be done meticulously, for pages that are the slightest bit crooked, unbalanced, or uneven look like the product of an amateur—and that can spell the death knell to sales. (This is a big reason vanity publishers' books often look more professional than self-publishers' products.)

COVER DESIGN AND ART

You may not be able to judge a book by its cover, but everybody tries. No matter how valuable the words inside may be, if the cover looks chintzy, your sales may suffer dramatically. In commercial publishing houses a great deal of editorial and marketing effort goes into choosing the best cover title, the relative sizes of type, the font (style of type) that will produce the right emotional reaction, the placement of all the design elements, even the colors and their effect when seen at a distance and up close. Artists Milton Glazer and Seymour Chwast made their names and fortunes when their Pushpin Studios designed successful covers for major publishers.

The cost of a professional designer can be high, but it may be money well spent. At the very least, you should extensively market-research every possible cover design until you're confident you've found one that not only says what you want to say but has an appearance potential customers respond to favorably.

PRINTING

This may be your biggest cash outlay. Research it carefully. One self-publisher living in Chicago, one of the printing capitals of the world, got the best deal down in Tennessee. Local printers, no matter how cheap, do you no good if they don't understand book printing. In small cities you can sometimes talk a local printer into a preferred rate (or no charge at all) in return for a percentage of the potential profits. If you're paying for printing, you must figure out the most economical run; the more copies you print at once, the cheaper each copy—but they're not cheap at all if you can't sell them.

One of the first self-publishers we ever met wrote college study guides in his bedroom behind a Brooklyn storefront. In the store itself he printed them on an ancient Multilith offset press he'd bought secondhand. You can do the same, if you have the aptitude and the time. At the very least, you ought to understand the technology, terminology, and especially the economics of the printing business so that you're an informed buyer.

BINDING

The company that runs paper through a press to print the inside of your book is not necessarily the best company for binding those pages into a finished product. Since this is another major cash outlay, study the subject, then cost it out carefully: analyze the prices you can realistically expect people to pay for your books in paperback, spiral, loose-leaf, and hard-cover bindings. Compare the potential prices with the equivalent costs of production.

WAREHOUSING

Where are you going to store the books once the printer and binder have finished with them? The printshop will probably not let you store them there (unless you've swung the deal in advance). Many basements and most garages are not dry enough to be suitable long-term book warehouses. Assuming you order 5,000 copies of a 6 inch × 9 inch book, and pack them efficiently and stack them 6 feet high, you'll need about 36 square feet of floor space.

SALES

Let's face it, it takes a certain kind of personality to be able to sell things. The enthusiasm of selling your own pride and joy of a book will carry you just so far. Then your native aggressive sales instinct—or lack of it—will take over.

Often, it's a good idea to hire someone else to sell to bookstores for you. But who will you choose? How much will it cost? How much do you have to add to your cover price to pay for sales help? These questions have to be answered *before* you put the first page into your typewriter to start writing the book.

Speaking of sales, don't think only in terms of selling your book copy by copy. If you have a great idea that a company or association might want to use, maybe it'll buy thousands of copies. The time to find out about that is *before* you write the book. The company might be inclined to make a deal only if its own products are mentioned. That's something you can't take care of after the printer has shipped you the finished copies.

You can also sell subsidiary rights to your self-published books. If your material interests their readers, few magazines care if you or Random House contracted for the printing. Book clubs are generally looking for a publishing-house pedigree, but Jan Venolia sold her *Write Right!* to both the *Times-Mirror* and *Writer's Digest* book clubs.

COLLECTIONS

Okay, you've sold some copies to bookstores and shipped them off. What do you do when they don't send checks by return mail? Don't be surprised. Bookstores are used to dealing with publishers on credit, and to returning unsold books up to a year later for full refund. You'll probably have to offer the same terms. Add to that bad checks from occasional mail-order customers. We don't mean to discourage you, but plan ahead.

BOOKKEEPING

When you're in business, you have to keep books so you know how you're doing, and so others know how you're doing: your state sales tax agency, IRS, state unemployment tax agency, federal unemployment tax agency, Social Security Administration, state department of labor, city licensing authority, and so forth. Self-publisher Jerold Kellman warns that your financial bookkeeping had better be good. "You're going to be questioned closely. To the IRS, if you're a full-time publisher, you're a rich daddy, and if you're a part-time operation, it's a hobby and a lot of people like to show losses on their hobbies."

By now, if you're still thinking about self-publication as a business, you've probably jumped way beyond our elementary checklist. And if you're going at it as a form of vanity self-publishing, no doubt we've lost you already; you're going to publish even if you perish. So we'll just share with you one of those good quotes that's too abstract to work in anywhere else. *The Diary of Anaïs Nin* records the author's ecstacy at her own self-publishing experience:

> . . . an act of independence . . . a marvelous cure for anger and frustration. The insults of the publishers, the rejections, the ignorance, all are forgotten.

Anaïs Nin was born in a fashionable Paris suburb. She was aided in curing her frustrations by frequent and generous subsidies from novelist Richard Wright, who was born behind the great house on a plantation.

Chapter Sixteen

The Writer and the Law

I N THE CLASSES WE'VE TAUGHT, THE WORKSHOPS we've given, and the writers' conferences we've participated in, experienced as well as fledgling authors have been full of questions about copyright, libel, taxes, privacy, slander, and defamation. But when you get right down to it, the law seldom affects authors directly, except in several limited ways:

> You should know about libel and privacy laws in order to write defensible books.
> You need to know a smattering about copyright law.
> You must live with the tax laws, like it or not.

16·1 Libel

To excerpt a definition from Harold Nelson and Dwight Teeter's textbook, *Law of Mass Communications*: Libel is defamation that occurs by written "communication which exposes a person to hatred, ridicule, or contempt, lowers him in the esteem of his fellows, causes him to be shunned, or injures him in his business or calling." Not many years ago, we were able to tell students that if they wanted to deliberately libel somebody, they'd almost have to hire a good lawyer as co-author. Now, however, the pendulum has swung against journalists again. You have to be a great deal more cautious when you write about real people or institutions.

In almost every libel suit, the publisher is only one of the defendants; another is the author. Furthermore, you can't count on publishers to know what's libelous; you can't even count on them to hire lawyers to read your manuscripts for libel. They may send controversial ones out for legal opinions, but it's not always the controversial manuscripts that give the most problems.

There is no way we can cite chapter and verse on what the law says you can and cannot say in print. Libel law isn't like a traffic law that says you can drive no faster than 55 mph, period. Libel statutes vary from state to state, and libel case precedents change not only from state to state but from year to year. Any time you write anything about anybody, libel law can be involved.

That's the bad news. The good news is that as an author, you are protected by the First Amendment. Along about 1964 the courts suddenly recognized that authors subjected to frivolous libel actions were suffering at least the temporary loss, if not the permanent erosion, of their First Amendment freedom of the press. Since then, judges have often tossed out libel suits that the authors or publishers could demonstrate were unlikely to succeed if they went to trial.

What all of this boils down to is that as authors, we have to exercise our freedom of the press as fully as each of us chooses to, but that as pragmatists we may want to—or under pressure from publishers, have to—exercise it in the most easily defended way. As any good writer knows, there are many ways of calling a crook a crook, a fact too many zealots overlook—and some ways are more defensible than others.

Let's borrow a page from law textbooks by spinning a parable about four different ways we can write about something rotten in the state of New Jersey. The facts are these: Joe So-and-So, perennial president of the Hoboken Civic Improvement Organization, has been the subject of a Senate Committee on Organized Crime investigation. Their published report says that committee investigators have seen Joe frequently in the company of known criminals and, because of that, he's now under investigation.

> If your book states that, because he's been seen in unsavory company, Joe So-and-So's crookedness is now being investigated by the Senate Committee on Organized Crime, you'd stand a good chance of ending up in court and paying huge libel damages.
> If you matter-of-fact quote from the Congressional report that says Joe is under investigation because he's been seen in the company of unsavory types, you might still get into a libel action, if Joe's the suing kind. But you'd stand a very good chance of having it tossed out before the lawyers' bills outpace the national debt.

In both the above suppositions, you'd leave readers convinced that Joe was not your run-of-the-mill hard-working next-door neighbor. Both, since they identify Joe, would leave you fair game for a libel suit (and for wearing a pair of concrete overshoes next time you go for a swim in scenic New York harbor).

> If your article were about New Jersey or civic leaders and not about Joe, you could simply write that one New Jersey civic leader whom Congressional investigators have seen hanging around with known criminals is himself under investigation. Unless Joe has been pretty

well identified publicly as the New Jersey hood cum civic-leader the feds are laying for, this approach is the second-best way to protect yourself and your publisher from a suit.

If your book were about scenic New Jersey and you felt Joe was not one of the scenes but merely a way to exercise your Woodward and Bernstein urge, you could ignore Joe and he'd do likewise to you. This, of course, is a foolproof way to stay out of court.

The above series of situations is *not* meant to point out that the coward's way is the safest—a truism we don't have to remind you of. What it does show—and if you missed this, go back and reread it more carefully—is that one of the most important defenses against libel is the author's intellectual honesty in evaluating his own research and in drawing conclusions for readers.

Although nonfiction authors are most prone to libel suits—and we'll concentrate our discussion on their problems—fiction authors must be careful that their characters' names and characteristics are far from any true-life models who might be tempted to sue.

A nonfiction author's first rub with libel problems may come in writing the book proposal. Don't promise anything, no matter how juicy and sale-clinching, that you might later decide to renege on because of libel considerations. The editor can hold you to delivery. Trapped in their own initial overenthusiasm, a number of authors have delivered libelous manuscripts and embroiled themselves and their publishers in sticky legal messes.

Next comes your research. Whether it's for nonfiction or for contemporary fiction, of course you're going to do it carefully and keep good documentation as you go along, and even preserve all of your notes until the libel statutes of limitation have expired (in some states two years after the last edition has been published). But let's be realistic. As you're sitting at the typewriter pecking toward that engulfing deadline, you'll wish you'd dug deeper and made better notes. So what do you do? If you write a stronger nonfiction statement than your research substantiates, or delineate an amoral character who's altogether too much like your ex-husband, you're possibly in deep legal trouble. (In the former case you're also offering the public a dishonest book.)

How honestly do *you* assess your research? Even though you've always thought to yourself that Henry Psychic must have doctored his experiments, when you sit at your typewriter, be sure you report what your notes show and not what your imagination conjectures. Henry and his lawyers will sue and collect if you say *on your own authority* that Dr. Psychic doctored experiments.

Now, if an ex-employee told you that the results were doctored, you can share that little detail with your readers: reporting her attributed statement doesn't mean that's the way it is, only the way she says it is. But you'd better also tell whether she's a disgruntled secretary or a top scientist about to blow the whistle, and not lead the reader to believe a statement is authoritative when it isn't.

Don't let the lure of a well-turned phrase turn your text from factuality. Whoever writes press releases for Senator William Proxmire apparently didn't pay careful enough attention to collecting or reporting on his research notes. In writing up one of our Wisconsin Senator's famous Golden Fleece awards to alleged wasters of government funds—in this case a Michigan scientist who conducted behavior research on monkeys—the Senator's aide wrote, "In fact, the good doctor has made a fortune from his monkeys and in the process made a monkey out of the American taxpayer." In fact, the doctor was on a salary from state institutions and not directly profiting much, if at all, from government grants. He sued Proxmire for libel—and won what any reasonable person *could* call a "fortune."

Returning to our hypothetical example, let's say that you sense that Dr. Psychic doctored his results but you can't find anyone who's seen proof. Your conviction led you to other labs, whose researchers reported that they'd tried to replicate Psychic's findings and failed. Report it just that way: "Dr. Psychic's published reports say . . . but researchers in labs at Texaco Tech and Brooklyn Biofeedback have tried to replicate his results and failed." If that's all the facts you've got, that's all you can report.

On the same day the U.S. Supreme Court "fleeced" Senator Proxmire, it also decided the following case: A one-time public figure, named in a book as a KGB agent, felt that the author had not presented his information accurately enough. The author swore that when he identified the plaintiff as a Soviet agent in the United States, he had relied on an FBI report. What he overlooked was that the FBI, like all police agencies, only investigates and offers *allegations*. Since the FBI report did not *prove* the named man was a KGB agent, and a court had never decided on the truth of the allegation, the author lost his case.

Stating an allegation as fact is libelous. However, nothing says you can't share your *opinions* with readers. This writing technique is overlooked distressingly often; some nonfiction authors have gotten the notion that when they became journalists they gave up the right to express opinions. Readers of nonfiction don't expect an author to spin 60,000 words of unopinionated prose. On the contrary, they welcome glimpses of your personality. If your opinion is that Dr. Psychic fudged, you can say so. It's your constitutionally protected right.

Dusty Sklar's book *Gods and Beasts* dealt mostly with cult groups in Nazi Germany; its final chapter mentioned the Unification Church. The "Moonies" sued for libel. But Edward Miller, vice-president and counsel at Harper & Row, Dusty's publisher, countered that what Dusty had said there was clearly her own opinion, which she had a right to express. That, along with several other arguments, was enough to convince the judge to issue a summary judgment, throwing out the case early in the proceedings.

On the other hand, Dr. Psychic and other possible libel plaintiffs have won in the courts the right to make you separate your opinion clearly from your facts. That's only good journalism, anyway, but the separateness you must keep is open to judicial interpretation. Heather Grant Florence, Bantam Books' vice-president and general counsel, said in *Publishers Weekly,* "Because the distinction between a fact—express or implied—and an opinion can be far from clear, a welter of rules and precedents have grown up around that issue." She delineated some variations in opinion: (1) Some courts have required that facts, whether published or not, fully and fairly justify an opinion. (2) Some have said that opinion is actionable when coupled with a clear but false impression that the author is privy to generally unknown facts. (3) Some have said that opinion is protected so long as it is honestly held and reasonable.

These three options, and probably many more, exist at local levels. But attorney Florence added, "The Supreme Court has not adopted any of these rules. Indeed, in the 1974 *Gertz* decision it appeared to give full protection to opinion: 'Under the First Amendment there is no such thing as a false idea. However pernicious an opinion may seem, we depend for its correction not on the conscience of judges and juries but on the competition of other ideas.' "

Let's move our hypothetical treatment of Dr. Psychic into an even more nebulous arena: *context.* You've carefully presented your facts so you don't claim there's more to them than there really is, and you've scrupulously kept opinion separated from fact. So far so good. But let's assume your book is a radical assessment of how scientists like Dr. P have helped the Pentagon's war-crazed generals plot to overthrow the United Nations. Some might regard your *author's viewpoint* as kooky, unpatriotic, or unconscionable. In fact, the people who've volunteered

the most information about Dr. P in interviews, Dr. Ex and Dr. Why, both of them conservative as a maiden uncle, might not like being thrust into the context of helping you put down fellow conservative Dr. P. They might hire a lawyer and sue you for libel. How do you avoid that kind of suit?

The fact is, if you want to ward off libel actions brought about through matters of context, you may have to let your research sources know not only your book's subject, but your own viewpoint about that subject. At the very least, you are not entitled to misrepresent your viewpoint. This limitation promises to cut down on the ease with which you can research difficult topics, but it's a limitation that's part and parcel of the overall honesty with which you should approach the research and writing of your book.

After *The Amityville Horror: A True Story* came out, two TV news reporters sued for libel. They didn't deny that Jay Anson quoted them accurately in his book. However, they did allege that the book was a hoax and that Anson defamed them in naming them as contributors of fact to the project. In another case, the scientist whose work was used for a book on cloning also cried hoax and said he was libeled by its author by having his name associated with the book. It's educational to note that neither case was dismissed by judges as being frivolous or without merit.

But you're going to take the ultimate protective step in your hypothetical book: you won't name Dr. Psychic or his detractors Dr. Ex and Dr. Why. You'll rely on your fictional skills and spin a yarn about three characters whose names you'll pick at random from the Manhattan telephone directory. Doesn't that cover you?

These days even fiction may not be protected from libel. First of all, if Dr. Psychic is the *only* real person known to have performed a total brain transplant, and your despicable fictional character also shoehorns in new brains, you might be in the same kind of trouble as if you were writing nonfiction. A California court did find that a novelist libeled a therapist with a highly visible specialty, nude encounter groups. Even if Dr. Psychic is not the world's only brain transplanter, if he could be identified as the inspiration for your character by people close to him, you still might not be in the clear. The law in this area is fuzzier than in most, and it's changing—a fact that underlines why authors and publishers ought to work together to make a book legally defensible. Unfortunately, the adversary relationship that develops between author and publisher often carries over into this arena too. In fact, difficulties between the novelist and her publisher were a major

stumbling block in defending against the California therapist's libel action.

We've found that many editors can be valuable in double-checking authors' documentation. (They're not all valuable, however, which is why we recommended in Chapter 6 that you insist the indemnity clause be changed to keep you free of any libelous additions your publisher may make or insist that you make.) Good copy editors are even more valuable than acquisition editors because they're such lovely nit-pickers that they could have made brilliant lawyers.

The attorney who keeps Bantam Books on its toes, Heather Grant Florence, advised in *Publishers Weekly:* "If investigative journalism is involved, the publisher should make it a point to be satisfied with the research behind it, including the sources, or at the least, the author's assessment of them and the basis for that assessment." She went on: "With fiction, in order to know when disguise is necessary, the publisher must talk to the author about the background for the novel. What is the town, really? Who are the characters? Where did the idea for the book come from?" She concluded, "As a rule, the publisher can and should take steps to gauge whether reliance on the author is well-founded."

We would like to add that authors should take the same steps, before the same axe falls on them that clobbered a colleague. After she authored one controversial book, her publisher submitted her next to an outside attorney, who read it for possible legal problems, discovered none, but submitted a bill for $5,000. The publisher deducted the sum, with no warning, from the author's royalty account. What could our friend do about it? Sue!

16·2 Privacy

Becoming more and more important to writers all the time is the concept known as the right to privacy. As long as they keep themselves from becoming public figures, people have the right to be left alone. Somebody who is not newsworthy *at the moment,* who is not a government official, and who doesn't comment publicly or for publication about anything of any sort of public concern, has the right not to be quoted, pictured, or named in print. This has potentially serious ramifications for most writers.

If you ask your neighbor—or a total stranger—how she raises her kids, and then quote her in your manuscript, you are invading her

privacy *unless* she's given you permission to (1) interview her, (2) quote her, and (3) use her name in your book. How can you be sure that in a year or two, when she sees your published book and reads what she said earlier about her lousy brats, she'll remember that she gave you broad consent? You can't, unless you have her sign a release. Asking interviewees for written releases is not standard operating procedure for authors at the moment, but it may become common if the privacy pendulum swings further against us.

To date, most serious privacy cases to reach the courts have involved people who were once in the news but had faded from the public eye. (The cases most often used to illustrate privacy problems involve magazines and newspapers, but the principles apply just as harshly to books.) For example, a onetime truck hijacker said that he'd gone straight for eleven years by the time his name was smeared by a *Reader's Digest* article on hijacking. In another case, a sixteen-year-old math prodigy had lectured to eminent mathematicians amidst great publicity; 25 years later the *New Yorker* profiled the grown-up math genius and said he was living in a seedy flat and was employed at menial labor. In both cases, the courts sided with the magazines and authors, saying, in essence, "Once a public figure, always a public figure *to some extent.*" In the latter case, the judge wrote: "At least we would permit limited scrutiny of the 'private' life of any person who has achieved, or has had thrust upon him, the questionable and indefinable status of 'public figure.' "

But in 1971, *Sports Illustrated* profiled a body surfer. He granted the writers long interviews and many photos, which in the court's eyes constituted his consent to the story's being published. Just before publication the surfer decided there were some aspects of the story that he didn't want published. He withdrew his consent. *Sports Illustrated,* on advice of lawyers, ran the story anyway but lost its day in court. The judge wrote that if consent is withdrawn prior to publication, "the consequent publicity is without consent."

The appeals judge gave *Sports Illustrated* a limited reprieve; it didn't have to pay damages to the body surfer. But the appeal decision haunts journalists, publishers, and constitutional lawyers to this day, since there's no telling when it will be used as precedent to decide another privacy case. The decision reads:

> In determining what is a matter of legitimate public interest, account must be taken of the customs and conventions of the community; and in the last analysis what is proper becomes a matter of community mores.

The line is to be drawn when the publicity ceases to be the giving of information to which the public is entitled, and becomes a morbid and sensational prying into public lives for its own sake, with which a reasonable member of the public, with decent standards, would say that he had no concern. . . . (Virgil *v.* Time Inc., 527 F 2nd 1122, 1124; 9th Cir. 1975)

In light of decisions such as the ones just quoted, Paul Gitlin, a lawyer's lawyer on literary matters, advised us once at an ASJA meeting to use a simple release form like the one he designed for Cornelius Ryan:

I hereby consent to publication of the interview conducted by Cornelius Ryan and consent to its publication by Simon and Schuster and its subsidiaries throughout the world.

There's no doubt that using a release form for all of our face-to-face interviews would be a fine safeguard. But we haven't started using them. Only one of our colleagues has, that we know of. It must be because, in the past, we enjoyed the giving and receiving of mutual trust that went with being authors. It's going to take something mighty dramatic to shake us out of that romanticism.

16·3 Copyright

There are at least two reasons for knowing rudimentary copyright law: (1) to know what your rights are so you can maximize your protection and your income; (2) to know how much of somebody else's copyrighted writing you can incorporate into your own.

As drafted by Congress, the 1976 Copyright Act is quite simple and straightforward, as laws go. It grants an immediate, automatic, and almost unlimited copyright on your work the instant you write it. You do not have to register your book with the U.S. Copyright Office before submitting it to a publisher. You do not have to type a copyright notice on your manuscript (although it doesn't hurt if you do). Your publisher must print a copyright notice such as *Copyright © 1986 George Washington* in the proper location in your book; and in all the contracts we've seen, the publisher is responsible for submitting the proper copyright forms to the U.S. Register of Copyright.

The copyright law is very protective of creators of artistic work of all sorts: poets, magazine writers, book authors, lyricists, painters, sculptors, even composers of rock-and-roll music. In case publication takes place without a copyright notice, the law allows five years for you to correct the error. You don't lose copyright protection if you (or your publisher) don't fill out the Copyright Office's forms, although you can't sue for infringement until you do fill them in. Also, the new law makes it clear that you may sell bits and pieces of your overall copyright: English language rights, Spanish rights, movie rights, cassette rights, and so on.

With this new improved copyright law, authors seem to be having problems not with protecting *their* books, but with figuring out what they can borrow from *other* authors. We'll devote the entire next section to that.

16·4 Fair Use

Fair use is concerned with *somebody else's* copyright on words you want to use. Both the old and new copyright laws allow authors to copy parts of copyrighted works without having to get permission, if they're within the limits of fairness to the author you're copying. But what is "fair" is left pretty much to your discretion, and to a judge's if the original author wants to challenge you. The law itself offers only vague guidelines; here's how it reads:

> In determining whether the use made of a work in any particular case is a fair use the factors to be considered shall include—
>
> (1) the purpose and character of the use, including whether such use is of a commercial nature or is for nonprofit educational purposes;
>
> (2) the nature of the copyrighted work;
>
> (3) the amount and substantiality of the portion used in relation to the copyrighted work as a whole; and
>
> (4) the effect of the use upon the potential market for or value of the copyrighted work.

To help our students stay within the parameters of fair use, we tell them that they need keep in mind just the following simple guidelines:

> You cannot copy so much of somebody else's work that you significantly diminish its commercial value.

> You cannot copy so much of somebody else's work that it noticeably enhances the commercial value of your own writing.
>
> You should not copy any part of somebody else's work without crediting the other author.

Publishers have their own varying interpretations of fair use. Their requirements are sometimes spelled out in contracts or in separate printed or oral guidelines. Many scholarly and educational publishers do not ask you to obtain written permission from authors so long as you copy only a line or two, or sometimes even an entire paragraph or two if they're essential to the point you're making. Trade publishers tend to require written permission from every author you copy no matter how short the quotation. Most publishers have standard printed permission forms for you to use.

When you mail your permission request form, the publisher may respond with its *own* form. You must make certain that the rights being granted in that form match the rights you've asked for. You will probably be asked to pay a modest fee to obtain the permission. If you expect to use many quotations in your book, try to arrange—before the contract-signing—to have your publisher pay permission fees. Often the publisher refuses but agrees to lend you the money and charge it against your royalties just as if it's part of your advance money.

In general, we feel safe using something copyrighted by another author if it definitely figures into the subject we're writing about. However, we use it sparingly, with credit, and only if it's the best literary device we know of to make the point we have to make. In short, we don't copy somebody else's words out of laziness, and we never copy surreptitiously.

It's important to remember that copyright protects *words*—the specific words and the sequence in which they're used. Ideas, concepts, philosophies, facts, observations, and similar cerebrations are *not* protected by copyright. On many an occasion, an author has gone to court to try to prove plagiarism and copyright infringement when somebody has borrowed his idea or has built a new book out of the unique research he conducted for his own earlier volume. But the courts have repeatedly ruled that ideas are there, like the sun and the air, for all to enjoy gratis.

A recent test of the free nature of ideas came when A. A. Hoehling, who wrote the 1962 book *Who Destroyed the Hindenburg?* sued Michael Macdonald Mooney, author of the 1972 book *The Hindenburg,* which became a movie starring George C. Scott. Hoehling stated that in his book he'd presented his own original concept that an anti-Nazi crew member blew the balloon out of the New Jersey sky. (All previous investigators had blamed it on God.) When Mooney's more recent work suggested a similar culprit, Hoehling claimed copyright infringement.

Judge Irving R. Kaufman of the U.S. Court of Appeals in New York disagreed: "Such an historical interpretation, whether or not it originated with Mr. Hoehling, is not protected by his copyright and can be freely used by subsequent authors." Judge Kaufman explained his verdict: "The rationale for this doctrine is that the cause of knowledge is best served when history is the common property of all, and each generation remains free to draw upon the discoveries and insights of the past."

Nonetheless, we always credit another author whose unique discoveries or insights we borrow, not because of legal strictures, but out of fair play.

16·5 Taxes

It's fruitless to point out that governments used to support their artists instead of the other way around. Authors enjoy neither the lobby of big business nor the protective paternalism the government gives to small business. Nonetheless, many provisions of the tax laws have been interpreted to help us in our continuing struggle to keep groceries on the table. But since full-time authors are as rare as bald eagles, you may have to teach your local tax auditor how his provisions apply to you.

In the first place, every full-time professional author has to accept—and make the doubting tax auditor understand—the principle that *everything we do* is income-producing. The following examples may sound familiar to you.

If you're at a party and somebody says, "Hey, you oughtta write about . . ." and the book makes money, you have to pay tax on the money. You are within your rights to deduct the cost of giving and going to parties if you find they lead to sales.

Likewise, you travel to North Dakota on what you've told the kids is a vacation. But your intent is to take pictures of buffalo that will end up eventually in a travel book; you also meet a crusty old-timer who talks about uranium mining and later make his story part of your novel's plot. You are within your rights to deduct most of the cost of your trip, since you certainly are going to be required to pay taxes on the income from the resulting photos and books.

The principle that you must keep in mind, as a full-time author, is *intent*. If you can show that you consistently go to parties *intending* to find book material, that's all the law really asks for. The same is true for your trips. The fact that you pay taxes on the income resulting from the parties and trips, and do so *before* being audited, helps to document your honest intent. And keeping records of book or article ideas developed at parties, on trips, or during other forms of research backs up your serious intent.

Part-time authors can take part-time advantage of deducting expenses. The key philosophical point there again is intent. You have to have offered for sale the books for which you ran up research and writing expenses. You do not have to have sold them, only offered them for sale. There are limitations on how many years in a row you can claim to have lost money—spent more than you took in—but rules on this change so often, you'll have to research them yourself.

As important as your intent, which you can demonstrate only circumstantially, are your records. You have to prove *where* every penny of your expense money went; and you have to prove *why* it went, as well as *when, how much,* and *to whom.* For expenses below $25, Uncle Sam used to take your written entry in a diary as sufficient proof for almost everything. (Check on current regulations for this changing guideline.) In whatever diary you choose to use, make a habit of jotting down books you're working on, people you're meeting, trips you're taking, money you're spending. You'd be surprised how fuzzy your memory gets about why you went to Hawaii, what you did there, what you wrote about it afterwards, and who published (or refused to publish) it.

Authors, like all professionals, have to hold on to their records until there's no chance the IRS wants to see them. For instance, if you buy a house or condominium apartment to use as your office, and depreciate it over a twenty-year-period, you must keep all pertinent records for twenty years plus *at least* the three additional years during which the IRS can audit those tax claims. Noted tax writer Julian Block recommends that you routinely hold on to all records for at least three years after you've used them in filing a tax return. That includes letters and proposals offering books for sale. How else do you substantiate that you were in the business of selling the writing for which you claim the expense deductions?

An accountant may be able to help you. However, we've tried a number of different accountants, all highly recommended by lawyers and business friends, and so far haven't found any who could cope with the peculiarities of the business of being an author. Julian warns, "The

IRS is one place to get information. But be aware that you can't absolutely rely on them. Even in the IRS's own book, *Your Federal Income Tax,* mistakes are inevitable, and the IRS is not bound by them."

Apply your research skills to all your tax questions, as we've done most of the time we've been in doubt. We locate books and articles with tax (and other) advice for businesses and tailor the tips to our own peculiar craft. Although it's worked for us so far, we're a long way from writing a book called *Tax Tips for Authors.* Maybe you can write that one.

Chapter Seventeen

Coping with
the Writer's Life

I N THE DECADES WE'VE PRACTICED OUR CRAFT, WE'VE met a great many would-be authors. As each eager aspirant approaches us for advice, or simply to rub our tattered elbows for luck, we wonder if he'll be someone who makes it or one who drops out somewhere along the way. We can't predict and don't expect anybody ever will.

Some start out so pathetically ill-prepared, we wonder what malady paralyzed their teachers. But even some of *them* learn the craft of writing with incredible ease once they see the need for it. Others start out with the gift of spinning flawless sentences and quotable paragraphs but they never learn to put related passages end to end. Saddest, to us, are those who have an obvious flair for writing and have learned the craft well, yet can't cope with the personal and social hazards of an author's life.

There are many hazards not often revealed to the reading public, or even to novice writers who try to learn by reading such books as the *Writers at Work* series. In fact, even writers sometimes don't learn the whole truth about writing colleagues until they're gone. Two close friends, who died a year or two apart, come to mind. Each wrote a great many major magazine articles and successful books; you'd know their names if we mentioned them. Both lived in fancy New York suburbs, but there the similarities end. Their stories in many ways exemplify the extremes to which a writer's lifestyle and self-image can carry him and his family.

We'll call the first author Karl. For as long as we knew him, he drove the same powder-blue Cadillac convertible; it had become his personal calling card like Truman Capote's roses and Tom Wolfe's white suits. His $150,000 house was paid for, he had a fat portfolio of blue-chip stocks, and he kept so much cash in the bank that his bankers took him to lunch periodically just to stay on his best side. Yet he was paranoid about going broke, as had happened to so many writers he'd watched. His wife complained bitterly about what a tightwad he was. He rarely entertained, and never traveled outside the United States unless he could do it on assignment.

Karl was eager to steer young writers down the straight and narrow. He proudly showed them how he jotted down every fact and anecdote onto 3 × 5 cards, which he spread out on his king-size bed when it came time to organize a book or article. "That way it goes 1, 2, 3. You can't work any other way," he'd admonish them, "or you're going to start procrastinating." Procrastination was his biggest sin: we knew whenever Karl was working against a tight deadline, because he'd phone the few of us who were a local phone call away and talk for hours to put off the dreaded confrontation with that first blank sheet of paper. Still, he always met his deadlines.

Underneath his gruff, materialistic exterior, Karl was the softest touch around for any writer with a hard-luck story. Some paid back their debts. Most didn't have it to pay back and, out of embarrassment, avoided Karl forever after. It prompted him to tell us, "I hate when someone asks to borrow money, because I just know I'm going to lose a friend."

To his dying day, Karl blustered and bragged to colleagues. Only to intimates did he reveal that deep down, he felt he was an incompetent hack. Yet his will endowed a prize for writers, and his widow lives comfortably on the interest from what he invested "to take care of her after I'm gone."

Konrad, as we'll call the second writer, drove only the current year's model of the flashiest car. But he drove into more than his share of concrete abutments because he always took Johnny Walker along for the ride. He was the life of every party, and if nobody had a party scheduled, he'd throw one.

Konrad could sniff out a story halfway across the world, which was where he'd always rather be. He roamed back roads and bayous looking for just the right material, but once he found it, his typewriter fingers would freeze up. Konrad couldn't make deadlines. Still, he managed to keep signing contracts and grubbing advances from book and magazine editors.

One time, the muse told Konrad he couldn't write unless he went to Brazil. Nothing could stop him. He packed his bag, left his wife a forwarding address, and paused only long enough to pick up Johnny Walker (Black Label) and this year's girlfriend. When Konrad got into a scrape in Brazil, he called Karl—who, being Karl, bailed him out. When Konrad died, his legacy surfaced slowly: a secret second mortgage on the family house, two Household Finance loans in arrears, a repossessor looking for the car, and advance money owed to publishers on two long-overdue books. (Even death doesn't excuse you from repaying the advance money. In fact, if the publisher can find someone else to finish your manuscript, the fee may be charged against your estate.)

17·1 The Writing Habit

One of the crazy contradictions created in the name of the craft straps the freest of the world's free spirits to rigid schedules. Publishers insist on deadlines. Therefore, authors who want their writing to reach the reading public need to develop self-discipline.

It's not easy. The headiness of writing your first book will more than likely carry you along as you race to meet your first deadline. After that, the novelty will probably have worn thin. Then you'll have to invent ways to conquer deadlines. Nearly every writer wrestles them with the same stubborn resistance.

DEVISING A SCHEDULE

For undercutting resistance, a schedule is the best initial device. We calculate the number of working days between our starting date and the day we must complete a manuscript. Next, going by prior experience, we estimate the percentage of time we'll have to spend on research, on typing the first draft, and on revisions and final typing. Then we type up a schedule. When it comes to allocating time for each draft, we lay out the days on a chapter-by-chapter basis. We leave space on the schedule to fill in the date when we've actually completed each assigned task, and the number of pages we've typed for each chapter.

Devise a schedule that suits your personality; just don't treat the matter lightly. The care you take with the schedule can determine whether you stick to it or not.

> If you're well-organized, are businesslike, and don't mind people looking over your shoulder now and then, post one copy of your schedule above your desk, put another copy over your spouse's desk, and mail a third copy to your editor.
> If you enlist these concerned individuals to ask periodically how you're doing, that might be all it takes to keep whipping yourself toward your deadline.
> If you like to be pampered, pamper yourself along the way.

For each milestone, schedule a major or minor treat, depending on how much pampering you need. Some writers take long vacations after every book is turned in, and that's enough incentive. Others need dinners out after every chapter.

Many pros simply hold a race: in Lane One is the bank account, slowly draining away; in Lane Two is the manuscript, slowly growing. To win this race, the author must finish before his checks bounce.

You may have to use several methods to stick to schedule. In fact, if you stay with writing as a career, you may find yourself devising more and more outlandish regimens with each new book because they only get harder to finish on time.

THAT FIRST PAGE OF THE DAY

There's a block that affects almost every writer we know personally or have read about: that blank piece of white paper, looking so much like a pale, fallen angel's wing, that you have to roll mercilessly into the typewriter to begin each day. We all have to devise ways to fill it with type, or we'll procrastinate.

Dodi Schultz reorganizes her files first; another friend sharpens each pencil on the desk; others file every scrap of paper, or make phone calls. Terry Morris takes a more direct approach: she ends each day in the middle of a sentence that urges her to finish it the next morning. Some friends retype the last page they wrote the day before, or answer a letter to get the mind and fingers moving. We often think that the only reason we still write so many magazine articles is that we write query letters to avoid having to start the day's work on the book.

Writers live with the contradictions in our craft because *we're* so full of contradictions. The same muse that keeps us from plunging into writing also makes us keep on long past quitting time. If you're to be an effective writer, you'll learn when it's time to knock off. It's not easy to learn, either. Under pressure of deadlines, we've often sat past dinnertime at the typewriter, only to regret it the next day when, as we glance over our output, it's obvious to us that the inspiration shut down long before the fingers.

THE CARE AND FEEDING OF EDITORS

Our aim in this book has been to stick to the unvarnished truth in describing the problems as well as the joys of being an author. Some of the problems that can't be avoided come in dealing with the people on whom you must depend to publish your books. We haven't whitewashed the difficulties you may encounter. We've even provided a number of horror stories to illustrate our points.

But it's important to remember that, on the whole, editors are bright, creative, cordial individuals who try to get a fair shake in the marketplace for the books they take on. They want to be friends with their authors, and if they find one who's a pleasure to work with, they attempt to work with him again and again—even if they move to other publishing houses. Although there are times when you can't avoid being your editor's adversary, there are even more times when cordiality and thoughtfulness garner results. Do negotiate toughly on contracts; do hold onto your integrity and assert your rights; but do separate the problems from the person. Keep in mind that your editor may be your book's best friend.

17·2   Living on a Writer's Income

It may be true that God looks after dumb animals and writers, but not with Her checkbook. A few successful authors we know have had the foresight to marry psychiatrists or Wall Street attorneys—for love, we're sure, but nonetheless it freed them to write what they want and when, without undue concern about feeding a family and paying the mortgage. The rest of us generally strike a balance between artistic instincts and workaday worries. Our writing can't help but suffer in the short run but, long-range, maybe our way of life benefits. We'll share some of the ways we've learned over the years to balance the two contradictory needs.

BE SURE YOUR TIME IS PAID FOR
Early in your career, it's unrealistic to expect that your book advances will make you rich. But do try to ensure that they cover your basic living expenses during the time you research and write your book. If an advance doesn't cover you, know beforehand where the extra cash is going to come from. Nothing freezes the creative juices faster than having to rush through a book just to raise next month's rent.

Many people decide to write the first book after they've been employed awhile, and the job provides a comfortable cushion—if they work out whatever problems that combination presents. A friend who holds a full-time editorial staff position while mothering two young-sters feels like she's drowning in work since signing her first book contract. And there's no doubt that she is. She writes evenings, weekends, even the Fourth of July, and her family is beginning to become impatient with her. If you need a salary to supplement your income, pick your jobs carefully.

If you are looking for a full-time job to cover you while you write your book, keep in mind that writers almost universally consider certain jobs worse than others. Surprisingly, writing positions get the lowest marks. In an interview with Richard H. Goldstone, Thornton Wilder warned that if you have to use the English language in almost any structured way in your job, "you will have a double, a quadruple difficulty in finding *your* English language at night and on Sundays." He went on to say, "When I had to earn my living for many years, I taught French. I should have taught mathematics. By teaching math or biology or physics, you come refreshed to writing."

If you do have to pay the rent by working at a salaried writing job, try doing what Frank did early on: drag yourself out of bed before sunrise so that your writing gets your freshest energy before you shower and rush for the office.

DON'T GET IN A RUT

Every so often, pause to see if you're further along in your career than the last time you took an assessment. If your ultimate goal is to get filthy rich, have you managed to increase your earnings geometrically with succeeding books? If you're not advancing, you'd better pick a new goal or go at the present one in a new way. We moved a thousand miles away from New York City, after Judi's entire lifetime spent there, just for the enriching experience of a different environment. We've never regretted it.

A lot of people who've always wanted to write novels get a foot in the door by writing nonfiction. If you're one of them, do you know when you intend to make the switch? The longer you put off the step, the harder it becomes. Murray Teigh Bloom might never have gotten his *Thirteenth Man* written and published if he hadn't taken his own advice to take a flyer every ten years. Salt away enough money, by hook or by crook, that you can take a year off to write your dream book.

LIVE YOUR OWN LIFESTYLE

Don't live some fairy-tale existence you think says you're A Writer.

Being a writer sometimes does funny things to perspective. One minute, you sit at a table with fellow wordsmiths complaining bitterly about how little authors get paid, and the next minute you feel obliged to prove that you've really made it by living in high style.

We all start out thinking that the ultimate objective is to author a book. Then just a book's not enough; it must be a book that gets noticed. Then only a really important or best-selling book will satisfy us. Finally, unless we keep our perspectives, the products of our words cease to symbolize success. Instead it's going to the Hamptons for the summer, to Jamaica for the winter, and to the Plaza when we have to spend a few days visiting New York. After all, the authors who've made it, we hear, all live that way.

Self-discipline is hardest when the money comes in chunks. When your signed contract comes with a $7,500 check, it's hard to keep in mind that it may be your last $7,500 for many months. We've learned enough to admit to family and friends that we have to pay for copies of our own books. Our parents get one free copy of every book we write. If they want more for their buddies, they pay, same as we do.

17·3 Nourishing Your Self-Confidence

One of the greatest blocks to a writer's craft and career is lack of confidence. Self-doubt attacks us all at one time or another. But unlike sports figures, neither our managers nor our fans do much to reassure us. Your track record for delivering on deadline, for needing little editorial guidance, for helping with promotion and sales—all these gauges of professionalism are buried like Pentagon secrets. Of all the editors who worked with our previous manuscripts, only one bothered to write and say she appreciated our effort to get a clean manuscript in on time. And our experience, we've been told, is typical.

A recent diet book, into which the authors had put much promotional effort, had been on all the national hard-cover best-seller lists for almost six months. Was the editor delighted with its runaway success? The book's co-author confided to us that, instead, the publisher was playing tricks with royalty statements by withholding, as reserves against returns, bigger sums than anybody in this business has ever seen. In order to rationalize this trickery, the editor was continually degrading the book as a literary bomb.

When a colleague's book became a record-breaking best seller and was sold to the movies, she was still on the road, promoting the book eloquently enough to help build up an even larger kitty of royalties for herself and her publisher. (Never forget that the publisher's gross is always about five times bigger than the author's.) Yet the publisher tied up every penny of royalties—which ran into six figures—for several years on the lame grounds that a nuisance lawsuit was pending and that part of the earnings might have to pay for settlement of that suit. Instead of offering support or at least sympathy, the editor railed at the author as if she had personally gotten them into the mess.

If you share stories like these with family, friends, neighbors, attorneys, and even some agents, you'll find that they seldom empathize. Outsiders view being an author as one of the most glamorous callings this side of Hollywood. Where *can* you find the continued support to keep renewing your easily deflated self-confidence?

AWARDS

One type of ego-fulfillment is what we call the Wizard of Oz technique. Remember how old Oz convinced the cowardly lion he was brave by giving him a medal for courage? Well, various public relations departments, professional associations, and writers' organizations fulfill the same function. Annually they award literally thousands of prizes, plaques, and public mentions to writers for doing good jobs. Some of them are self-serving public relations ploys, but never mind. Go after them, frame them, and hang them so that whenever an editor calls you a dunce, you'll have your certificate of merit over your desk to help remind you that you're not. The East Paducah Literary Guild's annual meritorious award may elicit snickers, but only from people who've never seriously tried to write a book.

WRITERS' CONFERENCES

Another institution that's received more than its share of giggles is the writers' conference. We confess to having giggled too, before we discovered the many kinds of satisfactions to be gained from some of the better conferences: marketing tips, craft guidelines, career models, encouragement, enthusiasm, professional contacts, friendships with other writers, and more.

Choose your conferences carefully. A properly conceived conference can pack you with useful tips and insights and charge your psychic batteries with enough energy to carry you through a couple of tough months. But the simple fact that a happening is billed as a writers' conference doesn't guarantee that it'll be of use to writers seeking professionalism. A great many seem designed to do little more than provide ego trips for the speakers—even some that are sponsored by big-name publishing companies. Price is no criterion, but some thought about the following can help you figure out which conferences best match your needs.

Are panel members professional writers and editors, or professional teachers? We've heard mostly sour reports on conferences that rely heavily on college faculty.

Have most panel members established themselves as solid pros? Are their careers at least several years ahead of yours? Too many conferences rely on panel members who are themselves struggling to get started. Their information is either secondhand (having been picked up at other conferences) or amateurish.

If you want to write novels, will there be editors and published writers of fiction on the panels?

If nonfiction is your bag, will editors and published authors of nonfiction be on panels?

If you're seeking personal advice, does the conference schedule time for that? Few conferences specialize in hands-on workshops and manuscript critiquing. If the conference offers critiquing, who's going to read and comment on your prose—the big names on the front of the brochure? If it's some unmentioned English student who's never written for publication, that's quite another matter.

If you need sales tips, does the conference stress marketing? Many conference planners think that writing to sell is a dirty subject.

Will there be time set aside for informal get-togethers among panel members and participants? We've found that informal shop-talk sessions are often fully as valuable as the formal meetings.

Is the conference likely to be cost-effective? If it's a serious financial drain, give long consideration to whether you'll be spending your money and time in the best way. You can't expect quick answers to big problems, only unstructured alternatives to gnawing puzzles. You can't expect to sell manuscripts at conferences, although it has happened on rare occasion.

COURSES

Much of what we've just said about writers' conferences applies equally to courses. You can't learn how to write in a brief course, although courses with the right instructors can help you polish what you already do well. In the seminars we run every year at the University of Wisconsin, the hard-working enrollees measurably improve their own styles by editing photocopies of classmates' articles, poems, and book chapters. The students who don't work so hard don't get so much out of the classes.

Classes can also impart marketing skills and information. This assumes, of course, that the instructor has more than a second-hand knowledge of the subject. In fact, every one of the questions for assessing conferences will prove useful in assessing courses.

Unless you're taking a course for companionship, expect to put in lots of writing hours outside class. To learn as much about marketing as possible, *write* queries and book proposals; don't just follow along as someone else's work is critiqued. To get the most out of any class, workshop, or seminar, turn in some manuscripts—and not old stuff out of your files. Unless you've stopped developing, the instructor or your classmates will be critiquing the writer you were a year or two ago, not the one you're trying to be.

TEACHING

After you've made it as a writer and feel you have little more to learn, try teaching a course yourself. Among the members of the American Society of Journalists and Authors, almost one in four teaches a writing course. You can't get rich, but you can be richly rewarded by meeting eager, mature students who want to learn. Many writers never know how much information they've packed into their heads until motivated students help them express it. It does wonders for the ego.

There are other rewards in teaching. For one, most of us write instinctively—only sometimes instinct isn't enough to figure out what's gone wrong on a page. But you can't teach writing instinctively; the students won't let you. In figuring out for them how you've solved various writing problems, you also figure it out for yourself.

Virtually every college and technical school in the country has a writing curriculum of some sort, and many deans are savvy enough to recognize the merit of hiring experienced writers to teach composition, brush-up English, magazine writing, book writing, creative writing, poetry, short stories, self-publication, interview techniques, research techniques, copy editing, you name it. If somebody doesn't have a course in it, suggest that you teach one yourself.

TAKING A TEACHING PART IN WRITERS' CONFERENCES

Experienced pros absorb a lot of psychic energy being panel members at carefully chosen writers' conferences. Some conferences pay panel members, some do not. For years we've co-hosted the annual Midwest Nonfiction Writers' Conference in Madison, Wisconsin, and have never had trouble finding panelists among top pros from coast to coast, even though they've had to pay their own expenses. Panel members, like conference attendees, come for several reasons. First of all, there's the chance to tell your horror stories to other pros—always valuable and cathartic. Then there's the knowledge you yourself gain. If the other panel members prepare as well as you do, you learn other ways of attacking common problems. Besides, you and some editors will sit side by side as peers, which is a fine way to make their acquaintance.

Finally, there's the tradition among writers of passing on what we've learned. We all got our start somewhere, generally at the cruddy bottom of the ladder, and we might not have made it any closer to the top if some kindly writer or editor hadn't given us a nudge. Taking part in writers' conference panels is one way to fuel the tradition. During the preliminaries at our last conference in Madison, we discovered that of the previous year's 200 participants, four had sold books based on what they'd learned at our conference. We introduced the new authors and had them stand up, and the pleasure of their peers, old and new, echoed for the rest of the two-day event.

WRITERS' ORGANIZATIONS

Fellow writers can always be depended on for psychological, social, emotional, and professional reinforcement. One of the best ways to meet them is through writers' organizations.

Years ago, we joined the American Society of Journalists and Authors (ASJA) because we wanted to gain marketing and professional insights through contact with pros who'd already made it. Sure enough, our careers took off once we were sharing drinks and swapping war stories with the likes of members Flora Rheta Schreiber (*Sybil*), Betty Friedan (*The Feminine Mystique*), Al Toffler (*Future Shock*), Bill Hoffer (*Midnight Express*), and Alex Haley (*Roots*). But we benefited most, professionally and personally, from talking rates and contracts with less well-known members, who, like us, were scrapping mighty hard to make it. If we complained about dropping everything to get a short-deadlined book in on time, only to watch the editor putter around with it for over a year, family members would only smile. But over drinks late at night in the Algonquin's lobby, ASJA members nodded knowingly and shared similar battle stories. It reassured us that we weren't at fault, the profession was. Because of the open sharing of information, whenever we were exploring a new book project, we knew which were the good publishing houses and which to submit to only as a last resort.

Now that we've moved out of the New York City area, which half the ASJA members call home, almost every month we drive to Chicago to kibbitz with the couple dozen midwestern ASJA members. Writers' experiences have no geographic boundaries. We suggest you apply for membership (to ASJA, 1501 Broadway, New York, NY 10036) once you're selling regularly to substantial magazines or have published at least one book. The organization's monthly newsletter alone is worth the annual dues.

The Authors Guild (234 West 44 Street, New York, NY 10036) provides another safe haven for published writers. Although it's not a social organization, its militant industry-wide agitation for better terms and conditions more than makes up for that. The Guild has been especially vigorous and effective in bringing reforms to outmoded and confiscatory contract clauses. The newsletter is helpful, too.

For face-to-face contact and encouragement, local writers' clubs can be as useful, especially if you're not yet eligible for either national association. In the Minneapolis area, for example, we know of three clubs that regularly meet for shop talk and encouragement. One meets twice a month to critique members' works, brainstorm ideas, cheer story assignments, boo unfriendly rejection letters, and generally help its members cling to their writing careers.

Writer's Market lists a great many local and regional clubs, but even that listing just scratches the surface. Some libraries keep track of community organizations. If you can't find a club in your part of the world, think of starting one. Barring that, do what one of our students does: she and a writer she met at a conference on children's books swap tips and encouragement by mail.

THE POWER OF POSITIVE THINKING

If you're going to make it as a writer, you have to be your own best friend—your steadiest, most dependable source of ego enhancement. All the courses, conferences, and clubs in the world won't help you on Wednesday when you're stuck figuring out how much you need to disguise your adulterous neighbor before you can use him in a book, or on Thursday when an editor offers you $3,500 less than you need for a book you've wanted to do all your life, or on Friday when that first sheet of paper just won't hold ink and it's deadline day.

At times like these, that old best-selling Norman Vincent Peale truism will have to do. If you're going to make it, you're going to have to know that you're good. You're going to have to believe that you're good enough to handle the job you've gotten yourself into, and you're going to have to believe it every day of your working life.

Chapter Eighteen

A Few Words About Word Processors

I T'S ALMOST IMPOSSIBLE TO TALK TO WRITERS THESE days without getting into a discussion of word processing. If you're just starting out, our advice is to forget about word processors until you're sure you're going to write long enough and hard enough to make one pay for itself. But if you're a professional writer, or a serious amateur who can afford one, you may want to give the matter serious thought. The time and aggravation you may save by computerizing your efforts may actually recoup the investment within a few years.

18•1   How to Shop for Word Processing Equipment

Computers and word processors are so different from the old-fashioned electric typewriter that we'd be wasting our time and yours if we tried to write a comprehensive description of all that these electronic packages can do for you. You've got to actually play with one yourself to know whether it's for you. First find friends or colleagues who've made the investment and try out their machines. Then shop around in computer stores and try out their machines. We spent six months shopping for our system, comparing various features in competing equipment ("hardware") and in the programs ("software") for each manufacturer's products. We finally settled on an NEC outfit as the best for our needs. (And we do mean *outfit*; a computer can have a number of separate components and fill a large desk.) We found the following guidelines helpful in making our selection, and pass them on to you.

1. If you buy equipment that's designed only for word processing, you're missing out on the valuable business uses offered by any small computer: bookkeeping, research telecommunication with data banks, and file maintenance of such things as editor's names and addresses.
2. The *software*—the computer program that tells otherwise ignorant circuits to copy your words and to help you edit them—is as important as the *hardware* you purchase. Unfortunately, you gener-

ally can't interchange programs among the many brands of computers. Writers ought to concentrate on selecting the best word processing program, not the hardware. No matter how inexpensive or cleverly designed, some manufacturers' computers do not come with easy-to-use word processing software. Some of the programs offered on lower-priced units (and on at least one expensive model) can't perform many of the following functions, which we consider basic to quick and effortless writing:

Transporting chunks of copy quickly from one place to another.

Copying text, without destroying the original, onto another computer disk or onto another spot on the same disk.

The following editing modes: *revise,* to make permanent changes in our copy, with the option to store the earlier version or erase it; *view,* to make changes that can be printed out for our consideration without permanently losing our original manuscript copy; *replace,* to change just the few words we want edited; *search,* to go quickly to a selected word or phrase in the manuscript; *append,* to add one set of pages to another and repaginate automatically; and *merge,* to add one piece of manuscript copy to another. And each command that calls up these wonderful operations should require one or two keystrokes on easy-to-use, easy-to-hit keys.

Good word processor programs add individualized flexibility by permitting the user to insert her own library of commands. Ours permits us to file 52 separate page formats or blocks of text, each up to 1,500 characters long. We can call them up, magically, to appear in our manuscript with just two key strokes. When we hit "E," for instance, our pre-programmed machine automatically sets up the correct alignment for Express Mail forms, prints in our name and address, prints $1,000 in the value square, and then prints in the recipient's name and address with just one more command—at 200 words per minute!

Some word processing programs don't leave anything to chance. They flash onscreen whenever you need to hit another special button. Having all those prompts and menus is valuable only for beginners. Later on they get in the way of seeing the maximum amount of copy, and that's the most important consideration for most writers. You may want to keep that in mind when you're shopping around.

3. For writers, the computer's printer is the one most important piece of hardware. Book publishers welcome manuscripts printed on

the less expensive *dot matrix printers* that are most often sold in computer packages. But for business letters, the more expensive *letter quality printers* are usually *de rigeur*. It's the printers that are most likely to suffer breakdowns, so don't chintz on this item.

4. The computer retailer will be a VIP during your first weeks. She'll hold your hand while you set up your purchase and learn to use it. If your time is money, pick a retailer you're comfortable with.

18•2 How to Use a New Word Processor

Most manuals that come with computers are abominably written. But they're all we have, and they do disgorge valuable tips once the user relaxes at the keyboard. The advice given in many manuals is to fool around with unimportant projects while you learn, but we haven't seen anybody really learn anything that way. Instead, try starting with an actual piece of writing and allow an extra week to complete it. Be extra careful at first to keep backup copies of everything you write—on disks as well as on paper, and plunge right in with the manual close at hand.

Switching to word processing really is easier than most of us used to believe. Frank's equipment arrived by UPS on a Monday. He unboxed it, found outlets for all its plugs, started it working, and wrote his first computerized letter on Tuesday. On the following Monday he packed away his obsolete electric whatchamacallit. Judi's machine arrived on a Thursday. She spent the weekend catching up on her personal correspondence to learn the computer's quirks, and on Monday morning she began the next book manuscript on her NEC. That book took *one-half* as long as it would have taken if she had written it on a typewriter.

Index

DATE DUE